My Jesus Year

My Jesus Year

A Rabbi's Son Wanders the Bible Belt in Search of His Own Faith

Benyamin Cohen

HarperOne
An Imprint of HarperCollins*Publishers*

HarperOne

HarperCollins books may be purchased for educational, business, or sales promotional use. For information please write: Special Markets Department, HarperCollins Publishers, 10 East 53rd Street, New York, NY 10022.

HarperCollins Web site: http://www.harpercollins.com
HarperCollins®, ■ ®, and HarperOne™ are
trademarks of HarperCollins Publishers

FIRST EDITION

Designed by Level C

Library of Congress Cataloging-in-Publication Data is available upon request.

ISBN 978–0–06–124517–6

08 09 10 11 12 RRD(H) 10 9 8 7 6 5 4 3 2 1

To my parents for the past
and to my wife for the future.

Author's Note

Hi.
Thanks for buying my book.

And since I've somehow convinced you to read this page by alluringly titling it "Author's Note," I might as well live up to my end of the bargain and let you in on a little secret, some ounce of information that allows you to ask your friends, "Hey, did you read the author's note in that awesome new book by Benyamin Cohen?" So, in the interest of honest reportage and full disclosure, I offer you this little nugget. Although everything in this book actually happened, some of the names, places, and other pieces of incriminating evidence have been changed to protect the innocent. And me.

Contents

My Jesus Year

THE NOISE IS thundering. The floor is shaking. My ears are pounding. It feels as if God is giving the commandments atop Sinai. Yet I couldn't be farther away from that holy mountain if I tried.

"Give me a 'Praise Jesus!'" the bishop screams into the mike.

"Praise Jesus!" the crowd shouts back in unison as they rise to their feet. The woman next to me, swaying to the blaring music, is smashing her hand against a tambourine she brought from home. The guy in front of me, I'm not quite sure why, is moaning and wildly flailing his arms in the air. It's like being at a rowdy rock concert—except for the undeniable fact that it is morning, the opening act is a heavyset black woman belting out Baptist hymns, and the main attraction is the Lord Almighty.

Here I am, a five-foot-two bespectacled Jewish kid, in a mosh pit of faith in a sea of fifteen thousand roused African Americans at the New Birth megachurch in Lithonia, Georgia. It's Sunday, prime time for prayer, and I am just trying to blend in, hoping I won't stand out too much.

Just as such hopeful—and unfortunately fleeting—thoughts are swirling through my mind, one of a dozen camera operators focuses on me. And before I know it, there I am, my face twenty feet tall on the two screens hanging from the ceiling in front of the amphitheater. My Jewish face on Jesus' JumboTron for all to see.

Oh, God, forgive me.

ONE

Son of a Preacher Man

*The boys grew up, and Esau became a skillful hunter, a man of the open
country, while Jacob was a quiet man, staying among the tents.*
—*Genesis 25:27*

THERE'S A STORY about my birth, and I'm told it's not an apocryphal
one. Eight days after I entered this world, the morning of my circumcision,
my father and I had our very first bonding experience. Just me and him in
the back room of a butcher shop. Allow me to explain. Please.

I was a tiny baby, and our rabbi was unsure if I weighed enough to med-
ically handle a circumcision. My dad, a man who holds multiple graduate
degrees, was getting medical advice from our rabbi. That's like getting a
chef's opinion on Middle Eastern politics. Or Paris Hilton's thoughts on
anything.

Nobody in our neighborhood, the story goes, had a proper scale to weigh
a baby. So my dad took me to the butcher.

Early on the morning of my circumcision, in the dark stillness before
daybreak, my dad drove me in our family's brown Plymouth Volare to
Sam's Kosher Meats and Deli. This was a depressing place. Sam was a can-
tankerous old man, always yelling at his wife in his thick eastern European
accent. The place was in a constant state of disarray. Bad vibes abounded.
Don't bring babies here. This is not a manger.

In the back room, deep inside the frigid meat locker, my dad took my
little baby body and placed it on the ice-cold metal meat scale. The scale
read 5.2 pounds. At least that's what he thought it read. It was 1975, and
digital scales wouldn't appear on the scene for years.

For years afterward, members of our tight-knit Jewish community would come up to me, pinch my cheek, and call me "Butcher Boy." At my bar mitzvah, the Jewish rite of passage into manhood, someone brought a rubber chicken to the party thinking it was funny. It wasn't.

My dad called the rabbi and woke him up.

"Five point two pounds," he said. "Will that work?"

"Yep," said the rabbi, in a bleary daze. He was surely still half asleep and completely oblivious to what he was agreeing to. And in that moment, my fate was sealed. There was no turning back.

Circumcision is more than just a minor surgical procedure. It is what ties a Jew to his ancestors. It's a remembrance of the covenant between Abraham and God made back in Genesis. The only difference between Abraham and me is that he had a choice. I didn't. At eight days old, I wasn't given a vote. And now I'm stuck with this religion for life.

Hours later, in the company of a couple hundred of our closest friends and family, I officially became a member of my people. The ceremony involved a scalpel, a lot of pain, and an emotional dent that would leave me reeling for years to come.

This was how I was introduced to religion. It was forced upon me, beginning in the frigid meat locker of a kosher butcher.

THE COHENS ARE a clan of rabbinic rock stars. My dad's a rabbi, and from the very beginning we were brought up to join him in the family business. Of us six kids only my younger sister and I didn't either become a rabbi or marry one (although, for the record, she does work in Jewish education).

Religion was served to us on a silver platter—whether we wanted it or not. We kept kosher, we observed the Sabbath, we prayed three times a day. No questions asked. These were all givens. I went to a preschool called the Garden of Eden. Except in this kindergarten, sin was not an option.

What's more, as religious as we were growing up, I never actually understood Judaism's fundamentals. After I was circumcised, like a prepackaged product coming off an assembly line, I felt haphazardly heaved into the deep end of the Jewish religious pool with the rest of them.

I tried to rebel at every turn. In preschool, I'll now finally admit, I tasted the sweet nectar of forbidden indulgence by gobbling up nonkosher Nerds candy behind my school building, crumpling its sin-soaked box back into my knapsack just before my carpool ride arrived. My dad once caught me yanking my *tzitzit* off one hot summer morning when I was about ten. What are *tzitzit*? you ask. The term literally means "fringes" and refers to the heavy wool garment with string and fringes on its corners that Jewish males are supposed to wear under their clothing at all times. Yes, let's say it together, *that's crazy.* I know.

In my childish eyes, my dad was someone who treated my siblings and me all the same, trying to raise us all in the same mold—with what appeared to me to be an ironclad fist of religion. With clenched teeth, he told us not to overdose on television, not to talk a lot with those of the opposite sex, and to avoid just about anything else that sounded like fun to a prepubescent kid. My brothers and sisters seemed to be fine with the religion we were born into. I, on the other hand, felt it as an unbearable weight upon my shoulders.

The fundamental basis of Judaism is that we're the chosen people. But what if we didn't choose to be chosen?

Don't get me wrong. I still did everything I was told (well, except for the now infamous Nerds candy incident of 1980). To the outside world, I was the rabbi's son, and no one would think otherwise. But a look inside my psyche yielded a different picture—one glossed with a gnawing sense of envy of those who could have what I couldn't. No bacon cheeseburgers. No girlfriends. No *Cosby* show.

Alas, these were the halcyon days of my childhood. And yet, I wondered: Why was I being denied a typical American upbringing? What had I done to deserve this?

My mom played good cop to my dad's Dirty Harry. She let me watch television. She didn't make a big deal when she found out about the crush I had on a girl at school. She treated me and my siblings more like individuals, encouraging each of us to embrace our strengths, whatever those may have been.

Unfortunately, this loving maternal parenting philosophy didn't gain much traction, as my mother collapsed suddenly and died on a bleak January morning when I was only thirteen years old. I had just come off the religious high of celebrating my bar mitzvah, yet with her sudden passing I instinctively reverted to an emotional fetal position. I felt crippled and woefully unprepared for the adulthood that lay before me.

•   •   •

WHILE I WAS growing up, my dad served as the principal of a Jewish high school in Atlanta. He felt bad that, come Saturday morning, the students went their separate ways to their individual synagogues. He longed for a place where the students and teachers could pray together on the Sabbath. So just before my mother's death, he decided to build an addition onto our home—a thousand-square-foot synagogue for them to pray in, with my dad leading the services. The construction contractor, a shady Israeli businessman, asked my dad for all the money up front. Apparently they don't teach Business 101 in rabbinical seminary, because my dad gave him the money. All of it.

Not surprisingly, the contractor fled the country with my college nest egg. My mom had a massive brain aneurism shortly after the incident. She was pronounced dead two days later. I guess you could say that even as a kid I never really had a positive association with synagogues.

Don't get me wrong. I indeed had moments of true religious verve and vigor as a child. I did in fact have genuine moments of spiritual inspiration. I remember fondly the day the synagogue attached to our home was finally completed nearly three years after the original contractor broke ground. It was a Friday afternoon. In a few hours, with the setting of the sun, we would usher in our Sabbath and inaugurate the sanctuary with its very first prayer service.

I entered the large room, alone for a moment, and took it all in. It was magnificent, a sight to behold. The new contractor, this one more honest than the first, had capped off the ceiling with a window-filled dome that allowed rays of sunlight to beam down into the sanctuary. They were like rays from heaven, perhaps my mother smiling down upon us. The room's construction may have contributed to her untimely death, but I was sure her spirit in heaven was full of joy now that it was finally complete.

I closed my eyes and pictured being the first to give my mother the grand tour of the new edifice. My father was an avid book collector and had lined nearly every wall of the sanctuary with bookcases as high as the eye could see. The hundreds of Jewish books, neatly stacked on each shelf, infused the room with intellectual warmth. In the front of the room, on a raised dais, stood the ark protecting two Torah scrolls inside. I almost wished that we didn't have to "open for business" in a few hours and that the room could remain in this virgin state forever.

Judaism didn't always suffocate me; there were periods of my life when my faith made me feel whole. Growing up in that synagogue, in the confines of those walls, I actually felt God's presence. Spirituality was *real* for me. It was tangible—in my prayers, in my thoughts, and in my daily life. I felt I could ask God, I could supplicate, I could cry, whether it was asking for divine assistance with getting a girl to like me, praying for an "A" on the next day's math test, or wondering why God had decided to rob me of a mother during my adolescence. Entering my teens without the aid of a mother would be the foundation of an eventual psychic distance between myself and God, one that would later blossom into full-blown cynicism.

The synagogue, with all it represented, brought some stability into my young psyche. The pain that its construction wrought on our family dynamic eventually gave way to a peaceful plateau, a place where I could feel close to my mother's long lost spirit and heal my wounds ever so slowly. But right before my eyes, whatever little stability my life had was about to be yanked from under me.

Less than two years after my mom's passing my dad remarried, this time to an artist from San Diego whom he didn't bother to introduce me to until they were practically engaged. I immediately assigned her the role of the proverbial evil stepmother, even though I hardly knew her. I met my future stepbrothers when my dad was showing them around our home shortly before they were to move in. The younger brother took up residence in the bedroom built underneath the synagogue and lined the walls with his Tony Gwynn posters and other sports paraphernalia.

After my mom died, even though I wasn't the oldest child, I had taken over many of the household duties. I had gotten into a comfortable routine that was shaken up by my new stepmother. She brought new rules and a new set of systems into the house. This was not the blessedly, blissfully blended family of *The Brady Bunch*.

I blamed my dad for all of this disruption. I despised him for doing this to me. I didn't care about his feelings or his need to move on after my mom died. I was an angry teenager who had lost his mother, and I blamed my dad for giving me this lot in life. After all, if he hadn't been an overly enthusiastic rabbi, I never would've been brought up in a wacky family that builds a synagogue next to their dining room. If it wasn't for him, I could lead a *normal* life, one free of all these ridiculous religious strictures.

No longer was it enough to just be mad at my dad; I also began to resent everything he stood for (Judaism) and everything that I believed had sent my mother to her early grave (the pressures of being a rabbi's wife).

It's true what they say about Jewish guilt. It's intoxicating and all-encompassing. As much as I thought I wanted to, I couldn't just stop doing the Jewish commandments cold turkey. No, that wasn't going to work. Ironically, I knew enough not to do that. I had been taught that, despite what we may be feeling inside, we are commanded to do these things. Judaism had my hands tied.

So in lieu of actual heresy, my spirit began to ebb and flow. My emotional connection to my religion began to vacillate. Prayers, the Sabbath, and a myriad of other Jewish commandments became less important. And, ever so slowly, my spiritual connection to God began to fade.

My growing religious apathy soon became coupled with an even greater vice: envy. Envy of those with things I couldn't have.

For years I had looked longingly at the church across the street from my house, its pristine landscape looming just outside my bedroom window. I watched, with transfixed eyes, each Sunday morning as the khaki-clad parishioners and their always smiling progeny emerged from their shiny minivans and walked into the sun-dappled, stained-glass sanctuary.

Pastor Duffey, the minister of the church, was my sole tangible entrée into this mysterious world of Christianity. During the few occasions he came over to our home—to shut off our oven, for example, after we had forgot to turn it off before the onset of the Sabbath, when Jews are prohibited from using electricity—I tried desperately to get a glimpse of who this man was. What was his life like? How did it feel to not be strangled by the myriad rules of an Orthodox Jewish lifestyle? How did it feel to flick on the light switch on the Sabbath? Where was he going after he left our house? To a football game? To eat pork?

While my upbringing was defined by what I couldn't do, it seemed to me that Christian kids had it all. In my eyes, they were wealthy, happy, and able to watch TV whenever they wanted. They had a choice. Should we watch *Transformers* or *He-Man*? Should we watch anything at all?

It was as if I had left the uterus with a yarmulke on my head and a Talmud already in my hand. All I was missing was a beard. A certain prescribed lifestyle was all I knew. I was brought up with certain expectations of who I was and who I should become.

Average Christian children seemed to just have it easier, unencumbered by the history of persecution we felt as Jews. In my eyes, they seemed to go through life with a laissez-faire attitude I could only dream about. They didn't have to worry how long their sideburns were (another Jewish law). They didn't have to wear *tzitzit*. They could eat at any restaurant, no matter how unkosher.

I felt lost, a traveler without a compass. I didn't feel a connection to my own religion. What's worse, the religion of others was tempting me, so close and yet so far away.

As I entered my college years and moved away from my dad's house and his overbearing ways, I felt an uncontrollable sense of freedom. Probably the same way Ben Franklin would have felt if he'd had the opportunity to shop at Circuit City. Forget the kite. This hi-tech wonderland would have been too much for colonial Franklin to grasp. He wouldn't have known where to begin.

I considered McDonald's, it's famed Big Mac and cheese the sheer embodiment of all that's unkosher, but it's utter and unbelievable unkosherness enveloped me in guilt. I thought about something less dramatic, perhaps a visit to a seedy bar. But after five minutes in the smoky joint, I gasped for some fresh air. Apparently, my feeble Jewish body wasn't built for blaring music coupled with an unhealthy dose of carbon monoxide. (Indeed, years later, a doctor confirmed what every Jewish male already knows—we're allergic to everything.)

This reminded me of a reality show I watched called *Amish in the City*. As a rite of passage the Amish send their teenagers on *Rumspringa,* a vacation from religion lasting several months to many years. During this time the kids are supposed to decide if they indeed want to lead an Amish life. The producers took five Amish teens and plopped them into a Hollywood home with five mainstream teenagers, including a stereotypical jock, a vegan, and a gay guy. They spent that summer dancing at rock concerts, getting their GEDs, and attending red-carpet events—you know, the usual stuff non-Amish kids do in their spare time. At the conclusion of the show, not one of the teenagers wanted to go back to an Amish lifestyle. I could relate to that.

As for me, I wanted to date a *shiksa,* a gentile girl, wrapped in bacon, but all I could do was order cable. My big defiant act was watching the Cartoon

Network, something that had been denied to me as a kid. We didn't have cable when I was growing up, so I was oblivious to miraculous inventions like its twenty-four/seven lineup of animation. What kind of heretic was I when I was in my midtwenties and my biggest vice was watching *The Smurfs*?

What's more, all of this freedom (while initially enjoyable) was in fact very limiting. The ease of a lifestyle free of religious strictures was tempting, but I had been taught otherwise. I knew this would be an unsatisfying way for me to go about my life. I knew I needed more. I yearned for a closer connection to something deeper, something more meaningful.

Again, I found myself looking to the Christians across the street. Not only did they have a life that was more fun and exciting than mine, but they seemed to be enjoying—nay, embracing—their religion all at the same time. It was a paradigm shift for me. Religion equals happiness. How could that be? I had to sit down.

We all, by nature, are riddled with personal uncertainties. They surround us on a daily basis. Our country is at war. Terrorism is a real threat. Our nation's political philosophies are divided. People are looking for certainty, some kind of stabilizing factor they can grasp onto. They want to have a concrete basis to build their lives upon. Enter religion.

For most Americans, church serves as that stabilizing factor. The sacred congregational community serves as a foundation on which they can rely upon in troubled times and a welcome place where they can feel they belong. And clergy is their bedrock, an unshakable force from which they gain strength, confidence, and fortitude.

To many, that's what religion is *supposed* to be. The irony was that, for me, religion was anything but. My religion was what was making me feel less certain about the world around me. Yes, I believed in God. But the conduit through which I connected to Him—my faith, my Judaism—wasn't resonating with me. And that troubled me even more. I felt that the religion I was given wasn't allowing me to access God the way I wanted. Maybe God made a mistake when He made me a Jew. Was I supposed to be a Mormon instead? Maybe a Baptist or a Pentecostal? I don't know. I just know this didn't feel right. Instead of being a stabilizing force in my life, my religion was what was shaking me to the core.

Was I alone in these thoughts? I certainly couldn't be the only Jew to have negative feelings toward my religion. America is replete with Jews who are apathetic at best. Indeed, I'm sure people from all walks of life, from all religions, have the very same issues at one point or another during their lives. After all, we are all pilgrims on our own individual journeys toward faith.

This realization—that I was not alone—was a start. Misery, as the saying goes, loves company. Now what?

Using my new cable TV service, I flipped on a Sunday morning church service. Christians were already cooler than us. They had televised prayers. The pastor, a tall black man in a shiny gray suit with an inordinate number of buttons, was rousing. The audience was enraptured. But I didn't get it. All he was doing was shouting aphorisms. Basic ones, too. "God loves you!" "Be good!" "Don't lie, cheat, and steal!" How could such fundamental tenets be inspiring to people? It boggled my mind.

It almost seemed shallow. Wasn't religion supposed to be this deeply fulfilling experience between us humans and a Higher Power? In college I had minored in religious studies and had learned of the Tao of the Eastern religions, of the deeply philosophical nature of humankind's place on this planet. How could this be transmitted by a slickly dressed showman shouting rudimentary one-liners?

AFTER THREE DECADES in Atlanta, my dad had found employment elsewhere and packed up our home. He sold it to a real estate developer who turned around and rented it to a bunch of college coeds. It has since become a frat house; the synagogue room now hosts keg parties.

As happens with most families, my siblings all left the nest and moved to other cities for college and to start families of their own. I was the only one who stayed.

So this is where I found myself. I felt abandoned by my family. And, even more, I felt abandoned by God.

This was not the way I wanted to lead my life. My actions were being fueled by anger and resentment. My decisions—to not visit family, to gain little from religion—were being dictated by years of friction and ill will. I so wanted something positive to live for. I needed some compelling, proactive reason to move forward on all fronts. This spiritual stagnation was eating me up inside, and I had to do something to fix it.

At the time, I was twenty-six, an age at which most of my Orthodox friends were already married. Some even had kids. They were starting their own lives and, I assumed, creating their own new connections to Judaism through the support system of spouse and children.

Thoughts of marriage became my cure-all. Surely, a nice wife I could bring home to my dad would show him I wasn't a completely lost cause. Wistfully putting all my hopes in the dream that getting married would solve all my problems—with my family and my religion—I began to think about it constantly. It became all-consuming. It was what got me through the day.

How to Find a Wife in a Hundred Dates

So Boaz took the convert Ruth and she became his wife.
—*Ruth 4:13*

DELTA FLIGHT #506 from Atlanta to New York was making its final descent into LaGuardia. This was the second time this month I had taken this flight, and already the seventh time this year—and it was only April. But I had to make the trek because if I ever wanted to find a single marriageable Orthodox Jewish woman, it just wasn't going to happen where I live in Atlanta (I had dated all five of them already). So I had no choice but to hop a plane to the Big Apple twice a month for my very own version of *The Dating Game*. I couldn't complain. After all, the biblical Jacob spent seven years enduring backbreaking labor for his true love, just to be told by his conniving future father-in-law that he would only be allowed to marry Rachel after an additional seven years of hard work. That's fourteen years. Working for your father-in-law. The least I could do was visit Manhattan—a place, mind you, my proud Southern heritage had taught me to despise with every fiber of my Confederate being.

But I didn't fly up just for one date—or even just one girl. I had worked out a system that allowed me to date a lot of women in a relatively short amount of time. During a five-year dating spree in my twenties, I went out with more than a hundred women. And they all seemed to be various versions of a sitcom cliché.

One girl was actually married and didn't bother to tell me until after I had paid the tab for dinner. In her defense (though I'm not sure why I need to be defending her in this book), she was technically "separated." That made me feel a little better, I guess, although I'm not quite sure why she felt the need to use air quotes when she said "separated." Was she not *really* separated? Was she only somewhat separated? Was she still married? That meal was the last time I saw her. As far as I know she's still married, still going out with unsuspecting single men, and still relying a little too heavily on air quotes.

As for me, my typical New York itinerary looked something like this: Fly up on a Sunday morning, go on five dates (coffee, lunch, coffee, coffee, and dinner), then fly back on the last flight out Sunday night. I boarded the plane those evenings so hopped up on caffeine that I was jittery as I handed my boarding pass to the flight attendant. It was really no way to lead a life.

But this is what my Judaism had taught me. Like my ancestors before me, I would marry inside the faith. The future of my people, I was told, lay on my gawky shoulders. It was the burden I was to bear. As if that hadn't shrunk the dating pool enough, I knew I could only marry someone who was also Orthodox. Someone who—like me—waited six hours between eating meat and milk, didn't turn the lights on during the Sabbath, and adhered to all the other unbelievably strange laws that I'll explain in the next chapter. Despite my almost lifelong frustration with my faith and the myriad laws it obligated me to follow (again, next chapter), I actually *wanted* to marry someone who was observant like me. This was because the lifestyle had become so ingrained in me I knew no other alternative. And I was actually fine with that. I just wished I could appreciate this Judaism I was so monotonously doing.

So for the most part, I seemed to be dating girls with backgrounds similar to mine. We had each been force-fed Orthodox Judaism growing up, and we were each being told who we should date and marry. And we each felt resentment toward Judaism because of it. It was perfect up to that point. Our only major difference was that I was from the South, which made me more chilled and laid-back. The girls were from Manhattan, which made them talk a mile a minute and have a tough exterior that I didn't find too attractive. They were looking for Woody Allen in his twenties. I was looking for Scarlett O'Hara in a *shtetl*.

A friend once set me up on a date with a girl in New York who was less religious than I was. Midway through the date, she grabbed onto my arm as we were walking and held it as we crossed the street. Run-of-the-mill activity in the nonreligious dating world. But in my universe touching before marriage was a cardinal sin. And we were smack in the middle of Times Square, with some of the busiest street corners on the planet. I was mortified.

Okay, I realize at this point I should briefly explain why a girl holding my arm is the religious equivalent of a Catholic skipping Lent. It's just not done in our circles. Segregating the sexes is an integral philosophy used ubiquitously with observant Jewish children from the time we're in elementary school. And by the time we reach high school, when faith often takes a backseat to our raging hormones, we're told not to have girlfriends or boyfriends. "Told" is a polite way of putting it. In no uncertain terms, my dad informed me, was I to fall in love during my formative teenage years. Well, needless to say, I took that as my cue to start lining up potential girlfriends.

I fancied myself a Casanova of sorts, flirting with all the girls at the private Jewish high school I attended. But, instead, I ended up feeling like another literary legend—Romeo. Beth Schwartz was the girl I thought I was going to marry. We were going steady on and off throughout high school. I would say we were dating, but I don't think we ever went out on an actual date because of the aforementioned ban on girlfriends. Both sets of parents forbade it, and that made us want to hang out even more. In that youthful state, we really did believe our forbidden love was akin to that of Romeo and Juliet. The uphill battle our religion provided added to the "up against all odds" gestalt.

This Shakespearean comparison was compounded by the fact that I would actually sneak out of my house in the middle of the night, ride my bike to Beth's house, and throw pebbles at her bedroom window. The Montagues and the Capulets became the Schwartzes and the Cohens. All we needed was an apothecary and this would turn tragic.

But it didn't. I had worked out a system to sneak out of my house each night. I would tiptoe through the dining room and into the synagogue attached to our house. The one good thing about having a large sanctuary built onto your house is it gives you the perfect back exit. This irony—that it was the synagogue door that aided me in my escape in the middle of the night to visit my forbidden girlfriend—was completely lost on my teenage mind.

This went on for most of high school until I was caught, finally, during my senior year. After hanging out with Beth most of the night, I rode my bike back home as the sun was coming up. There, to my horror, were my dad and stepmom in the kitchen window. The jig was up. My dad had taken the spare key I kept hidden under the welcome mat, and I was locked out. Feeling like a fugitive turning himself in, I knocked on the door.

My dad went ballistic. He went on about trust and about what people would think if they knew the rabbi's son was spending time with a girl in the middle of the night. With just a few months left in my high-school career, I felt I was robbed of those formative years—at least the way I had pictured them playing out in that wonderful video loop in my head.

Anyway, as my dad was yelling at me, his skullcap tilting to the side from his swift movements, something came over me. I don't know why it happened just then, but I began to smile. This really got my dad upset. Here he was trying to scold me, and I looked as if I had just won the lottery.

For some reason, this is the moment it hit me. If Jews had epiphanies, this would've been one of them. My smiling was a primal response. I finally realized that my dad was not God and could not dictate what was right or wrong when it came to religion. Beth and I were in love, and I knew deep down that God approved of this union. So who was my dad to forbid it?

And so I smiled. I smiled knowing full well that from this day forward my relationship to God was my own and no one—not even my dad—could hijack that.

"Yell all you want," I told my dad. "Who cares? You can ground me. You can do whatever you want. But just know this. You can't stop me. Because when you go to sleep at night—and you can't stay up forever—I'll just sneak out again and again."

I felt as though I had just given that speech from *Braveheart* to rally the troops before the big battle. Except (a) that epic film didn't actually come out until many years after this seminal incident and (b) taking a cue from the allegedly anti-Semitic Gibson on how to deal with my rabbinic father was probably not the best source of inspiration. Regardless, it worked. My dad left the room in a huff, and I felt, for the first time, that I had won.

This act of utter defiance was the epitome of what we Jews call *chutzpah,* a word Jewish theologians have spent centuries trying to translate into English, but I'll just call your basic "eye-popping gall." That's what had come over me when I lashed out at my dad. It may be true that he wasn't, as kids tend to say, "the boss of me," but I shouldn't have told him that. In so doing,

I had stripped him of the notion that he was in charge. That upper hand is critical for all parents to believe they have and also critical for every child who wishes to rebel.

HERE I WAS in my twenties going out with girls who had the same religious neuroses I did. To be honest, these matches between two people cut from the same cloth are usually a disaster waiting to happen. It's a little like dating someone you met in Alcoholics Anonymous. Pairing two addicts together, two people with the same predisposition toward acting out, can ultimately lead to serious trouble. In many couples made up of a husband and a wife who both grew up in Orthodox Jewish homes, I've seen the two partners rebel exactly same way.

I didn't want a girl as screwed up as I was. I wanted a girl who would inspire me to be more religious. I was looking for salvation.

Unfortunately, the place I was looking was a breeding ground for this split, "Metrodox" personality. Most of my friends lived on Manhattan's Upper West Side and were setting me up with people they knew. This seemed like the ideal place because, according to some estimates, there are more twenty-something Orthodox Jews on the Upper West Side than there are in the entire rest of North America. A seemingly perfect dating pool for me to dive into.

But all is not as it seems. In a thirty-five-block area nestled comfortably between Riverside and Central Park, knit yarmulkes and modest skirts are de rigueur. Not a surprising sight in New York, but when you consider the skirt is tight and low-riding and the knit yarmulke has creased folds from being in a pocket all day at work, then it's a whole different story.

Safely away from their families, these thousands of like-minded Jewish singles have created a unique counterculture all their own. Although they may keep kosher and pray three times a day, they also go clubbing and are involved in physical relationships with those of the opposite sex. Being tugged in one direction by the secular world and in another by the religious world, they have styled their own compromise. Although they may feel a sense of connection being around so many like-minded young people, they also feel an unbearable sense of loneliness and despair.

And these were the people I was being set up with. Their cognitive dissonance was certainly not the antidote for my own religious angst.

So, what was my dating scene like? Picture a Jewish Melrose Place where everyone just wants to get married. With thousands of young Jews packed into the same neighborhood, Metrodox dating had become a phenomenon unto itself. There's an old saying in this community that's kind of reminiscent of prison terminology: "You're here for either six months or six years." Which leads to the obvious question: If there are so many singles, why does it take so long to find a mate?

My friend Ari, who has lived on the Upper West Side for nearly a decade, calls it the menu theory. "Every time I go to this restaurant with a pretty large menu, I have a hard time figuring out what to order," he says matter-of-factly. "People have this ADD mentality where you see everything at once. That's why you need less selection."

This weeding-out process doesn't happen at a bar, but at the epicenter of Jewish life on the Upper West Side, Congregation Ohab Zedek. The synagogue is the Jewish Gen-Xer's answer to Studio 54. It's a kosher meat market.

I spent several Sabbath weekends there and witnessed firsthand this dating ritual. On any given Friday night, a couple hundred young men dash into the synagogue's sanctuary, hair still wet from recently applied gel. The women are in attendance, but not as prompt; they begin to fill their separate section two at a time, in pairs, as if Noah had called them in from the rain. The architect of O.Z., as the synagogue is lovingly nicknamed, was a pure mastermind. The women's section is located on a horseshoe balcony surrounding the men's section, making eye contact between the sexes impossible to avoid. Sure, it's not what God intended, but it draws a crowd.

As the service comes to a close, I join the crowd—now three hundred strong—as we make our way through the front foyer out onto the steps and into the street. The mere volume of Jewish singles in attendance makes it almost impossible for me to exit the synagogue in less than a half hour. It is on these steps, these legendary steps, where the real service begins. Guys who have been scoping out their prey inside now make their move. It's like watching a Discovery Channel documentary on wild hyenas in their natural habitat. *The male hyena,* the voiceover intones, *after completing the ceremonial prayer service to the wildebeest gods now confidently approaches the female.* It's a deadly mix of testosterone and Torah.

The sheer size of the dating pool wasn't my only problem. The ones I was going out with all seemed to be from the Jewish *shtetl* known as Crazy-town. There was Anorexic Jenny, who spent the first few hours of each day with a hot water pack attached to her rumbling stomach. After dating Psychotic Ellen for a couple months, I flew her to Atlanta. She dumped me on day one of her visit and was dating someone else by day five. About a year later, she called out of the blue and asked why I stopped calling. And there was Midget Deborah. (Okay, technically she was a little person. Or a dwarf. I don't think she really liked being called a midget. Especially by me. Which is what I did when I first met her. It just slipped out.) She was the only girl to make me feel tall (which is good), but she also made me feel as if I was dating a kid (which is bad).

I never found out what happened to Anorexic Jenny, Psychotic Ellen, or Midget Deborah. Or the probably still-married air-quotes girl. My years of flying up to New York to find my future wife had led me nowhere.

WHILE I WAS going through all of this, my future wife was traveling a markedly different journey. The blond, blue-eyed daughter of a Methodist minister, Elizabeth was having her own crisis of faith that somehow landed her on the path to Orthodox Judaism even before I met her.

Her dad was one of two ministers at a nondenominational church just outside Atlanta. He loved God and loved teaching the Bible, but he didn't love the politics of working in a church. He was not cut out for a minister's calling and eventually left the church disgruntled. He grew a ponytail, bought a convertible sports car, and compulsively collected Civil War figurines. They say fanatical people replace one obsession with another. In this case, Jesus was replaced by General Lee.

Even when her parents took a step back from organized religion, Elizabeth felt as though she was missing something without it. Although she has never questioned the existence of God, she has frequently pondered the best way to cultivate a relationship with Him.

In her father's theological library she found *The Jewish Book of Why,* a basic primer to the chosen people. (Questions answered in this 1981 classic include such odd gems as "Why is Tuesday a favorite day for marriage among some Orthodox Jews?" and "Why does breast-beating often accompany prayer?") The book opened her eyes to another way of approaching the Almighty and religion in general. She wasn't even aware that Jews existed in the modern world. In school and in church, she had heard about the ancient Israelites, the so-called Hebrews who are discussed in the Bible. She had no clue they were still around and living in far-flung places like Atlanta, Georgia.

Like any teenage girl looking to do something she probably shouldn't, Elizabeth turned to the chat rooms of the Internet. It's there that she eventually bumped into Jewish boys her age. More specifically, she found some who lived nearby. For the remainder of high school, she hung out with these Jewish teenagers and their families. She joined them for Sabbath meals, attended synagogue with them, and even started practicing Judaism to some degree. All the while still being a Gentile, the daughter of a lapsed minister.

Once in college, Elizabeth began to explore the feasibility of converting, which is a lot harder than you would think. Christianity is a proselytizing religion and seeks converts in any way possible. In many churches, people can accept Jesus and become a Christian in under an hour. It's like Lens-Crafters for the soul.

Judaism, on the other hand, doesn't missionize and could basically care less if someone wants to convert. Indeed, when potential converts to Judaism approach a rabbi, the rabbi is required to rebuff them at least three times before agreeing to actually help them. But once people do convert, our religion holds them in incredibly high regard. The biblical Ruth eventually converted and became the progenitor of the Davidic dynasty; hers is the maternal line from which the Messiah will ultimately come. Not too shabby for someone who wasn't born into this religion.

By now Elizabeth was, for all intents and purposes, a practicing Jew. She observed the Sabbath. She prayed three times a day as prescribed. She kept kosher. At home, her parents bought new dishes and kept a separate part of the kitchen for her new dietary requirements. She was just as, if not more, religious than many Jews. The only thing was she wasn't actually Jewish.

She eventually connected with a rabbi who agreed to convert her, just not right then. It took another couple years before she would dunk in the holy waters of a *mikvah,* a ritual bath, and emerge a member of the Jewish nation. Shortly before she took that plunge was when I met her. In synagogue.

Despite the fact that she wasn't yet Jewish, she had been attending services for years. I had seen her across the room a few times (men and women sit separately in Orthodox synagogues) and had always thought she was a high-school kid. At some point, we actually introduced ourselves after the service one Sabbath, and I realized she wasn't a teenager (a good thing), but that she wasn't yet Jewish (not a good thing).

Here I had been flying to New York for years and going out with more than a hundred women, and the girl I was going to marry was right in my own backyard. But had I met Elizabeth years ago when I first began looking for a mate, it wouldn't have been the right time. Well, for starters, back then she *was* a teenager. And, oh yeah, she was still jonesing for Jesus back then. Now she was making moves on Moses.

The rabbi who performed our wedding ceremony made mention of this propitious timing. In the Jewish tradition, we believe in a concept called *beshert,* which is literally translated as "predestined one." Before we are even born, our sages teach, God knows which two people should spend their lives together in holy matrimony. There is such a bond between these two souls that God has to use all of His strength just to keep them apart until the appropriate time for them to find each other. Standing under the marriage canopy, the rabbi told our gathered friends and family that it was like God pushing apart the waters of the Red Sea with all His might. Only when the time is right are the two brought together. Finding each other is not the hard part. It's waiting until the right time.

For nearly three decades of my life, God already knew that (odd as it may sound) the rabbi's son was going to marry the minister's daughter. And how perfect that match would be. Elizabeth was stronger in her new-found faith than I ever was. My wife came to Judaism not because she was forced to or merely because, like me, she was born into it. No, she chose it of her own volition.

Ironically, I found a minister's daughter who was the beacon of spiritual inspiration that I had been so desperately seeking. My religious cynicism finally had a worthy opponent.

As being Jewish was new to Elizabeth, I felt compelled to step up to the plate and perform each Jewish commandment with a renewed sense of verve and vigor, as if it was my first time as well. I didn't want to be the putz who screwed this up for her.

But my hopes of her conversion waters somehow inundating me as well weren't the best-laid plans. Yes, she was inspiring to be around. Yes, she brought a fresh outlook to my years of tired Jewish observance. I had finally found my soul mate, but something about me still felt empty.

Elizabeth and I got married in the very same synagogue in which I had my circumcision, the event that had originally tethered me unwittingly to this faith. And therein lay the inherent problem. I'd found a partner, but I was seemingly stuck in the very same place. My spiritual apathy today was just as strong as it had been back then on that fateful morning. I quite literally hadn't moved an inch.

As much as I wanted her to be, Elizabeth was not going to be the magic pill for my spiritual ails. I couldn't take two of her and call the rabbi in the morning. In Hebrew the book of Genesis describes Eve, the quintessential wife, as an *ezer knegdo,* which is literally translated as "helpmate opposite him." Elizabeth would be my Eve. She would assist me in my journey, in my search to find new meaning in Judaism.

But she alone could not solve all my problems. After all, she herself found inspiration outside her inherited religion; perhaps I would need to do the same. She peeked behind the curtain of a foreign religion to help reconnect her with the Almighty. I wasn't planning on converting, but maybe I needed to examine Christianity to see how it could make me a better Jew. For me to reach a renewed sense of faith in faith, I would have to follow her unusual path. She worked at it. She grasped Judaism and made it her own. She had chosen it. Yes, she would help me. Indeed, she would be my muse. But it was me who had to take that elusive first step.

THREE

Mission Impossible

God said to Abram, "Go for yourself from your land, from your relatives, and from your father's house to the land that I will show you."
—*Genesis 12:1*

LET'S SAY, FOR argument's sake, you're in a college philosophy class. Your professor has been on a kick lately about the concept of "what if" to get you and your classmates to start thinking outside the box. Stuff like what our world would be like had Al Gore become president in 2000. What it would be like to fly. What it would be like if you were a cartoon. You know, normal stuff like that.

Now, clearly delusional, he's given you an assignment that opens up the Pandora's box of all Pandora's boxes and asks you what it would be like if you started your own religion. What would your theology be? What laws would you mandate of your followers?

Ideas begin to bounce around the classroom. Someone gets the ball rolling and starts off with the basic monotheistic mantra—an invisible God, one who's all-knowing, all-powerful. Yada, yada, yada. We've heard this all before. Nothing new here. So much for this classroom discussion.

But then your classmate, the really sinister one, gets it going. Let's force our people to be really obsessive-compulsive. Make them tie their left shoelace before their right one. Make them wash their hands twice on the right and twice on the left anytime they eat a piece of bread. But not cookies. Or fruit. Just bread. Oh, and make them recite a specific blessing—in a foreign language—before they eat anything. And also when they're finished eating. And speaking of blessings, let's make them say one every time they see lightning. Hear thunder. Glimpse a rainbow. See a dwarf. Put on new clothing. Smell a spice. Cross a river. Yeah, and make them say a blessing every time they go to the bathroom.

This is getting interesting now.

Okay, enough with the blessings. How about for one day each week they can't shower. Or use any hot water. And for nine consecutive days each summer they can't do laundry. And one day a year they can't sit on a chair.

How about a Sabbath. Anyone got some ideas to throw around about their day of rest? Yeah, forget rest. Let's create so many intricate laws regarding the Sabbath that they'll just feel as if they're walking on eggshells the whole time. For starters, they can't use cars on their Sabbath. For twenty-four hours they just have to walk everywhere. And if it's raining, they can't carry umbrellas. Forget umbrellas. They can't carry *anything*. No umbrellas, no purses, no books, no strollers, nothing. Not even a key to their house. It'll be like they're homeless.

Okay, there's not much time left in class. Let's move on to prayers. Prayers can't be in English. How about ancient Hebrew? Sure, sounds good. Hey, can we throw some Aramaic in there too? Don't see why not.

Anyone else? In a moment of utter genius, you decide to make your people pray the exact same words each day of their entire life. No room for change. Every day, every week, every month, the prayers won't change. Same words. All the time.

Class is dismissed. You and your classmates do not, thank the Lord Almighty, possess special powers that allow you to create a bizarre "choose your own adventure" religion. But what if you did? What if it were all true? What if I told you this fake religion you just created, this faith-based *Dungeons and Dragons* alternate universe—it actually exists.

Look back at the last couple pages. Everything your philosophy class came up with? All Jewish laws. Let that sink in for a moment. Seriously. I know. It's scary. The thing about saying a blessing after going to the restroom? True. Oh, and that thing about tying your left shoe before your right one? Sadly, also true.

This is how Judaism appeared to me growing up. Just swap your philosophy classmates for a cadre of rabbis, my father being one of them. But everything else matches the doomsday scenario described above. All the myriad mind-numbing laws. A bunch of dos and don'ts. To be exact, 613. That's how many laws are delineated in the Five Books of Moses. There are

248 positive (do this) and 365 negative (don't do that) ones. And don't even get me started on the oral laws. Jewish tradition teaches us that in addition to the Old Testament God gave oral laws to Moses. These laws were eventually written down. The result? Twenty tractates of the Talmud with thousands of pages of esoteric discussions on laws relating to everything from menstrual blood to cattle ranching. In Aramaic.

Before we take this discussion any further, I should point out that not all Jews are crazy and law-obsessed. We don't all tie our left shoe before the right one. The worldwide Jewish community can basically be divided into three groups (they can obviously be subdivided into many more and entire books can be written about each one, but for the purposes of our conversation, three shall suffice). The strictest group, the ones who adhere to all of these laws, are known as Orthodox Jews. I had the good fortune of growing up in this denomination. Then there are the Conservative Jews, who follow some but not all of these laws. And, finally, there are Reform Jews, who consider themselves culturally Jewish but follow very few of the laws listed in this chapter. And then, of course, there are the majority of American Jews—those who are unaffiliated with any of these groups.

Everything we do in Judaism is ensconced in a long litany of laws. My childhood friend Chaim, now a Villanova law professor, is an expert on the intersection of law and religion. He recently published a paper that, among other things, compares theological and legal differences between Christianity and Judaism. At one point he compares baptism to the Jewish *mikvah,* a ritual bath we use for things like conversions, married women, and—I kid you not—new dishes.

In discussing baptisms he writes that Christian scholars mostly agree that "ritual technicalities should not interfere with the process of spiritual conversion; it's the conversion of the heart that matters most." But when it comes to talking about a *mikvah,* the rabbinic sages "address nearly every question that an imaginative lawyer might direct at a rule requiring immersion in a pool of water (what counts as *immersion,* what defines *in,* what qualifies as a *pool,* and what constitutes *water*)."

Read that last sentence again. Nowhere are the theological issues mentioned. Where's the spirituality?

Just for kicks, here's another example Chaim gives. When discussing the prohibition against cooking on the Sabbath, he explains: "What constitutes cooking? What is the minimum heat (of either the dish or the water) required for something to cook? How long must something be on the fire before it is considered 'cooked'? Is direct heat even needed? What about leaving an egg near a bubbling kettle or in the hot sun? Is defrosting something equivalent to cooking it? Is salting vegetables equivalent to preserving them and thus too similar to 'cooking'? And what is the scope of the prohibition? If A brings the fire, B brings the wood, C brings a pot, D fills it with water, E adds spices to the water, and F stirs the pot, are they all liable? (Yes.) Would the answer be different if the fire came at the end rather than the beginning? (Yes.) Does it matter if one is unaware that cooking is prohibited on the Sabbath? Or if the cooking is an inevitable, potential, or incidental by-product of some other action?" It's like one of those Russian nesting dolls, but this is worse. Every time you open one, there are *two* others inside. They metastasize in an absurd geometric progression.

Are you starting to get the idea? The Talmud is not discussing how to make the day of rest a more spiritually uplifting experience. On the contrary; its meandering questions instead ask us to compulsively obsess over every bit of minutiae. Ironically, figuring out what work we can and cannot do takes a lot of work, rendering this period of time anything but a day of rest. Of course, I'm not the first to make this connection. Freud, a Jew, who as a child regularly attended Catholic Mass with his Czech nanny, believed that religion was the "universal obsessional neurosis of humanity."

This is exactly how I felt growing up. As if I was in jail, imprisoned by a faith that favors deed over creed. Judaism is a religion in which actions trump faith. Checking lettuce for bugs (another weird Jewish law and a real party favorite) is just as important as belief in God. This type of religious conviction is completely anathema to most Christians. They *merely* want you to accept Christ. They don't care if you examine your salad before you eat it. (But it wouldn't hurt, since we actually do sometimes end up finding microscopic bugs in store-bought lettuce. Just an FYI.)

This conceit is evident in a Hebrew concept known as a *shayla*. The term is basically translated as "question," but it refers to a more specific type of question. When we ask a rabbi a question about Judaism, more often than not it's a legal question, not a theological one. For example, we're not allowed to mix meat and dairy food. To be extra careful, we keep two sets of dishes. Let's say I used a dairy spoon with a meat pot by accident. I need to ask the rabbi what to do with that spoon. Do I throw it away? Is there a way to make it "kosher" again? Most likely, he'll respond with a litany of follow-up questions. What was in the pot? How hot was it? When was the last time the spoon had been used? And so on. Compounding this problem is that asking a different rabbi will often garner you a different answer.

I'm not asking the rabbi, as a Catholic parishioner would a priest, how many Hail Marys I need to say in order to be forgiven for this transgression. That's not the point here. I'm asking a practical question. What the hell do I do with this spoon? I'll ask the obvious. What does this have to do with spirituality? Because once we go down this road, there's no natural place to stop. Forget the spoon. What about the pot? What about the food that was in the pot? What about the stove this tragic episode happened on?

In many ways, it's like trying to measure ever smaller units of distance. First you start in miles, then you go down to feet, then you go down to inches, then to centimeters and on to millimeters. There's no stopping. You can always divide something up one more time. There's always another layer of precision. So too there are volumes of Jewish case law, each one more refracted than the one before. Before you know it, you're talking about the social behavior and disposition of a theoretical ox.

Allow me to explain. Please.

Imagine this. I'm a kid playing ball with my friends, and I'm called inside to study the Talmud. It's a dense section about the laws of damaged property. If I had an ox (which I don't) and if I lent it to you (which I wouldn't) and during that time my ox gored you (which I don't think he would since he's such a fun-loving animal), am I liable for the damages? The Talmud dives into a difficult discussion on such a case. Has this ox ever gored before? If so, when? How often? What type of damages occurred? I didn't get it. Why would an eight-year-old boy have to learn about oxen? After a few hours of this, I was the one who wanted to damage some property.

Yet we were taught that studying this was the most important part of our religion. But this back-and-forth exercise in intellectual gymnastics seemed more like a law-school class than a theological discourse. And those who master the Talmud, out of all the other texts in the Jewish pantheon, are considered the most brilliant. I didn't understand how this had become the barometer of saintliness in my religion.

Maybe I'm crazy, but I thought religion had something to do with belief in God and being nice to your neighbor. I wasn't aware it had anything to do with oxen or pots or spoons, and even if it did, that those things would be of paramount import.

Why was this educational activity of studying an arcane Aramaic text like the Talmud so critical to being a good Jew? What kind of religion was this that worshiped minutiae over meaning?

Don't get me wrong. There are brilliance and beauty in this faith. I just haven't found them yet.

THERE IS ONE area of Judaism that is particularly troubling. Yes, the oxen rank up there, but they're not my ultimate summit. For me, that would be prayer.

Our sterile prayer services have literally hundreds of laws surrounding them—exactly when they can be said, when to sit, when to stand, what you need to be thinking about, what can be in the room with you, which direction to face, what to wear during prayers ... and the list goes on. Not following just one of these laws can negate the entire prayer you just recited—which means you've got to say it all over again. It takes years to learn all the laws. I should know. After a lifetime of saying these prayers, I've spent the last four years *relearning* them with my friend Joel during weekly study sessions. It's this nearly scientific approach that basically sucks all the spirituality and joy right out of conversing with God.

All of this perhaps explains why synagogue attendance is at an all-time low. There is nothing outwardly exciting or even enjoyable about this experience. Many Jews pay their synagogue dues, but only attend a few times a year. Merely paying for membership makes people feel good about themselves. In his book *Bowling Alone,* political scientist Robert Putnam makes note of this trend, decrying the decline of what he calls "social capital" in America. He writes, for example, of how senior citizens join the AARP but don't actually attend meetings; they merely pay a membership fee. To stem the tide, he suggests it's high time we reassert the human connections between us.

Nowhere is this more apparent to me than in houses of worship. Most American Jews only attend services twice a year, on Rosh Hashanah (the Day of Judgment) and Yom Kippur (the Day of Atonement), which are collectively referred to as the High Holidays. Meanwhile, church parking lots are filled to capacity every Sunday morning. I begin to wonder: What are they doing in there that's so much fun it's bringing people back week in and week out?

Instead of lifting my spirit up, instead of inspiring me to feel a closer connection to the divine, instead of making me feel that being a member of the chosen people is the ultimate blessing, my religion has been smothering me. Instead of Jewish pride, the cloistered environment I grew up in bred envy of those of other religions for what was being denied to me. How come they got to have it easy? How come they could eat at McDonald's and I was forced to eat *matzah,* the proverbial bread of affliction? Indeed, ever since I was a child, I've found that my eyes and spirit have been wandering across the street from my childhood home, to the packed parking lot of the Cokesbury Methodist Church—my snake, my apple, my Garden of Eden all wrapped into one.

But I never dared enter to see what actually went on in this Wonka factory of faith. Perhaps too scared or too guilt-ridden, I remain, as my religion has for millennia, the outsider.

My New York speed-dating spree, which lasted through most of my twenties, was a low point in reconciling my faith, but the real challenge was coming to terms with my future. I now had seemingly everything an Orthodox Jew like me covets. I had married Elizabeth, the beautiful blond daughter of a minister. She gave me unique first-class access to this Christian world I felt so deprived of. She even came with a doting evangelical grandmother who wanted to pay for my ticket to Israel for the Second Coming of Christ. By marrying Elizabeth I had hoped to quash the envy that had gnawed at me as a kid. But, alas, something was still missing. I needed to actually pry open the doors to the Wonka factory and go inside.

Recent polls show that 40 percent of Americans, more than in any other country, attend church regularly. In the United States more people pray to Jesus on Sunday than attend all the weekend sporting events combined. And here in the Bible Belt, where I've lived my entire life, a street corner is more likely to have a place of Christian worship than a Starbucks. In Atlanta, there are no fewer than fifteen megachurches with more than ten thousand congregants each, the most in the entire country. Go figure. Nationwide, congregations are ballooning, and pastors take over football stadiums to spread their message weekly, in multiple services, to as many as forty thousand in a weekend.

Meanwhile, synagogue attendance is flagging; for that matter, Judaism as a whole is struggling just to keep its followers interested. Studies indicate that Jewish philanthropists in this country spend more money on what's called "inreach" than any other cause—including that catchall cause, support for Israel. Fueling all of this is an alarming fact: 50 percent of Jews in America are now intermarrying into other faiths. The Jewish community in America is hemorrhaging; we're a dying breed. And, even though I had not intermarried, I wasn't doing much to help either. My spiritual malaise was not allowing me to embrace Judaism the way I knew I should.

So this is where I find myself: an Orthodox Jew looking for spiritual meaning in the American Bible Belt. If only I could spend a year immersing myself in Christianity. I would pray with a whole host of churches, celebrate their holidays, and enjoy their culture. I don't merely want to be the Jack Kerouac of religion, traversing the vast Bible Belt landscape in search of wild spiritual experiences. I'll embark on this journey because I want to know the true appeal of Christianity to Christians. What are they doing so right that we Jews are doing so wrong? Is their church experience simply more fun? Do they just have better PR? Or, as I suspect, is there something deeper going on? Mind you, I'm not looking to convert. I'm just in search of universal answers and common truths about the way we all experience faith in America.

And, as crazy as this sounds, I'm looking to Jesus to make me a better Jew. I want to reconnect to my Judaism. Throughout my childhood and even into early adulthood, I honestly did have moments of true spirituality. Like the day of my bar mitzvah. Graduating into Jewish manhood gave me a sense of pride and purpose that I didn't have the day before. Or my experiences in my dad's synagogue attached to our home. The prayers I prayed in that room were some of the most meaningful ones I've recited my entire life. I was always the last one finished. Nowadays, I can barely sit through the whole service. Back then, I actually felt as if I were talking to God—and He was listening.

But time has distanced me from those rare moments. As well, even as a child, I don't think I was ever taught the true meaning of being Jewish, and of religion in general. Yeah, I was taught to wear a skullcap and to follow the thousands of rules of being a good Jew. But I never understood my religion on a deeper level. This immaturity, this lack of understanding, led to a spiritual apathy that was troubling to me. All of my brothers had become rabbis. My older sister married one. I knew there was wisdom to all of this (after all, I was still a practicing Jew); I just needed to find a way to appreciate it.

I want to be a good Jew, but I fear I lack the necessary tools. And rather than go down the normal path—study the Torah, speak to a rabbi, watch a Mel Brooks movie—I will seek to find a renewed appreciation for my Judaism in the last place anyone would look: the hallowed halls of a church.

So I tell my new bride, still dripping from the conversion waters, that I want to go on a religious road trip through local churches of different denominations to finally see what is going on in them. I guess I half thought she would find the idea charming. After all, she had explored a religion outside the one she was born into. What would be so bad if I did the same? And another thing: She needn't worry that I might leave Judaism. I had no intention of doing any such thing. It had nothing to do with a newfound fondness for Christ, but as a means to an end. I know it sounds crazy, but it's true. I'm hoping to find something in a church that will reconnect me with my Judaism. Common sense be damned.

Well, this doesn't go as well as planned. I broach the subject with her, and she thinks I'm certifiably insane. Who would blame her? Here she had just spent half a dozen years working to convert to Judaism and now her dear husband wants to go to church.

I want to experience synagogue specifically and Judaism as a whole with the same virgin eyes that attracted Elizabeth to my religion. The only way for me to do this is to go to church, to taste the forbidden fruit. As the artist M. C. Escher once said, "Only those who attempt the absurd will achieve the impossible."

"Church is not as exciting as you think it's going to be," she tells me one night. "It can be just as boring as synagogue. I'm telling you, but if you want to see it for yourself, go right ahead. Knock yourself out." She says I can go on two conditions: I can't tell anyone I'm doing this and she won't go with me. It may not be a ringing endorsement, but it's the best I'm going to get from her.

But Elizabeth is only half the problem. Technically, Jews aren't allowed anywhere near a church, let alone inside during Sunday services. It's yet another Jewish law, one that I was taught over and over again as a child who lived across the street from a church. "Don't go over there. It's dangerous," I was told, as if Cokesbury Methodist was the home of a child predator or the haunted house of the neighborhood witch.

So I open my Rolodex and start calling all the rabbis I know. This is how my mind works. I am so frustrated with Judaism that I want to spend a year gallivanting through Jesus' house. Yet the one thing that's now stopping me from doing so is a seal of rabbinic approval. The irony of this doesn't faze me, and I keep dialing. Rabbi after lenient rabbi gives me the no-go, saying this is strictly prohibited. I want to grow spiritually, and here my religion is holding me back. This feeling is all too familiar.

I'm about to give up on my planned mission, my big out-of-the-box idea to reconnect with my Judaism by stepping foot in church. With nowhere else to turn, I ask a rabbi whom Elizabeth is close to and has known for many years. Surely he, of all people, will understand where I'm coming from. After all, he had helped Elizabeth understand Judaism when she was still a Christian.

Barely hesitating, the Orthodox rabbi surprises me and gives me his blessing. He lauds the idea and encourages me to go to as many churches as I can. As Jews we need to look beyond our peripheral vision, he tells me. There's much we can learn from other religions. As well, he says, I can help explain Judaism to and break down the myths and preconceived notions of those I meet along the way.

Like my wife, this rabbi also gives me two caveats. One, I must wear my press pass so that everyone who sees me knows that I am there to observe and not to pray. I'm a journalist for a Jewish publication, so that shouldn't be too hard. Second, he says, I must wear my skullcap so that people know I am Jewish. He wants me to stand out and not blend in with my fellow faith-based compatriots.

Armed with his rabbinic approval and riddled with Jewish guilt, I start to map out which churches I'm going to visit first. There are so many to choose from—Episcopalian, Baptist, Catholic, Pentecostal, and on and on. It's July now, and I'm going to give myself an entire year, a complete cycle of seasons and holidays, for this adventure. I not only want to finally see what has been denied to me all these years, but deep inside me I so want to feel spiritual again. I want to find God all over again. I want to own my religion and get out of this fog of faith.

As excited as I am to get started on this quest, I've got to admit that there's a part of me that's not itching to go. I'm scared. Growing up in a cloistered Jewish neighborhood and going to private Jewish schools, I always encountered Christians as the minority—the occasional science teacher, the teller at the bank, maybe a family friend. My parents had created an odd environment for me. In America, where Jews make up less than 2 percent of the entire population, I had been raised in a subculture that showed just the opposite—Jews were the majority and non-Jews were the minority. I didn't realize it at the time, but I was living in a *Twilight Zone* episode.

I was scared to venture out into this unknown territory. What if I wasn't welcomed at these churches? If centuries of Jewish persecution had taught me anything, it was that I should be wary when cavorting with Christians. I try to think of some common ground and the only thing I come up with is Jesus. They seem to like him, and he was once Jewish. So maybe I have a fighting chance.

Another scary thought: Religion has bred some pretty nasty folk over the years. Forget about Pharaoh, Nebuchadnezzar, and other villains throughout biblical history. I'm talking about modern-day whackos. Like David Koresh going down in a blaze of glory with his fellow Branch Davidians in Waco, Texas. Or the Jonestown cult members who gulped cyanide-laced Kool-Aid in a mass suicide. Come to think of it, people have done some pretty odd things in the name of religion. Maybe I'd have trouble coming out of this alive.

The bottom line is that I have no idea what to expect, and I don't like walking into places where I have no idea what to expect. It's like a perpetual first date. And nobody I know likes first dates. To be perfectly honest, I was kind of hoping no rabbi would even allow this venture to take place, thereby giving me the best excuse not to go church hopping.

But a rabbi did approve this pilgrimage. He may be punished in the afterlife for giving me the go-ahead, but I have no justification for dragging my feet any longer. My soul is yearning for something deeper, and I owe it to myself to start the process. Like the wide-eyed Don Quixote in search of adventure, I will leave my comfort zone and enter into uncharted territory.

My religion has come, some say tumbled, a long way from the Judaism of yesteryear. The Garden of Eden is overgrown with weeds and bitter fruit, its pristine paths trampled by decades of religious persecution and plain old fashioned apathy. We no longer live in a Polish village, and we certainly don't live in biblical times. Fiddler is no longer on the roof, and Moses has long since left the mountaintop. Even God, some say, has left the building.

Which is why the rabbi also said, "Come back and tell us what we can all learn from going to church, so we can make synagogue life better. It's important for Jews to know." He wanted me to be the skullcapped guinea pig, learning from the ways of our Christian neighbors. He recognized the usefulness of this journey for myself and others like me. As if my personal quest wasn't enough, here I am saddled with an extra burden—that of my entire people. Leave it to Judaism to pile on the extra work. But the rabbi was persistent. "Our people, they need you," he said in his best Jedi master impersonation.

So now it is my leap of faith into the unknown abyss of Christian life that will help bring my people back. At least that's what the rabbi wants. As for me, I just hope it will function as the antidote to my own spiritual ills.

So with my doubts, fears, and Orthodox Judaism in tow, off I go to church.

FOUR

Welcome to God's House

Take the anointing oil and anoint the Tabernacle and everything in it;
consecrate it and its furnishings, and it will be holy.
                                        —*Exodus 40:9*

THE NOISE IS thundering. The floor is shaking. My ears are pounding. It feels as if God is giving the commandments atop Sinai. Yet I couldn't be farther away from that holy mountain if I tried.

"Give me a 'Praise Jesus!'" the bishop screams into the mike.

"Praise Jesus!" the crowd shouts back in unison as they rise to their feet. The woman next to me, swaying to the blaring music, is smashing her hand against a tambourine she brought from home. The guy in front of me, I'm not quite sure why, is moaning and wildly flailing his arms in the air. It's like being at a rowdy rock concert—except for the undeniable fact that it is morning, the opening act is a heavyset black woman belting out Baptist hymns, and the main attraction is the Lord Almighty.

Here I am, a five-foot-two bespectacled Jewish kid, in a mosh pit of faith, in a sea of fifteen thousand roused African Americans at the New Birth megachurch in Lithonia, Georgia. It's Sunday, prime time for prayer, and I am just trying to blend in, hoping I won't stand out too much.

Just as such hopeful—and unfortunately fleeting—thoughts are swirling through my mind, one of a dozen camera operators focuses on me. And before I know it, there I am, my face twenty feet tall on the two screens hanging from the ceiling in front of the amphitheater. My Jewish face on Jesus' JumboTron for all to see.

Oh, God, forgive me.

After Catholics, Baptists are the second-largest Christian denomination in America with nearly fifty million members and growing. And they have more churches—thirty-seven thousand—than the Catholics. Today I'm at one of them.

I figure if you're suddenly going to church after thirty years of attending synagogue, you might as well jump head first into the deep end. New Birth Missionary Baptist Church, in Lithonia, Georgia, boasts more than thirty thousand members, which makes it one of the largest megachurches in the nation. At Easter, so many people are in attendance that services have to take place at the Georgia Dome, where the Atlanta Falcons normally play to sell-out crowds of seventy thousand fans. The church is more than just a house of worship and is widely recognized for its charitable work, including paying off the debt of several congregant families (the church has even opened its own bank), tutoring students, leading parishioners in massive weight-loss programs, and even giving away cars to single mothers. Sounds like a reality TV show. Or Oprah.

And now the gospel of New Birth has spread beyond Georgia's borders. No fewer than eight other New Births have been founded in places like Tennessee and California. Those without a New Birth nearby need not worry. Services are broadcast not once, but six times throughout the week on various cable outlets. The church has an international reach through radio broadcasts, books it publishes, and streaming services on its Web site.

Pulling into the parking lot, I realize this place is like a small city. The campus contains several buildings. The parking lot alone is the size of several football fields. That's in addition to the *actual* football field next to the parking lot. People are being bused in. Those who drive their own cars have New Birth flags hanging from their antennas.

This is the type of church I dreamed of before embarking on this journey. Congregants as far as the eye could see. I'm not really sure how the concept of "strength in numbers" first came into play with regard to worship. On the one hand, this seems completely foreign to me—synagogues are infamous for having breakaway factions, and Jewish neighborhoods are littered with the synagogues some won't attend. There's a classic Jewish joke. A man is found on a deserted island, and the rescue team sees that he has built for himself two synagogues. When asked why, the stranded man replies, "One is the synagogue I regularly attend. The other is the one I'd never step foot into."

So tiny synagogues dot the landscape. Part of what's intriguing to me about Christianity is the megachurch trend. According to a 2006 Hartford Seminary study, 49 percent of the nation's megachurches are located in the South, on my own home turf. And a 2005 survey found that there were 1,210 megachurches in America, more than double what there were just five years earlier. Why would someone want to pray among thousands? Isn't it easier to connect with God in solitude?

No one can say for sure where the first megachurch started. For all intents and purposes I guess you could call Mt. Sinai the world's very first megachurch. Think about it. By some estimates, there were at least three million people there when Moses received the Ten Commandments, all gathered together to worship the Almighty. And God revealed Himself. It must've been one helluva service. All they were missing were some ushers and massive LCD screens to broadcast the prayers on.

But if you don't buy into my Sinai theory, then you have to wait until the nineteenth century, when you can give props to a British preacher by the name of Charles Haddon Spurgeon. This guy's nickname was the "Prince of Preachers," so you know he was good. He was prolific, to say the least. His sermons were published weekly and, by the end of his life, he had preached more than thirty-six hundred sermons and written forty-nine volumes of religious works. Even back then, megachurch statistics were mind-blowing.

This guy was the Rick Warren of his day. Warren, the founding father of modern-day megachurches and ministries, owes a debt of gratitude to Spurgeon. Warren's Saddleback Church, just outside Los Angeles, attracts more than twenty thousand people weekly and has paved the way for other American megachurches. According to *Outreach Magazine,* it is the fourth-largest church in America. (New Birth Church is number thirteen.) You may also know Warren for a little devotional book he wrote called *The Purpose Driven Life*. It's been translated into more than fifty languages and was the best-selling book in the entire world for three years in a row. And it's the best-selling hardback nonfiction book in American history. Those are numbers of biblical proportions.

As for Spurgeon, he frequently preached to five thousand people on any given Sunday. Some put that number closer to ten thousand. Either figure indicates a megachurch by any standard. The pinnacle of his preaching career came in October 1857, when Spurgeon supposedly preached to 23,654 people at the famed Crystal Palace in London.

Spurgeon died in 1892 due to a ridiculously unhealthy combination of rheumatism, gout, and something called Bright's disease. But his legacy lives on. He founded a theological seminary called Spurgeon's College and an orphanage, both of which still exist today. A collection of his hand-written notes is, for reasons beyond my comprehension, on display in the backwoods of Birmingham, Alabama.

If Spurgeon holds the title of the megachurch's Big Daddy, its matri-arch was most certainly Sister Aimee Semple McPherson. When the char-ismatic Pentecostal began preaching around 1915, her tent revivals often had standing-room-only crowds of thirty thousand. Legend has it that the National Guard was once called in to help with crowd control.

At first an itinerant preacher, Sister Aimee eventually settled in Los Angeles and built America's first megachurch—the Angelus Temple. The sanctuary could seat more than five thousand and reportedly had packed services three times a day, seven days a week. As if that wasn't enough, she also created her own denomination, the International Church of the Four-square Gospel.

Indicative of the eventual merging of media and megachurches to come, Sister Aimee started her own weekly newspaper called the *Foursquare Crusader* and a monthly magazine named *Bible Call*. In 1924, she became the first woman in U.S. history to purchase a license from the FCC for her own radio station. She used it to broadcast her sermons to an even wider audience.

Despite the fact that she was the mother of the megachurch, history had another footnote in mind for Sister Aimee's bio. She is perhaps most widely known for allegedly being abducted near Venice Beach in the spring of 1926. Most people assumed she had drowned, others thought she was kidnapped, and some believed she had orchestrated the perfect disappearing act. Indeed, a male colleague who was reportedly romantically involved with Sister Aimee coincidentally also vanished around the same time, and many conspiracy the-orists believed the two had run off together. This was huge news in the 1920s. It was the O.J. trial of its day, sparking intense media coverage for weeks not just in Los Angeles, but throughout the country.

About a month after she disappeared, Sister Aimee miraculously re-emerged from a Mexican desert claiming she had been kidnapped and bru-tally tortured. There were many holes in her abduction story—an immense lack of evidence about everything she claimed—and, indeed, many people say they saw Sister Aimee and her lover at a number of hotels during her monthlong absence.

So she may have faked her own disappearance. C'mon, who hasn't done that—or at least wanted to? But her work in the megachurch world is legendary. Without her we wouldn't have the likes of Joel Osteen, a pastor who bought for his church the forty thousand–seat arena where the Houston Rockets played professional basketball. Sister Aimee gave birth to scores of megachurches across America, including the one that I'm at today.

INSIDE THE SANCTUARY, I settle into my seat. "Let's give a big New Birth welcome to our Jewish friend Benyamin Cohen," the bishop shouts to the crowd. It's the first time I can recall being introduced as the "Jewish" Benyamin Cohen.

I'm trying to keep a low profile, but my co-worker Rita (a deacon in training here) had given the church a heads-up about the Jewish journeyman who would be joining them today. (I guess as a dorky white boy it wasn't much of a challenge to draw some attention to myself.)

Not quite sure what to do, I smile sheepishly and wave my hand to the thousands seated in the amphitheater-style seats around me. Before I know it, a dozen people are giving me hugs. "Bless you, brother, bless you," they say as they bridge the gap (a little too close and a little too tight) between two disparate religions.

My appearance apparently ignites another frenzy, as the music suddenly goes into overdrive. Two women perform an African dance in front of the hundred-person choir. I feel as though I'm at a Broadway performance of *The Lion King.* The Hebrew words *Bruchim habaim,* which mean "Blessed are those who visit," flash on the big screens. I'm a celebrity. Me and the Big Man. I'm going to hell for this.

Not whooping and hollering like those around me, I seem to be the only one among the fifteen thousand faithful not breaking into a sweat. People are literally jumping out of their seats, racked with divine spasms. Blue spotlights dance around the room as at a rock concert. I half expect to see people holding up lighters.

Behind the choir is quite possibly the largest gold cross I've ever seen. Positioned with the New Birth crest, it looks more like the world's most religious hood ornament.

A dozen uniform-clad members of the film crew, one of which is atop a crane shooting sweeping vista angles, are zooming in on praiseful congregants to display on the large screens. It's not hard to find those worshipers. I sneak out to use the restroom and don't miss a single bit of the action—the audio of the service is being pumped in through overhead bathroom speakers. Jesus in the john. Just what I need.

I'm in a state of utter shock at the moment. No, not because the service is broadcast in the bathroom. Although, I have to admit I find that a little odd considering doing anything religious in a restroom is strictly prohibited in Judaism. We're even taught to remove our prayer shawls before using the loo.

The prayers in the potty notwithstanding, I am in awe of my surroundings. All I can think is, "My God, I'm finally in church." This moment in time was three decades in the making. My entire life I had looked longingly at the church across the street. I always wanted to reach out and grasp a small piece of its Christianity just to see what everyone was talking about. I wanted to enter a church's doors and see the magic of what happened inside. I was so close and yet at the same time so very far away.

But now I am finally here, my feet firmly planted on Christian soil. I had dreamed of this moment for as long as I could remember. This was my spiritual summit. That being said, how in the world can the actuality live up to all the hype?

This whole experience is at once everything I hoped for and nothing like I expected. With the choir, the dancing, and the jamming, this is indeed the lively service I had been longing for. This is what had mesmerized me on the faith-based television stations that broadcast Sunday morning services. There was passion here, something I felt was lacking with my own prayers. My wildest faith fantasy could not have painted a more vivid picture than this.

Yet there is something gnawing away at me (beside the obvious fact that I am severely outnumbered). This singing-and-dancing light show in no way, shape, or form resembles anything roughly related to religious practice for me. To be perfectly honest, my idea of connecting with God bears little resemblance to services with tambourines and television screens. In some ways, this felt more like a concert performance than a religious service. I was brought up on a prayer diet of soft mumblings in a quiet contemplative service—in Hebrew—three times a day. A once-a-week jubilant celebration of these proportions is completely foreign to me. I realize now that I can look forward to a year full of such dissonant experiences.

The monumental scale of all this is jaw-dropping for a Jewish guy like me. The minimum number required for prayer at synagogue is ten people. So there are literally thousands of what we call *shteibels* that have cropped up in our communities around the world. They're mini-synagogues that are bare bones—a few folding chairs, some prayer books, and a Torah scroll. These *shteibels* can be in a hole in the wall—and often are. They're in basements and back rooms across America. I remember taking a high-school field trip to New York City and visiting the diamond district, a workplace haven for many Chassidic Jews. It was time for the afternoon prayer service and, like members of a secret society, we were ushered down a passageway that led to a small room. It may have been the break room or someone's office. I don't recall. But every day at this time, it turned into a mini-synagogue. There were no signs or demarcations. It was just there, and people who wanted to attend knew its location. Sort of like the synagogue attached to the dining room of my childhood home.

It's quite rare to find a synagogue with more than two thousand members. The synagogue I attend has about eight hundred, and that's considered large by Jewish standards. And those that do have more members only see full attendance on special occasions, not on a weekly basis as at New Birth.

The one place you would likely find tens of thousands of Jews gathered in one location is Madison Square Garden. Allow me to explain—for your benefit as well as for any neo-Nazis or KKK Grand Dragons who may be reading this chapter looking for a good potential target. Some Jews have a custom of studying a page of Talmud every day. But not just any page. Everyone starts with the same page and works through the entire Talmud together. Since the Talmud is ridiculously complex (possibly because it's in Aramaic, possibly because it's written cryptically, and possibly both), communities around the globe offer daily classes to study the page of the day. And for those who can't make it, there are daily-page podcasts you can download from the Internet. At this page-a-day rate, it takes seven years and five months to complete the Talmud. But when we do complete the cycle, there's a party that's been seven years in the making.

Jews in the New York area rent Madison Square Garden for this celebration, at which they read the final lines of the Talmud in unison and pray together. Even some not in the tristate area fly in for this event. The last time this event was held, in 2005, the seats at Madison Square Garden sold out so quickly the organizers had to also rent the nearby Continental Airlines Arena in New Jersey.

BACK AT NEW Birth, the woman with the tambourine next to me leans in to ask what brings me here today. In her fifties, she's dressed in a bright orange pantsuit and has closely cropped silver hair. I tell her that I've come to learn, and her face lights up. Christians, unlike Jews, are proselytizers and are eager to educate the uninitiated. She takes this as her cue to be my play-by-play commentator for the next three hours, explaining with unabashed enthusiasm each step of the service—the music, the fire-and-brimstone sermon, the next round of music. It's all so overwhelming.

It's time for the collection, and ushers pass me a few envelopes. A green one is marked "King's Offering." I'm not really sure what that is and, more specifically, which king it refers to. I guess it means Jesus, but don't Christians refer to him as the King of Kings? So who is this other king? Does New Birth have its own king? Is that like an administrative position? Whomever it's referring to, I don't want to skimp on my gift to him (or her). On the other hand, a purple envelope is marked "Love Offering." If I don't give a lot to that, will the church think I don't care for Christians? A blue envelope is simply marked "Together We Can," which totally throws me for a loop. Together we can what? This is all too confusing for me. I should've asked Rita these questions beforehand. But how was I supposed to know what to expect? I had just assumed a collection plate would be passed and I could throw a dollar or two in it. This is more like playing a spiritual stock market.

I recently read a news story about a church in Augusta, Georgia, that installed ATMs in its lobby. These units, cleverly dubbed Automatic Tithing Machines, allow the congregants to make contributions with a credit or debit card. Users can choose which church funds they want the money to go to, have a receipt printed out, and even get a confirmation e-mail. The congregants can do all of this privately and without multicolored envelopes. Sounds like a good idea to me.

(I wasn't sure where I had read this, so I went online later and found the original article. It's from the *Los Angeles Times*. Besides the ATMs for

Jesus, the article—which ironically quotes a critic of the kiosks as saying, "They're not kosher"—also discusses other ways this church is innovative, including holding a fellowship breakfast where the congregants discussed the "spiritual wages of lunching at Hooters." Note to self: Find out what really goes on at Hooters.)

After a couple hours of singing and preaching at New Birth, I have more than enough for my first day living as a Christian. I'm told a typical service here can last four hours. That seems excessive. I'm not quite sure why. Our Sabbath service at synagogue can easily go four hours. I guess I just thought this whole church thing was going to be easier.

I tell tambourine woman I'll be back more during the course of the next year and quietly attempt to sneak out as best I can.

I walk out past the gift shop packed with patrons buying Bibles, DVDs, and New Birth bling. I pick up some brochures, including one for Samson's Health and Fitness Center, located on the New Birth campus. Next to the logo of the biblical Samson tearing down two pillars with his bare hands is a photo of New Birth's Bishop Eddie Long in a muscle shirt lifting weights. He can pull it off. No disrespect to my Jewish sages, but that image, with Long's bulging biceps, is no match for a picture of my synagogue's rabbi. If this isn't a metaphor for Christian strength I don't know what is. Bishop Long could take down my weak, asthmatic Jewish body in a heartbeat.

At the gift shop, a visiting clergy member who traveled from Colorado just to be here this morning buys a gift basket and other goodies to bring back home. As a first-timer, I'm given a complimentary "Welcome CD" in slick packaging. Not a bad gimmick. It dawns on me that we don't have anything like this in Judaism. Maybe we should consider some multimedia visitors' packets. We can learn from the way churches reach out to new-comers. Heck, I even got preferential treatment in the parking lot—there was a spot labeled "First-Time Visitor" right next to the handicap spaces.

Why don't synagogues offer a goody bag of multimedia swag to take home with you on the way out? Hands down, Christians do a bang-up job at branding their religion, but we Jews—well, not so much. Supposedly we run the media, and yet we can't cough up a gift basket and a take-home CD? And the common excuse we give—well, Christians have more finan-cial resources—simply doesn't fly. Jews, per capita, are one of the wealthi-est populations in this country. Last I checked, the Rockefellers were all circumcised.

There is much we Jews can learn from our Christian brethren about mass-marketing our message. They are masters of outreach. Yeah, I know, we're not a proselytizing faith, but we do need to minister to those in our flock who have long left the spiritual path. Judaism, at its finest, is a bountiful and vibrant religion. Even a cynic like me knows that. Yet most younger Jewish Americans opt for the path of least resistance: a Friday-night bacon cheeseburger with their non-Jewish live-in girlfriend Christina Mary.

And we only have ourselves to blame. Some Jews' sole experience of Judaism, confined to the synagogue Sunday school classroom, gave only the guilt without the joy. They got only a watered-down version of a millennia-old tradition, and that resulted in some random combination of watching comedian Jackie Mason, whining, "Oy vey," and eating a deli sandwich on rye bread.

At New Birth, on the other hand, the Lord's spirit (in both the gift shop and the sanctuary) practically hypnotizes the audience into rapture.

New Birth is not *all* fun and light shows, of course. There are dozens of kids running in the halls, congregants streaming in late, and, I'm sure, plenty of participants who are merely going through the motions. Yet most of the people here are spiritual, and this is certainly a religious experience for them. Compared to the somewhat lackluster activity at Jewish services, the congregants at New Birth are doing something in their services, at least I can say that much.

The grand scale of the services may not be my cup of tea, but they seem to be serving a purpose. New Birth, for example, has recently branched out and started a Hispanic ministry—just one of the ways it is succeeding in reaching out to the many Baptists who are being underserved. Its services are indeed representative of strength in numbers.

I think it's kind of apropos that the first church I went to is called New Birth, because for me this was only the beginning.

FIVE

Pray Ball

You built a mound for yourself and made a lofty shrine in every public square.

—Ezekiel 16:24

I've only been a pseudo-Christian for a week, and already I have a confession to make. Is that a normal time frame? I'm sure everyone sins, but seven days after taking this yoke upon myself seems a little quick even for me. What is it with us Jews witnessing something spiritual and then sinning so shortly thereafter? How many days after miraculously crossing the Red Sea did my ancestors start complaining about the desert conditions? Pharaoh's henchmen drowned in the ocean, and no more than five Bible verses later the Jewish people started getting irritable.

In light of my ancestors' display of diva behavior of biblical proportions, my infraction doesn't seem so bad. So here's my confession. Going to New Birth was not exactly my first encounter with Jesus. I know I shouldn't have lied, and I'm sure that makes me an immoral and unethical person, but doesn't religion teach forgiveness?

It's not as though I had been to church before, however. That part was completely true. Okay, come to think of it, that part isn't technically true either. For a small period of time (maybe just for a few weeks) my mother attended an aerobics class held in a church auditorium. Even as an eight-year-old kid I had a desire to go to church. I pretended to be sick so I could skip school and hang out with her that day in the church. It ended up not being such a profound experience. I went and colored in my coloring book on a nearby bench. At the end of the day, it was just a plain old-fashioned auditorium. No sign of Jesus anywhere. I'm not really sure what I was expecting—the Son of God leading his twelve apostles in some Jazzercise? Bishop Eddie Long in a muscle shirt?

Okay, so my confession is that I had actually sort of started this journey a year ago, but it was only for a day. I swear. Can Christians swear? You see, last summer I went to the Christian Book Association's annual international conference, which attracts more than thirty thousand faithful. And, in my defense, I didn't go looking for a spiritual epiphany. I went as a journalist and at the invitation of—get this—a group of rabbis.

I didn't quite realize just how big the Christian publishing world was. Of course, I had driven past the Christian bookstore next to my dry cleaners, but I just assumed it was like our Judaica shops—some books, some artwork, some jewelry, and the usual religious knick-knacks. I even thought I was enlightened, since I had heard of the best-selling *Left Behind* series of Christian books, which paints a grim picture of a post-Rapture apocalypse and has sold more than sixty-five million copies. Although the film adaptations, which star 1980s *Growing Pains* stud Kirk Cameron as a journalist who tries to save Jewish souls, didn't fare as well. But Cameron needn't worry. His journey from sitcom to saved has been quite lucrative for him. His "Way of the Master Ministries" is a small media empire with books, speaking engagements, a radio show, DVDs, and an evangelical television show that's seen in seventy countries. Even *Growing Pains* isn't seen that far and wide.

Anyway, the Christian book market is huge, and it's more than just the *Left Behind* series, encompassing Bible-based diet books (*More of Jesus, Less of Me*), children's books (*God, Should I Be Baptized?*), and even romance novels (*A Fair to Remember*). According to a 2006 study by the Book Industry Study Group, although religious books only make up about 6 percent of the general market, their sales grew nearly twice as fast as secular books (a trend I hope translates to spiritual memoirs like the one you're currently reading). The folks here at the CBA convention say that Christian book and gift sales reached $4.6 billion in 2005; that's a half billion more than in 2000.

In a world where Christian pop culture is so mainstream that we often don't even know that the product we're looking at has religious overtones, it was heartening to see a fellowship of Jews coming to learn the craft, to see how they could improve Jewish products. Some rabbis who work for a

Jewish publishing company called Artscroll, and I've got to pat them on the back for this, were crossing over to the other side for some creative marketing ideas they could apply to their own books. And they asked me to tag along. I was floored by what I saw.

First, the sheer size. Imagine three football fields bursting with ministores full of new products. The floor was divided into three basic areas—music, books, and paraphernalia. It would literally take several days to look through everything. The registration area alone was the size of an airport terminal. There was so much going on—lectures, book signings, and product showcases—that the organizers had to print a daily magazine just to keep everyone abreast of the goings-on at the convention. And among the thousands of convention-goers, a handful of us men in yarmulkes stood out.

But, beside the sheer magnitude of it all, what was more intriguing was the mainstreaming of Christian pop culture. Located in the center of the convention floor was the Time Warner island, aptly titled "Warner Faith." A shrine to everything Christian, the area touted the company's latest books—hundreds of them, all titles you would find in your nearby Barnes & Noble.

In other areas there were rock bands, cartoon shows, and Stephen Baldwin DVDs. Yes, Stephen Baldwin. Of all the Baldwin brothers, he's the one who has become a hard-core Christian evangelist. I learned this from meandering by a booth at the convention hall that was screening a new action film starring Baldwin called *Six: The Mark Unleashed,* which is actually a modern-day prison retelling of the book of Revelation. Keep in mind we're talking about a guy who has starred in movies with less than holy names like *Sex Monster* and *Threesome.*

But you've got to give this guy some credit. Becoming a born-again has completely changed Stephen Baldwin's life. He's started his own skate punk ministry (although I'm not really sure what that means), has become a cultural adviser to President Bush, and wrote a 2006 memoir about becoming a born-again called *The Unusual Suspect,* an obvious play on the name of the one movie he's actually famous for appearing in. His hard-core fundamentalism is simple: Accept Jesus or you won't get into heaven. This is a guy who's ridiculed in the press, a guy who appeared on *Celebrity Mole* twice, yet his book actually made it onto best-seller lists. That's a testament if I've ever heard one.

Someone was promoting ThySpace.com, supposedly God's answer to MySpace. Another table had board games like Scattergories: Bible Edition. At the Scripture Candy booth, I spotted some faith pops and prayer jelly beans. Signs for Christian singles cruises vied for space with Bible software posters. Walking among the aisles upon aisles of Christian toys—Noah's pals collectible animals, Heavenly Harmony Karaoke, a Tower of Babel pop-up book, Bible puppet and trading cards, Almighty Heroes dolls featuring the beefy men of my Old Testament—felt more like a visit to the Disney store.

And that comparison extended into the animated-film genre. One of the major attractions at this convention was the VeggieTales area, where the line to take pictures with Larry the Cucumber and Bob the Tomato snaked around the convention hall floor. For those of you who have yet to be exposed to the phenomenon that is VeggieTales, allow me a brief sidebar. They're Pixar-quality animations, produced by a company called Big Idea, with moral lessons for children hidden (sometimes a little too obviously) within the story line. They include cartoons like *Minnesota Cuke and the Search for Samson's Hairbrush,* a story about dealing with bullies disguised as an Indiana Jones parody. Their slogan is "Sunday morning values, Saturday morning fun."

The company's bread and butter is adapting biblical episodes into cartoons featuring CGI vegetables—yes, vegetables—portraying the main characters. *Dave and the Giant Pickle,* for example, tells the story of David and Goliath. *The Wonderful Wizard of Ha's* is a takeoff of the biblical parable of the prodigal son starring an asparagus with bug eyes. Since the first video came out in 1993, more than fifty million copies have been sold.

Back in 2002 the company released its vegetable version of the Jonah story and in 2008 a pirate-themed flick as full-length feature films in theaters across America. The cartoons are now shown weekly on many NBC stations. (Interestingly, in an attempt to remain religiously neutral, the network first had all references to God edited out of the broadcasts, but eventually responded to public outcry and stopped leaving the Lord Almighty on the cutting-room floor.) The cartoons are only the beginning of this veggie empire. There are video games, plush toys, cell-phone ring tones, books, apparel, snow globes, mugs, nightlights, mouse pads, posters, dinnerware, and of course the obvious tie-in, vegetable seeds. There is even a VeggieTales amusement park ride at Dollywood.

I actually watched a DVD of theirs called *Esther: The Girl Who Would Become Queen*. I did this for anthropological reasons (after all, Esther is part of the Hebrew Bible) and not because I still enjoy watching cartoons. The story of how Esther helped save the Jewish people from utter annihilation is the basis for our holiday of Purim. So, for all intents and purposes, any cartoon about Esther would have to be a Jewish one.

But Jews don't produce good cartoons and, well, Christians do. And Christians, as I've found out, are fascinated with the Esther story. I'm not exactly sure why. The people I've asked say it's simply because she's one of the few female heroines in the Bible and she makes a great role model for girls everywhere. This makes perfect sense if little girls are taught only a very broad overview of the story. But if they dig any deeper, they'll find out that Esther was betrothed to a man not of her faith who was much older than she was and whom she really didn't love. Not to mention that Martin Luther, the father of Protestantism, once referred to the book of Esther as filled with "heathen corruption" and "bloodthirsty, vengeful, murderous greed." Not your typical cartoon fare. Although I should point out that the VeggieTales version of the Esther epic isn't nearly as dark. In the original Haman tries to commit genocide against the Jewish people; here he's merely trying to send Esther's family (no race or creed mentioned) to the Island of Perpetual Tickling.

And yet Esther is venerated throughout Christianity. She's remembered on the Lutheran calendar of saints. Françoise d'Aubigné, the sometimes Catholic, sometimes Protestant wife of King Louis XIV of France, commissioned a playwright to pen a tragedy called *Esther*. Handel later composed a classical piece based on that *Esther* play. In modern times, Christian families are naming their daughters Esther as if it were the new Britney or Christina. A woman with the unlikely name of Queen Esther Marrow is a famous church singer who has a musical compilation with the Harlem Gospel Choir. In 2006, a Christian film company released *One Night with the King,* a soap-opera rendition of the biblical Esther tale based on a novel by a Pentecostal preacher. To be honest, I'm not so sure I like the whole industrial Christian entertainment complex usurping Esther for its own purposes.

I STOPPED BY a booth for a Christian apparel company called Living Epistles, which was hawking irreverent T-shirts that looked as if they were being sold at a rock concert. Call it "Fashion of the Christ" wear. In a distressed font, one shirt touted the "Lord's Gym" and featured Jesus struggling to lift up the cross. The catchphrase? "Bench-press this." After all, what modern-day movement wouldn't be complete without some ironic, hipster T-shirts? I have a theory and it goes something like this: Christians do it better. I'm thinking about putting it on a T-shirt.

Although T-shirts may not seem like the benchmark for a successful enterprise, studies have shown that the mass-market commercialization of religion is working. Its tactics are actually helping bring people back into the fold. A 2004 article in the *New York Times* entitled "Christian Cool and the Generation Gap" had this to say:

> "My generation is discontent with dead religion," said Cameron Strang, 28, founder of Relevant Media, which produces Christian books, a Web site and *Relevant* magazine, a stylish 70,000-circulation bimonthly that addresses topics like body piercing, celibacy, extreme prayer, punk rock and God.
>
> "We don't want to show up on Sunday, sing two hymns, hear a sermon and go home," Mr. Strang said. "The Bible says we're supposed to die for this thing. If I'm going to do that, this has to be worth something. Our generation wants a tangible experience of God who is there."

I could relate to this guy. We're from the same generation and want similar things for our respective religions. He wants Generation X (and Y) to be crazy for Christ, and I want my people to be jazzed about Judaism. There were semantic (and Semitic) differences, but the overarching concept remains the same. Since reading that article, I've subscribed to Strang's *Relevant* magazine. It's fascinating reading, and I highly recommend it to any who want to learn how to spread the gospel of their religion to a younger audience.

Christians aren't the only ones hopping on the pop-culture bandwagon. Even us Jews are getting in on the action, although I'm not sure at what expense. Our parents may have grown up in the dark shadow of the Holocaust, but my generation is quite unfamiliar with that world of rampant anti-Semitism. We live in a country that welcomes us with open arms and, like no other time in history, we are not only being told it's okay to be Jewish but—be still, my heart—that it's actually *cool*.

This until recently unfathomable trend can be seen in the rash of Jewish content flooding mainstream media. It seems you can't turn the TV channel these days without hearing a Jewish reference. On *Boston Legal, Saturday Night Live, Curb Your Enthusiasm*. Or on reruns of *Friends, Seinfeld,* and *Sex and the City*. It's suddenly hip to be Heeb (which, by the way, is a name of a hipster Jewish magazine now on newsstands).

Nowhere is this more culturally relevant than on *The Daily Show with Jon Stewart*. Not an episode goes by in which the sardonic and quick-witted host doesn't reference his Jewishness—in a good way. This is an important show considering that, according to the Pew Research Center, more male viewers aged eighteen to thirty-four get their news from *The Daily Show* than from any of the network evening news shows. The fake news program, which frequently tops its late-night competitors *Leno* and *Letterman* among the coveted eighteen-to-twenty-four demographic group, is sending a clarion call to college-aged Jews everywhere: Stay in Hebrew school. It's cool.

This new Jew cool transcends television. In 2001, pop-folk duo and then MTV staple Evan and Jaron told Jay Leno that they have a "Sabbath clause" in all their contracts that exempts them from working on the Jewish holy day. Screaming teenage Jewish girls could be seen lighting Friday-night candles all across our fair land.

A new novelty beer came on the market called "He'Brew." And even something as materialistic as Jewish fashion is getting a much-needed makeover. Call it *Queer Eye for the Rabbi*. For years, Jewish fashion meant nothing more than Star of David necklaces and head coverings in synagogue. But now, T-shirts are coming out with phrases like "Jews for Jeter" and the *Jerry Maguire*–inspired "You had me at Shalom" printed on their fronts. There are even baseball hats with "Naughty Jewish Girl" and hot pink thongs with the word "Jewcy" emblazoned across them.

Even non-Jews are getting in on the act. Perhaps the most iconic example of the new Jew cool comes from the perennial purveyor of all things pop, Madonna. The once-staunch Catholic now follows the ways of the cultlike Kabbalah Centre, donating millions to the Jewish mystical group. She has given herself a Hebrew name (Esther, of course), written Kabbalah-themed children's books, and, perhaps most important, single-handedly brought an archaic and practically obsolete Jewish discipline into the public's consciousness. Not bad for a woman whose main contribution to society before this was a song called "Like a Virgin" and a coffee-table book about sex.

Speaking of raunchy coffee-table books, actor Leonard Nimoy (a.k.a. Spock from *Star Trek*) came out in 2002 with a book of photographs of nude women wearing Jewish paraphernalia. I had the opportunity to interview Nimoy during his fifteen-city book tour. "The book has awakened my own new interest in spirituality and given me a new pathway into it," the Jewish actor confided in me. "I've been doing more reading, more research, more studying and have gotten more out of my own spirituality by working on the book." Even this Vulcan was reconnecting with his faith.

A year later, in 2003, a movie came out called *The Hebrew Hammer,* starring actor Adam Goldberg as a Jewish Austin Powers–like superhero who fights Santa's evil son Damien Claus (played by the inimitable Andy Dick) and saves the holiday of Chanukah. It's a preposterous premise and the movie, obviously, doesn't take itself too seriously. It was all in good fun and was dubbed the first Jewsploitation flick. The film's writer/director, Jonathan Kesselman, tells me a sequel is now in the works in which the Hebrew Hammer and his partner in crime, Mohammed Ali Paula Abdul Rahim, must chase Hitler through time and prevent him from rewriting the Jews out of history. Val Kilmer is in talks to play Hitler.

Around the time of the original film's release, just about every publication in the greater New York area jumped on the same bandwagon and discussed this new "Jew cool" concept. As a young Jewish journalist, I was often asked to comment on this new phenomenon. And each time I said the same thing. "T-shirts and beer are great and they may get unaffiliated Jews in the front door. But then what? Is this just another fad? Will watching *The Hebrew Hammer* inspire them to raise good Jewish children? Will eating stereotypically Jewish food like bagels and lox make them more Jewish? If we want to keep these people interested, we've got to offer them something more meaningful than a cult movie or a gastronomic experience."

Looking back, who was I to make such a comment? Yeah, I cared about Judaism. But I was feeling just as disenfranchised as they were. I was just mad that they were attempting to reconnect by wearing a T-shirt proclaiming "Jon Stewart for President." And perhaps I knew then what I know now: It's going to take a lot more to find faith.

Echoing my concern is Tim Lucas, a pastor at an emerging ministry in New Jersey. He told a reporter, "Popular culture is a wonderful buffet to dine at. But it's easy to overeat."

I'm not even sure why I have such a fascination with Jews and pop culture. Elizabeth makes fun of me because anytime there's even the faintest whiff of a Jewish joke on a television show we're watching, I crack up. Recently I was watching a show that mentioned ever so briefly a synagogue class trip to a dairy farm. One kid was wearing a "Jews for Cheeses" T-shirt. Even if the joke's not funny, I laugh. I guess it's because I'm a little embarrassed by my religion. If I tell Middle Americans I'm Jewish, they instantly think I look as though I'm from Brooklyn or from the cast of *Fiddler on the Roof*, when, in fact, most American Jews look nothing like the stereotypes. We look like Jon Stewart and the bald guy who married Charlotte on *Sex and the City*.

So anytime a character on a TV show says something that's even remotely Jewish, I smile, knowing that they have just helped in my twisted personal crusade of mainstreaming Judaism for the masses. So when John Goodman in *The Big Lebowski* famously says he doesn't "roll on Shabbos," I'm filled with joy. When a Jewish character on Showtime's *Weeds* invokes the Hebrew word for "life" by wearing a T-shirt proclaiming he "likes to get chai," I jump with glee. (For someone who's never even puffed a cigarette in his life, I'm not sure why I just gave two stoner references.)

But for some reason, and I've yet to figure it out, Christians are more successful with their pop-culture outreach than we Jews have been. Christianity, like the product of any multinational corporation, has marketing challenges. But, from what I can tell, it is being promoted head-on—and to various niche markets.

After hearing a story on NPR about an evangelizing tattoo artist in Birmingham, Alabama, I did some additional research and found out that there's actually a Christian Tattoo Association with more than a hundred tattoo parlors as members. This sort of group is not an anomaly. It's fast becoming the norm. (Although looking to Christianity to see what Jews can learn from it is part of the point of this book, I've got to admit that I don't think we'll be seeing Jewish tattoo artists—and there are some—coming into the mainstream anytime soon. After all, getting a tattoo is technically forbidden in Jewish tradition. Which is why it makes absolutely no sense for a fan of Kabbalah like Britney Spears to have a Hebrew tattoo on the back of her neck.)

There are Cruisers for Christ, a self-proclaimed classic auto ministry, which holds car shows as a forum to minister to the unchurched. There is actually a Jewish equivalent to this. I once wrote an article about the Florida-based King David Bikers Club, whose members have their own motorcycle-riding rabbi and drive on "guilt trips" every Mother's Day. But they're not the only Jewish bikers. There are also the Chaiway Riders and Hillel's Angels.

A group calling itself the Christian Game Developers holds an annual conference to come up with new ideas for Jesus-themed video games for kids. Those monumentally popular *Left Behind* books I mentioned? They were turned into a video game—by three Jewish guys who converted to Christianity. Even our stereotypical Jewish technology nebs are leaving the fold to create Armageddon-themed video games. Why can't we Jews have something similar? A video game called *Son Slayer II: Egyptian Rampage* could be popular.

Of course, this discussion would not be complete without reiterating that Christians and Jews have different goals with their various pop-culture forays. When Christian communities host music festivals and car shows, they are trying to missionize, to spread the message of Christ to the public. They are trying to "save" people, to recruit new converts. Jews, on the other hand, have no such notions. We make campy T-shirts and motorcycle down I-85 to make us feel better, to promote Jewish pride among ourselves. It's not in our theology to seek converts.

So I guess it isn't very surprising that during the 2006 World Cup, the Full Gospel New York Church in Flushing, Queens, used the televised games to draw worshipers into the building. It worked. More than a thousand "fervent fans" showed up to watch the game, but also got treated to a pre-kickoff prayer, rousing performances by a dance troupe, and a gospel choir.

This is, by far, not the first example of the unlikely marriage between sports and religion. NASCAR, quite possibly a church unto itself, featured a studio-sponsored race car promoting Mel Gibson's *The Passion of the Christ* in 2004. And this summer, just as my year of living among Christians is getting under way, major league baseball introduced "Faith Day" at several of its Bible Belt stadiums—including that of my very own Atlanta Braves.

DON'T LET THE name fool you. Faith Day, at least according to the marketing geniuses in the Atlanta Braves front office, has nothing to do with the wide and colorful tapestry of the city's multifaith makeup. It specifically refers to Christianity, and not even Christianity as a whole. When the

Braves became the first team in major league baseball to hold Faith Day today, they were targeting a single faith—the evangelical niche.

I feel as if I'm in hell. It's a sweltering summer day here in Hotlanta, and I'm at Turner Field watching a baseball game. The temperature reading under the scoreboard shouts ninety-two degrees. But that's not why I feel as though I'm in the depths of damnation and dancing with the devil. That feeling comes courtesy of a harebrained idea I had to drag Mendel, a rabbi friend of mine, and his nine-year-old son to the game with me. There's nothing wrong with taking your rabbi friend to the ball game. In fact, I encourage it. But just not on Faith Day.

I told them it would be educational to witness pop-culture Christianity and that I would pay for the tickets. So they're sitting next to me as we watch the traveling cast of *Mama Mia* sing "God Bless America" before the game gets under way. What's worse, it's the "Three Weeks," an annual period of mourning held each summer when Jews are not supposed to go swimming, shave, listen to live music, or, in general, have much fun. (That's the shorthand explanation of this time of deep sadness for my people. We're actually commemorating something very serious, the days and weeks leading up to the destruction of both the First and Second Temple, which occurred on the exact same day in 586 B.C.E. and 70 C.E., respectively. This is a time when Jews postpone weddings, parties, and, I would assume, Christian rock jams at evangelically themed ballpark days.)

But I somehow felt it necessary to haul a rabbi and his innocent, cherubic son on my twisted Judeo-Christian tour. So not only does it feel like hell outside, but I have a sense that's where I may be headed after the game.

The commingling of baseball and religion shouldn't shock anybody. They're both national pastimes. And many people have long held a religious devotion to their hometown sports teams. Faith and fandom often go hand in hand. Sports allegories often exceed biblical metaphors. In his book *Touchdown Jesus,* author Scott Eden describes the pilgrimage-like atmosphere that permeates game days at Notre Dame, a staunchly Catholic university, calling the fans "congregants" and exploring the many pregame rituals that actually take place in a pope-sanctioned basilica.

Truth be told, the concept of Faith Day doesn't even seem that odd to me. It could be because, for the last few years, the Atlanta Braves have been hosting an annual Kosher Day at the stadium, during which they serve rabbinically supervised hot dogs and onion rings. The only difference is that this is more than just about food today. Indeed, unlike big plastic cup day, thirsty Thursday, Frisbee night, bat day, or "I Can't Believe It's Not Butter" day, Faith Day is more than just about giveaways. Today's specially themed outing is all-encompassing, with bands performing, booths promoting a Christian lifestyle, and your favorite baseball players giving testimonials about how they were saved by Jesus. I heard one guy refer to it as "Beer today, God tomorrow."

Faith Days have proved very successful for minor league teams, not necessarily in numbers of converts, but perhaps where it counts more—at the ticket office. When attendance is low, a Faith Day can be a godsend. The Nashville Sounds, a Class AAA baseball team, witnessed a 59 percent increase in attendance during a Faith Night program.

The Braves lose to the Marlins 6–1, but that doesn't dampen the mood for this revival. After the game, several thousand people stick around for the Faith Day activities and shuffle over to the left-field stands, where workers are already on the field constructing a makeshift stage.

The three of us find seats next to some vanilla-looking preppy teenagers, one of whom is sporting a "Satan is a punk" T-shirt. A local Christian radio station known as the Fish is throwing prize packs and a giant plastic Jesus fish to the excited crowd as banners promoting the event's sponsors—Focus on the Family, Toccoa Falls College, and Comcast among them—are unfurled behind the stage.

One of the sponsors is a group called United Potential, Inc.; its sole mission is to evangelize Christianity through baseball. That's a niche of a niche if I've ever heard one. The group's national director is Tim Cash, a former player for the Houston Astros, who now moonlights as one of the Atlanta Braves' chaplains. Every Wednesday evening, as churches across America are holding Bible study sessions, he studies the Good Book with a bunch of people who swing bats for a living. Last night, he tells the crowd, eight players attended his class.

One of them was John Smoltz. This star athlete is the first pitcher in major league history to boast 200 career wins and more than 150 career saves. But his stats weren't always on fire. He began the 1991 season with a pitiful 2–11 record and started seeing a sports psychologist for help. He returned from those therapy sessions and went a phenomenal 12–2 to finish out the season and helped the Braves get to the World Series for the first time in the club's history.

But ask Smoltz his greatest accomplishment, and he'll tell you it has absolutely nothing to do with the game of baseball. In fact, it has nothing to do with any physical prowess at all. "I currently have ten no-decisions," Smoltz says, taking the podium in front of the gathered crowd of three thousand Faith Day–goers. He starts his testimony about how he was saved by referring to the number of games he's neither won nor lost. "But because of the decision I made in 1995, I know where I will be after I die, and I can only hope and wish everyone here knows where they will be too."

Sounds a little morbid to me, but the crowd is cheering. One of my challenges during this year is trying to better understand Christians and their apparent fascination with all things death. (Jesus died for our sins, these crackers represent his body, this wine represents his blood.) Smoltz, dressed in a light blue polo shirt and khaki shorts, tells the story of how he came to find the Lord. "Baseball became my god," he admits. "I was so consumed by it and I wanted to be liked. I was a people pleaser, but I was missing the boat." Here's an adult who's confessing his "sins" to a group of mostly children. Sure, he's not regaling them with stories of prostitution, infidelity, or gambling, but the concept seems a little weird.

His roller-coaster career (countless injuries have sidelined him over the years) led him to look for answers, and the other believers on his team sparked in him an interest in Christianity. In 1995, while dining at a Bennigan's restaurant with the team chaplain, he was convinced to change his life forever. Bennigan's doesn't seem like the holiest place to have a born-again experience. Neither does Applebee's or the Olive Garden, for that matter. But, owing to my kosher restrictions, what would I know? I've never stepped foot in any of those places. But even in the few weeks I've been pretending to be Christian, I think I can safely say that I don't think Bennigan's is the coolest location for an "I got saved" story.

Bennigan's is a poor-man's substitute for a nativity location. Don't get me wrong. I'm not mocking Smoltz's newfound commitment to his faith. Not at all. In fact, I admire him for making such a bold decision and being so open about his faults and foibles. But I guess I just feel bad for the guy. I mean, for heaven's sake, he won the Cy Young Award. He deserves a proper epiphanal location.

In any event, the chaplain told Smoltz not to put off repenting, but to do it that very day. So Smoltz realigned his priorities, and he now considers himself a born-again Christian. Maybe there's something to the golden chicken tenders at a casual-dining eatery. Again, I'll never find out. Kosher restrictions and all.

"Do I want to live my life in a no-decision?" Smoltz asks rhetorically. "Don't be caught in the 'what if,' in the no-decision. And don't take my words as the absolute truth. Define them for yourself."

Smoltz takes his faith seriously. He's on the board of trustees at the Georgia-based King's Ridge Christian School, he's campaigned for the former head of the Christian Coalition, and he got embroiled in a local controversy when he made disparaging remarks about same-sex relationships, allegedly comparing them to bestiality. This is something he obviously does not bring up with this youth-centric audience. "Sharing my faith is the greatest thing I get to do," he says, wrapping up his remarks. "I'm just a vehicle. God works through me." Smoltz encourages us to ponder these thoughts as he leaves the stage to a standing ovation.

We all stay standing for Aaron Shust, a local pop star whose "My Savior, My God" is currently the number-one song on the Christian music charts and has become the most downloaded inspirational song on iTunes. I didn't realize iTunes had an "inspirational songs" category, but it seems I'm learning a lot of new things on this journey.

Shust is very clean-cut for a rock star, and it's indicative of the nature of Christian pop music in general. Much of the genre pretty much sounds like popular acoustic songs you'd hear on mainstream radio. The only difference here is that the front man, instead of singing "I love her," switches the words to "I love him," referring to Jesus. Which ends up sounding just a tad gay. That irony is apparently lost on this spiritual set.

Growing up, I was actually a fan of this easy-on-the-ears style of Christian pop music. I just didn't know that's what it was called. As a teenager, my musical tastes weren't yet honed, and I devoured just about anything my local Top 40 station decided to serve me. The Eurythmics "Sweet Dreams Are Made of This"? Loved it. In fact, I once stayed up until midnight knowing it was the number-one song on Casey Kasem's Sunday night countdown, so I could record it on my boom box. Mr. Big's cheesy "To Be with You"? It was the soundtrack to my eleventh-grade crush on Stephanie Feinstein. Milli Vanilli's "Blame It on the Rain"? No words can describe how much I liked this song. I danced to it countless times in the privacy of my bedroom. Anything by Boyz II Men? Sign me up.

But what I really liked was listening to a program called *Sunrise* on Sunday mornings. It was the highlight of my musical week. It played all fun pop songs with no sad love ballads among them. These were sugary pop confections, just the way I liked them. It wasn't until at least a year later that I finally realized this was a Christian music show. I'm still not sure what exactly blew its cover. The fact that it was on at 7 A.M. on Sunday mornings didn't clue me in. Maybe it was the disc jockeys quoting Bible verses between songs that finally caught my attention.

But listening to Shust perform brought back fond memories of those days, and I make a mental note to start listening to Christian pop again. Wait . . . it's the three weeks of mourning. What am I thinking? I shouldn't be listening to any type of music, let alone Christian tunes. What is wrong with me? I look over to Mendel and his son and feel horrible that I convinced them to come here today.

After a few songs I suggest we leave, partly because it's so hot, but partly because I feel so guilty. On the way out, we walk through what is being billed as "Sponsor Village"—essentially a row of tables and booths giving away everything from Moses bobbleheads to camouflage Bibles. Because we all know nothing screams faith like freebies.

One sponsor, World Vision, is asking me to adopt an African child. I'm not really sure how serious they are. Who do they think I am? Madonna? Angelina Jolie?

To THOSE GATHERED, this was a faith-based activity and by coming out today in the thousands they were, in essence, showing their support for their religion. I've got to admit that at first I didn't understand Christians' desire to commingle faith with baseball. This hybrid of church and stadium just didn't make any sense to me. It seemed heretical at worst, trite at best. But after experiencing it today, I'm walking away with a different perspective.

By bringing their faith with them into the ballpark, they were mixing the sacred with the mundane. And in a good way. They were able to transform baseball into something holy. And this was not God making the day a sacred one. It was through the efforts of human beings—through all those involved—that Faith Day was turned from a mere marketing gimmick to a place where the divine resides.

In Judaism, this idea is pervasive. We say blessings on just about every-thing we do (before and after we eat anything, when we see lightning, when we see a politician . . . shall I go on?). By doing this we are taking a run-of-the-mill task like using the restroom or eating a Snickers bar and transforming it into a holy act. Indeed, the Talmud teaches us that we should recite a hundred blessings each and every day. (Considering there are more than seventy in our daily prayers alone, you begin to see how we can pretty easily reach triple digits.)

As Rabbi Aaron D. Twerski writes in the introduction to his guide on the laws of Jewish blessings, giving thanks to God before every act we do is a "constant and unrelenting" reminder that we are put on this earth for one reason and one reason only—to sanctify God through everything we do. Each blessing we recite, Twerski writes, is "a testimony to a purposeful creation in which we are granted the privilege to play a role."

But what if every day was Faith Day? Would it still be special? This is a challenge I (like many observant Jews) find myself facing constantly. I recite so many daily blessings and so many daily prayers (not to men-tion the fact that they're the same ones each day), that I no longer look at them as something special. Take, for example, the paragraph-long Hebrew blessing Jews recite after we use the bathroom. In it, we literally thank God for making holes in our body so that we can relieve ourselves. But there's a problem. Imagine reciting that exact same formula five times a day, every day of your whole life. I can pretty much guarantee that after a while you're going to be daydreaming about whether or not you zipped up or if you have toilet paper stuck to your shoes, and not giving gratitude to the Almighty for creating openings in all the right places. In this light, it's a real challenge to make every blessing count and be relevant. It's just human nature.

Maybe I can learn a lesson from Faith Day. Maybe I shouldn't knock myself out for never concentrating on the after-bathroom blessing. Instead, maybe I should choose one time each day and make that my "Faith Day blessing." Try elevating the mundane just one time. It's what Jesus would do, and I'm starting to see that.

Christians, I'm slowly learning, have a remarkable desire to sport their religious pride at any turn, whether it's with a Christian tattoo, a Stephen Baldwin movie, or a baseball game. Maybe that explains the wild success of "What Would Jesus Do?" bracelets and bumper stickers. Christians want to be reminded of their faith constantly. But more than that, they want others to know how beautiful that really is.

I consider this as I drop Mendel and his son off at their house. Pulling out of their driveway, I look at the two of them carrying what's left of the kosher sandwiches they had brought with them. I hope I didn't scar them by taking them with me today. As for me, I feel better now than I did before going to the stadium. Not because I witnessed Jesus, but because I witnessed something far more inspiring—His people.

SIX

God's VIP Section

You shall observe the words of this covenant, so that you will succeed in all that you do.

—Deuteronomy 29:8

I GOT CURSED today. By God. And, I guess I've got to admit, I kind of feel I had it coming. You know, the whole Jew going to church thing and all.

Toward the end of each summer every synagogue in the world reads Deuteronomy 28 during services. If you've never read it, consider yourself quite lucky, as you are untainted by the knowledge that a benevolent God can sometimes have a split personality—loving-kindness one moment and blowing one serious gasket the next.

Deuteronomy 28 is the one chapter they don't tell you about in Sunday school. It's no wonder. Any child who hears the horrific curses for not following God's commandments contained in the latter portion of this chapter would most likely ditch religion altogether and sign up for Atheists of America. Put simply, these are quite possibly the most depressing fifty-five verses in the entirety of the Old Testament. And that's saying something when you consider other sections talk about being burned alive (Numbers 16:35) and having your corpse exhumed so your bones rot in the harsh heat of the sun (Jeremiah 8:2).

Each Sabbath morning at synagogue, people are called up to the Torah scroll to recite a blessing over the different sections that are read publicly. When it comes the time of year to read the text of curses out loud in synagogue, you can imagine that nobody's lining up to accept this honor. So, instead, we ask the prayer leader to take the punch for the rest of us. *Don't take it personally,* we tell him. *And if things don't work out, can I keep your Tivo?*

Little did I ever imagine it, but this morning at the service the person calling up members of the congregation to recite the blessings over the Torah scroll apparently had a mental hiccup and accidentally called me up for the curse section.

I had been attending church for a few months now, but nobody really knew. I hadn't placed a Jesus fish on the back bumper of my car. I had pretended to take Communion a few times, but those crumbs were long gone. And yet this random guy who invites people up to the Torah at my congregation had called out my Hebrew name in front of everyone. Was he in cahoots with the Lord Almighty? At least I wasn't being struck by lightning. But somehow, on some spiritual level, this felt worse. It was as if here I was, in front of my entire community, being called out for heresy, for apostasy, for being a Jesus freak. A bolt of lightning wasn't looking too bad right about then.

To be fair to God (and, at this point, I think that's not a bad idea), He actually started Deuteronomy 28 on a relatively positive note. A paragraph or two about some blessings you will receive for following His command-ments. It's as if God paints an opening scene of sunny vistas and serene prairies as far as the eye can see. A butterfly flutters by for added effect. Some band is playing pleasant acoustic tunes in the background. But then the butterfly smashes right into a tree it didn't see. Clouds form. The music stops. And the Bible veers into some pretty dark territory rather quickly. Think of it as if horror master Stephen King wrested the divine pen from God, tied Him to a bed, and unleashed *Misery* on Moses and the Israelites.

The latter portion of this chapter of the Bible explains, in somewhat punishing detail, what will happen to those who don't follow God's com-mandments. It's a doomsday scenario. *Independence Day, Armageddon,* and *The Day After Tomorrow* all rolled into one. There's a long litany of curses. Cursed will you be in your home (v. 19). Cursed will you be at work (v. 16). Your family will be cursed (v. 46). You'll get boils and hemorrhoids, and nobody likes boils and hemorrhoids (v. 27). You'll get the plague (v. 22). Your wife will cheat on you (v. 30). Your kids will hate you (v. 32). You will become tabloid fodder (v. 37). You will go stark raving mad (vv. 28, 34). Cannibals will eat your family (v. 55).

Each passing verse the prayer leader reads is like a dagger in my back. I know I don't follow all of God's commandments. I barely follow half of them. I'm fully aware that I'm not in the running for poster Jew of the year. I'm not even friends with people on the nominating committee.

And I'm sure my recent church-hopping adventures aren't making the Man Upstairs too happy with me either. But, really, did I need to be reminded so eloquently about all these curses—my wife having an affair, my unborn children being sold into slavery, robbers stealing everything I own including my beloved high-definition flat screen? Why was God having a problem with my mingling with those of other faiths? A little interfaith dialogue never hurt anyone. I was merely following a model that I had learned about from the Bible itself. Didn't Moses learn how to improve the Jewish judicial system from the non-Jewish Jethro? And Jethro is honored in Jewish tradition for this. He even has a Torah portion named after him.

It's not as though I was committing murder or eating pork. I was *merely* spending my Sunday mornings in church. After all, the whole purpose of my Christian endeavors was to make me a more spiritual person. Wasn't that, I justified, what God wanted from me anyway?

My twisted deal making and mind games with the Almighty were obviously not working. He was, apparently, in no mood for my shenanigans. He was upset. I had crossed a line. I had rocked the boat. And God was telling me very clearly I had stirred His anger.

What was it the famous eighteenth-century preacher Jonathan Edwards said? We are all but sinners in the hands of an angry God. I certainly was. Indeed, maybe I had gone too far. Maybe I was more than just another member of the sinners' coterie. Maybe I had become, probably much to the deep dismay of both my heavenly father and my earthly one, their proverbial mascot.

A WEEK GOES by and my growing guilt notwithstanding, I opt for spiritual suicide. I will continue my quest to come closer to my Judaism by hanging out among my Christian neighbors. If my God was going to curse me, if I was really going to incur His full and utter wrath (crazy curses and all), I might as well go out in a fiery ball of glory with guns blazing. After all, there's no sense in only doing something halfheartedly. My rabbinic father taught me that.

Which is why, at this precise moment in time, I find myself on the floor of the Georgia Dome, the home stadium of the Atlanta Falcons and the arena to attend if you wanted to rock out to the Rolling Stones. But I'm not at a football game or a Mick Jagger concert. I'm at Megafest, an annual gathering of the faithful that draws upward of two hundred thousand during the four-day event. And tonight I'm in God's VIP section.

As a Jewish journalist, I have media credentials, and they have, in the past, scored me tickets to screenings of movies before they come out and a seemingly never-ending supply of religious books to review in my magazine. But tonight my press pass has given me unfettered access to a sold-out event at which Jesus Christ is the main attraction.

But it's Pastor T. D. Jakes's name on the marquee. Who is this guy? The short answer is that T. D. Jakes is America's favorite pastor. But stopping there is like calling Picasso a scribbler and Michelangelo some guy who dabbled in Play-Doh. You get the point.

Jakes's Potter House church in suburban Dallas rests on twenty-eight acres of land and boasts thirty thousand members. He preaches to millions more on his weekly television broadcasts. *Time* magazine has, at one time or another, called him one of the twenty-five most influential evangelicals in America as well as the next Billy Graham.

He's also an apostle for the underprivileged. He's the driving force behind Dallas's Capella Park, a 230-acre mixed-use development that includes a Christian preparatory academy, green space, hundreds of homes, and a senior-citizen complex. After Hurricane Katrina, President Bush very publicly sought Jakes's support in reaching out to the African American community.

He's written more than a dozen books; many have topped best-seller lists and sold millions of copies. One of them, *Women, Thou Art Loosed,* was made into a movie and a regular seminar to motivate the fairer sex. His book *He-Motions: Even Strong Men Struggle* aims to do the same for men. He owns a Grammy-winning record label and has his own greeting card line with Hallmark. He runs worship cruises to Alaska, leadership conventions in London, and, of course, the annual Megafest here in Atlanta.

When I told Elizabeth about tonight's festivities, she actually agreed to come with me. Turns out even she was a little curious. I also bring along my former roommate Michael, who wanted to witness the spectacle. Together, the three of us are in the minority, just a few white faces in a sea of African Americans gathered here to witness the gospel of Pastor T. D. Jakes.

My media credentials get us led us through the bowels of the Georgia Dome, past the lockers of the Atlanta Falcons, and directly onto the field where we are escorted to a group of folding chairs to the left of the stage. There are tens of thousands of people here. Back in 1999, Jakes broke the single-day record for attendance at the Georgia Dome with 84,459 faithful clamoring inside to hear him speak. That's more people than came here for the Super Bowl.

This place is filled with lost souls desperate for a little salvation, a category in which I am beginning to include myself. I'm only a few months into my yearlong journey, and I'm hoping being surrounded by such praise and worship will do me some good.

Pastor Paula White, a blond woman who refers to herself as "just a messed-up girl from Mississippi," is Jakes's opening act. She grabs the microphone and discusses an Old Testament verse that talks about God blessing His people. It's Deuteronomy 1:11, which gives her the bright idea of telling everyone in the crowd to put $111 in the offering envelopes being passed around.

I look around at the rows of people near me. Many of these folks cannot muster up that kind of money, especially after they had to pay just to get in the door tonight. Pastor White knows this, so she suggests people pick a buddy and each donate half. I guess a partial blessing from God is better than none. I quickly do the math in my head. Even if only half the people here give the suggested contribution, that's still well over $3 million just at tonight's event alone. That's not including the entrance fee or the cost of any of the other many events being held throughout the weekend.

Echoing the proverbial notion that whatever you give to God, He will give back to you manifold, Pastor White assures the crowd, "You're gonna get that settlement. You're gonna get out of that apartment." It's as if everyone in the crowd is simultaneously dealing with both a lawsuit and a housing crisis. Then, for no apparent reason, she says, "Slap somebody upside the head." I feel as though I'm at a Madea family reunion.

Pastor White passes the baton to Derick Faison, an associate pastor at Jakes's church. "Give me a crazy praise in this house!" he yells into the mike. "You're too blessed to be stressed. I see a new season in your life. Slap somebody upside the head." Maybe that's their mantra.

During a performance by Grammy-winning gospel singer CeCe Winans, I walk around the Dome's floor taking pictures. There are signs all over for the sponsors of tonight's event—the Georgia lottery, CareerBuilder.com, a local rent-to-own furniture store. This is definitely targeting a financially strapped niche audience.

To its credit, Megafest is hoping to lift participants up into a better tax bracket. Throughout the four-day event, there are workshops in wealth and basic money management by financial gurus. Earlier in the day, I strolled around the convention floor and saw some of these seminars. But as the people exited the room afterward, they were bombarded with credit card offers and tables of Megafest paraphernalia like T-shirts and DVDs. I overheard one person say to his friend, "What can I spend my money on today?" as if everything he had just heard about keeping a tight grip on his wad of cash went in one ear and out the other.

I'M SLOWLY LEARNING that this notion of mixing faith with finances is not unique to Megafest. At the few black churches I've been to already, praying to God for things like more child support and help in securing a better job are de rigueur. Even bling gets a blessing. The bottom line plays a big part in spirituality.

Jakes, who himself drives a Bentley, is at the forefront of the movement known as the prosperity gospel, the notion that God wants His followers to be rich. This isn't a particularly new fad. Oral Roberts, perhaps the most famous televangelist of the last century, preached to tens of millions on his *Hour of Healing* show that "God ain't poor no more." He wanted people to know that having faith could lead to wealth, and there was nothing wrong with that. Donations to his church were dubbed "investments" and put into spiritual "accounts."

Besides Jakes, another leader in this movement is the appropriately named Pastor Creflo Dollar, who preaches the prosperity gospel at the World Changers Church International here in Georgia. By all measures, he practices what he preaches. He lives in a $3 million mansion near Atlanta and another $2 million apartment in Manhattan. He owns both a Hummer and a Rolls Royce. A November 2007 Senate investigation into his ministries' finances revealed that Pastor Dollar rakes in $69 million annually.

Dollar actually has two churches. On Saturdays he takes his private jet up to New York, where he preaches to about nine thousand people at Madison Square Garden, and then he flies back for Sunday morning services to preach to twenty thousand at his $7 million church building just outside Atlanta (which I visited).

He, Jakes, and others believe God wants them to be wealthy, often citing chapter and verse (e.g., John 10:10) to back this up. But others believe they are distorting the gospel. Al Sharpton, for one, condemns the prosperity gospel and so does the political activist Reverend Jim Wallis, who calls it a "biblical heresy." Pastor Raphael Warnock, of Martin Luther King, Jr.'s Ebenezer Baptist Church, calls it the "gospel of the bling-bling" and says it is dangerously out of line with Jesus' teachings.

Pastor Rick Warren, author of the popular book *The Purpose Driven Life,* is one of the movement's harshest critics. "This idea that God wants everyone to be wealthy? There's a word for that: baloney," he told *Time* magazine in a September 2006 cover story about the prosperity gospel called "Does God Want You to Be Rich?" "It's creating a false idol. You don't measure your self-worth by your net worth."

Although Judaism has similar notions about prosperity—our prayers often ask for sustenance—it is, by far, not the highlight of the service. We do not worship the almighty dollar. If we're asking for anything, it's usually for stuff like health or good tidings. But the focus of most of our prayers is praising God and actually has nothing to do with our wants and needs. This could be because Jewish prayers are merely a substitute for giving sacrifices. In Temple times, Jews didn't pray the way we do in modern times. They gave three sacrifices a day. When we no longer had the Temple, the rabbis instituted three prayer services in their stead. Nobody was bringing a bull to the altar in the hopes of getting better bling. A new job wasn't on the mind of the Jew who gave of his flock to the Lord. It was a way for the Jewish people to recognize God's dominion over the world, to say, *Here, you're the boss. Take my best animal. It's my pleasure. Enjoy.*

In fact many of the prayers we recite have more to do with esoteric topics such as cattle and animal husbandry than about asking for things. It is, perhaps, one of the myriad reasons why many American Jews do not get inspired at prayer services. After all, what's so enthralling about the slaughter of a ram? The congregants at a church have something to get excited about. At a synagogue? Not so much.

It's the moment we've all been waiting for. Pastor Faison does the introduction: "T. D. Jakes is an author, an evangelist, a philanthropist, a pastor, a teacher. He's a vessel of God." The crowd starts to cheer. "Can I get a witness?" The crowd goes wild. "Make some noise for our pastor, T. D. Jakes. Give it up!"

To the roar of the audience, T. D. Jakes takes the podium, howling into the microphone like James Brown enraptured. He's a bear of a man with a taste for big boxy suits. He squints, his eyes constantly at half-mast. "Bless that wonderful noise of Jesus," he says, flashing his famous gap-toothed grin. "By the end of Megafest, you might get a DUI arrest," he tells us. "Driving under the influence of the Holy Spirit."

He welcomes what he dubs the "pastors and potentates." I don't even know what that means, but it just sounds good rolling off his tongue. Jakes's Potter House church in Dallas is watching tonight's event live via satellite—as are various churches in Europe and Africa. As if that wasn't "mega" enough, the festivities are also being broadcast to nearly three hundred prisons.

One moment he's growling, the next he's speaking in a soothing Barry White–style baritone. His words are mellow and mellifluous, bouncing off the walls of the Georgia Dome as if in his own private cathedral. His nuggets of wisdom seem to combine to form more of a ballad than a sermon.

In a profile of Jakes, journalist David Van Biema describes his preaching mannerisms as follows: "Jakes's eccentric pauses, coy glances at his audience and the occasional odd, Holy Spirit–inspired stutter that sounds like a skipping CD might normally mystify or annoy the nonanointed. And yet, somehow, they do not. Like Brando's mumbling or Michael Jordan's outstretched tongue, they are pendants to an overwhelming gift."

Legend has it Jakes used to preach to an imaginary congregation as a child. And you can tell this guy has practiced. His speeches are absolutely mesmerizing. Before coming tonight, I Tivoed several episodes of his weekly sermons on the Trinity Broadcast Network. Like many black megapastors, he plays the role of the wise but fun-loving uncle. He tells you what you need to know, but often does so in a colloquial "Hey, I'm right there with you" way. He exudes camaraderie.

In one sermon I watched, he talks about temptation. "My wife and I are always trying a new diet," the barrel-chested Jakes tells the audience. "She likes bread pudding. I like peach cobbler. My body doesn't care. What I'm doing is just as bad as what you do." Shots of the crowd show people nodding in agreement. *He's one of us, he's real, he gets us.* Jakes jokes with the crowd constantly as if they're all one big happy family. Regarding his preaching style, Van Biema writes, "With its improvisatory electricity, ornate call-and-response cues and dramatic eruptions of prophesying or speaking in tongues, it is an unrivaled preacher's toolbox."

If you're ever watching a video of one of T. D. Jakes's sermons and you want to get to the really good part, fast-forward until you see the sweat beads build up on his face. That's when you should hit "play." He sweats profusely, repeatedly grabbing a cloth to wipe his bald dome. It's the sweat that indicates when Jakes kicks into high gear and starts his patented growl.

This is the point he's at now at the Georgia Dome. As large as he is, he crisscrosses the stage in almost balletic fashion, stretching to the tips of his toes to stress a particular point. "*Spiritual* people are not exempt from *physical* problems," he shouts.

"Praise Bishop Jakes!" audience members respond almost in unison.

Jakes speaks about people who go to church by routine, people who pray just by going through the motions, and my ears perk up. "Nobody forced you here," he intones, as if he's suddenly changed tonight's sermon to "Things Benyamin Cohen Really Needs to Hear." "You have to search the inventory of your resources," he exclaims, I swear looking directly at me. "Pray for a breakthrough."

I think about his words. *Pray for a breakthrough.* I look over at Elizabeth and Michael. For them, this is all pretty much just a fun spectacle, something they can chat about at the water cooler tomorrow. Michael, a self-proclaimed geek, may even blog about it when he gets home tonight. But I'm here for more than mere entertainment. I came here searching for something, something meaningful. Jakes, as if reading my mind, knew exactly that prayer was my Achilles' heel. I couldn't spend a year among Christians hoping, by some sort of spiritual osmosis, to absorb their religious exuberance. Unfortunately, it didn't work like that. I would also need to pray, to pray for guidance to an avenue that would lead me to greater Jewish observance. *Pray for a breakthrough.*

"Church is more than an orga-*nization*," he continues. "It's an orga-*nism*."

It's true. A house of worship is nothing more than bricks and mortar unless you have living beings in it who wish to pray. I wonder what that says about me and my synagogue. Is my lack of enthusiasm about prayer services bringing down the holiness of my synagogue? Surely the meaningful prayers of my fellow congregants are enough to make up for what I lack. Or, perish the thought, are they all just as cynical and uninspired as I am?

Jakes moves on, discussing how empty a house of worship can be if no one in it wants to pray. All the bells, whistles, and ornate architecture in the world don't make a sanctuary inherently holy, he explains. It's the parishioners. The most modest surroundings can be transformed into the most spiritual of sanctuaries. Too often we focus on the edifice and not what goes on inside its walls. As Jakes eloquently puts it, "We build a monument to where God *was,* but not where God *is.*"

His sermon moves me. I'm actually a little excited to go back home and put the lessons into practice.

There's no reason why a rabbi can't sermonize this way. Yes, our prayers are set in stone. But the few minutes of preaching that the rabbi does on Saturday morning are up for grabs. I sometimes feel we use our ancient prayers as a crutch. We choke ourselves with a "This is the way it's been done for centuries" mentality even though Jakes's stagecraft and "preacher's toolbox" of sermon techniques are wholly permitted in our religion. They're just rarely, if ever, employed. What kind of disservice are we doing to ourselves? To future generations?

I feel a natural high as we take the subway home. Michael snaps a picture of me and Elizabeth next to a big Megafest sign, one I will later frame and put on my writing desk. It will serve as a reminder that my goal for this year is to the leave the stagnation and comfort behind. In its place is an honest search for something enlightening that I can implement in my daily religious routine. Some nugget of faithful wisdom that I can, wholeheartedly and happily, impart to my children.

Jakes may have been preaching Jesus, but I was hearing Moses. I was hearing Abraham, Jacob, Isaac. My biblical namesake, Benjamin. Generations of Jews before me. Who am I to question it all?

SEVEN

Getting High on the High Holidays

And Moses declared the appointed festivals of God to the children of Israel.

—*Leviticus 23:44*

I HAVE A red-and-green Starbucks coffee mug with Christmas decorations drawn on it along with the phrase "It only happens once a year." I'm not really sure what that slogan means. Elizabeth thinks it refers to the special Starbucks holiday flavors—the pumpkin spice latte, the gingerbread latte, the Tazo chai eggnog latte, and the popular peppermint mocha—which are only sold during the Christmas season. My guess is it has to do with Starbucks' attempt to pull on people's heartstrings, reminding them ever so cleverly that the holidays they love and the traditions they cherish only happen once a year. So embrace them. Enjoy them. And have some smooth Arabica coffee while you're at it.

If only I shared such similar sentiments for the season of Jewish festivals known as the High Holidays. Held each fall, they are something that in years past I rarely looked forward to. For me, thank God, they only happen once a year.

Call me a glutton for torture, but Elizabeth and I belong to two synagogues, both just a few blocks from each other. They each have slightly different ideological bents (You love *Israel*? We *love* Israel), both of which speak to us on certain levels. So we've decided, like many in our community, to support them both. Which means that come the High Holidays, they each ask us to pay for tickets. In addition to their annual membership fees, which often exceed a thousand dollars, synagogues ask that their members pay for High Holiday admission. Just think of asking for God's mercy as a premium service.

Both requests came in the mail today. I tossed them both aside. I just can't go another holiday season pretending to enjoy these services. They're crowded (one synagogue actually holds the services in a nearby gymnasium), they're hot (which is not good considering Jews are forbidden to shower during the holidays), and they're long. All in all, it doesn't add up to a conducive environment for conversing with God.

The Jewish holidays of Rosh Hashanah (the Day of Judgment, also known as the Jewish New Year) and Yom Kippur (the Day of Atonement), which usually occur near the end of September or beginning of October, are the two festivals that even the least observant Jews celebrate. It's the Oscar season of Jewish festivals. Collectively known as the High Holidays, these two days are the holiest days on the Jewish calendar. Even the Jews who eat pork and intermarry 363 days of the year muster up the strength and fortitude to proudly proclaim their Jewishness and spend those days immersed in prayer at synagogue.

But not me. No, the guy who was born into a rabbinic superfamily and has said a blessing on everything he has eaten since the day he learned how to speak wants nothing to do with these holidays. Indeed, my favorite day of the year is the day *after* Yom Kippur.

In general, Jewish holidays can usually be boiled down to one simple formula: Somebody tried to kill us, God intervened, now let's eat. Although being divinely rescued from a death sentence is certainly something to celebrate, it doesn't carry the inherent festive mood of a day originally intended as a joyous occasion, like, just as an example, the birth or resurrection of a Savior.

The High Holidays, in particular, are very solemn days. It is on these days that Jews believe God determines our fate for the coming year. Will we be inscribed in the Book of Life or sealed in the Book of Death? At synagogue, we don a special white robe on these holy days so that we can approach God and beseech His mercy with a pure spirit. It is telling, though, that this is the very same white robe that dresses those from our religion when they lay in their coffins. It's as if God is telling us, *Be careful. You're already on thin ice. You're already dressed for your funeral. All I need to do is close the casket.* Indeed, these are heavy—not festive—times.

Yom Kippur is a Sabbath on steroids. It goes a little something like this. The night before, we stop eating a half hour before sunset. And that includes water. In fact, we won't be able to put anything in our mouths until the following night. That includes toothpaste, mouthwash, and Tic Tacs (although, technically, Tic Tacs are always forbidden since the gelatin in them renders them unkosher). We're dressed to the nines—except for our feet. We can't wear leather shoes because it's apparently not the best idea to proudly wear a dead animal on our feet when we're asking God for mercy. So you see men in fancy suits walking to synagogue in Chuck Taylor canvas high-tops. Or plastic sandals. Or just their socks. You get the point. It looks odd, to say the least.

So we head off to synagogue that night in formal wear and flip-flops and pray for at least two hours. We walk home (like the weekly Sabbath, we don't drive) and catch some shut-eye. We wake up, can't take a shower, can't even put on deodorant (all part of the laws meant to make us suffer during this holy day), and saunter off to synagogue again. And that's where we stay the *entire* day. Most synagogues' Yom Kippur service starts early in the morning and doesn't end until nightfall. Sounds like fun, doesn't it?

But this is only the beginning. The High Holidays mark the beginning of an entire month of Jewish festivals, ones that require us to be even more different than we already are. I don't like being different.

Take, for example, the festival of Sukkot. This is an eight-day holiday that begins a week after Yom Kippur. In commemoration of the booths the Jewish people inhabited during their time in the desert, during these eight days we are required to move out of our house and live in a hut. Indulge me while I repeat that. For eight days, we move out of our house and live in a hut. We eat there. We sleep there. We watch Monday night football in there. And God said to Moses, *Let's go camping.*

The difference between the customs of Jewish festivals and those of Christian ones can be summed up like this. Come December, you guys put a Christmas tree in your house. If this were a Jewish tradition, it would turn rather quickly and depressingly into a Talmudic dissertation on forestry. What kind of tree? How tall is it required to be? How many branches does it need to have? Can we outsource the purchasing of the tree or is the commandment itself the actual action of buying said foliage? But I digress.

Nonetheless, I still feel some of our holiday customs take the cake. Most modern-day Americans do not spend a week every year living in an eight-by-twelve-foot hut built on their driveway. Normal American holidays mean turkey. Presents. Garlands. Why couldn't I just be *normal*? That's really all I ever wanted. Can't a Jew get a little tinsel?

And yet it will never happen. There will be no tinsel in my future. Because I am, for better or for worse, burdened for all eternity by my religion. The yoke of heaven is squarely upon me, and my shoulders are starting to get sore.

Thank God, it only happens once a year.

I'VE MADE UP my mind that this year—a year when I am trying my hardest to actually reconnect with my religion—that I will try something different for the High Holidays.

Elizabeth mentioned to me that one of the synagogues is offering an alternative service. It's going to start early, move quickly, and forego most of the singing. We both decided that, although this may not be the ideal type of service for some people, it was exactly what I needed right now.

The alternative service is not anathema to synagogues the world over. Many synagogues, especially Orthodox ones, offer what's called a *hashkama* service, from the Hebrew word meaning "early." Jewish law actually encourages this, deeming it praiseworthy to pray the morning service just as the sun is rising.

It's supposed to be reminiscent of Abraham sacrificing Isaac. As the Bible states, "And Abraham woke up early in the morning and he saddled his donkey" (Genesis 22:3). Abraham thought that he was about to kill his precious son, the progenitor of the Jewish nation. Instead of reluctantly getting ready for this surely difficult trip, Abraham "woke up early," eager to fulfill the will of God. In addition, "he saddled his donkey." He had many servants who would normally have been involved in the preparations for such a trip. However, Abraham was so anxious to fulfill God's command, he himself went and saddled his own animal.

I don't yet have children, but even I know that no father wants to be on Abraham's mission. *What to Expect When You're Expecting* doesn't have a chapter on child sacrifice. And for good reason—it's something no parent wants to think about, let alone actually go through.

But Abraham was not just "some guy." He was Abraham, and when God spoke, he listened. *You want me to do what?* Abraham surely asked.

No problem. You want me to do it at 9 A.M.? No problem. But would you mind if I got a head start and did it even earlier?

That was Abraham for you, always the overachiever. He got up early, packed his own bags, and saddled his own donkey. If he was going to do this, he was going to do it the only way he knew how—the best way possible. He puts the rest of us to shame.

There are always two ways to fulfill a commandment. We can, like Abraham, go far beyond the letter of the law to perform it enthusiastically. Or we can, like most of us, perform a commandment with mediocrity and a blasé attitude. Unfortunately, I've been part of the latter group for far too long.

IT'S THE DAY before Rosh Hashanah. For a month leading up to this Day of Judgment we are taught to be in repentance mode, taking inventory of our actions over the past year and seeking forgiveness from those we may have sinned against. The Talmud teaches that on Rosh Hashanah and Yom Kippur we ask God to forgive us for those sins we may have committed against Him. But if we want to truly enter the new Jewish year with a clean slate, we must also seek forgiveness from other people.

In elementary school, the rabbi made each of us go around the room, round-robin style, asking forgiveness from our fellow classmates.

"Jason, do you forgive me?" I asked.

"For what?" Jason replied.

He was just supposed to simply respond "yes," so I could move on to Josh, Kim, Hallie, Kevin, Joey, Stuart, and Suzanne. I had a crush on Suzanne.

"Nothing. I'm just asking for your forgiveness."

"Why?"

Jason was making this hard. And Suzanne was waiting.

"Um, because the rabbi said so?"

Jason stood there, silent. He was making me mad. He should've been asking *me* for forgiveness.

For better or worse, this well-intentioned but scripted tradition spilled over to our family as well. My brothers and sisters and I all sought forgiveness from each other the day before Rosh Hashanah. It was like a big Cohen family intervention. Held every year. On the exact same day.

For the most part, these were hollow requests thrown into regular conversation.

So, how is school going? Did you take out the trash? Oh, by the way, do you forgive me for anything I may have said or done to you this year? Great. So did you watch Alf *last night?*

As we got older and moved to different cities, the in-person pleas for forgiveness turned into phone calls that started trickling in hours before sunset. My older sister, Rachel, was usually the first to call, followed by Dani, Elie, Chanie, and my stepbrothers, culminating with my brother Ezra texting me for forgiveness from his BlackBerry moments before the holiday began. And amid all of these long-distance calls whizzing across the country came the one I dreaded the most. The one from my father.

This was the Call of All Calls. We would exchange a few pleasantries. He even recited the traditional blessing a father gives to his son before a Jewish holiday. But then it would come.

"Do you have anything to ask me?" he would say.

Of course I did. Why did you force religion on me growing up? Why does it bother you so much that I'm not a rabbi? Is it really so bad that I didn't follow in your footsteps?

But that's not what he wanted to hear. He wanted me to ask for his forgiveness for the years of anguish I caused him. After my mother's passing, I had become emotionally if not geographically distant from him. We lived under the same roof and yet we couldn't have been further apart. I know that distance caused him unbearable pain. And perhaps that is why I continued down that path. Withholding love was the one way I knew how to hurt him, to gain control in our dysfunctional relationship.

I had rebelled in other ways as well—not attending his alma mater, a New York rabbinical college; not communicating with him the way my siblings did; disrespecting him; embarrassing him; mocking him; the list goes on. Let's just say I had something to apologize for. It all added up to a frayed and tattered connection at best.

In this instance, he was more than just my dad. He was my heavenly father calling from on high and exposing me for what I really was. A fraud. An observant Jew who simply went through the motions while failing to reach the spiritual depths of being a member of the tribe. It was the day before God would judge me for my past actions, and my dad, like any parent, wanted his child to walk into that situation with a clean slate. But

I was too stubborn. I remained, probably to a fault, like a little kid who wouldn't budge. I was a child of religious privilege, born into a family ripe with Judaism, yet I was still shunning that heritage.

Waiting for his call today is making me pace. How would I respond this year, a time when I am working to mend fences and grow spiritually? A time when I am trying my hardest to allow grace into my life.

I decide standing by the phone is not the most productive way to spend the day, so I fulfill a promise I made to Elizabeth's grandmother and take her to a Christian-sponsored museum exhibit called "From Abraham to Jesus," a touring display of sacred texts and artifacts from biblical times. She had been excited ever since I told her I could get us press passes to the event. Doing something religious, even if it is with my wife's evangelical grandmother, somehow feels like the right thing to do on the day before Rosh Hashanah.

As we're driving downtown, she tells me about a recent service at her church. Her church, she is constantly telling me, is like no other church. Ever since I started going to churches I've been asking her to take me, but she's afraid her house of worship is too "out there" and "odd" for me. She thinks I might mock it, which, I guess, is not completely out of the realm of possibility. Apparently, her church is a hybrid of evangelicalism, Pentecostalism ("Yes, we speak in tongues," she tells me), with some old-school tent revivalism thrown in for good measure. Sounds right up my alley, but she says I'll have to wait until she's ready to take me.

In the meantime, I enjoy our little chats about religion. Of all the Christians I've met, she seems the most fascinated by Judaism. And it's a genuine fascination. She appreciates Judaism so much because she looks at it as the roots of her own religion. Every time she comes over to our house, she goes directly to my shelves of Jewish books. She wants to read about the Dead Sea Scrolls. The myriad customs of Judaism. Even mysticism. When she sees my copy of *Kabbalah for Dummies,* she frowns. "That's not respectful," she says.

She's constantly asking me my opinion about the crisis in the Middle East.

"So, Benyamin, what do the Jews think about the president of Iran?"

"Well, we collectively discussed this at last week's Jew meeting, Grandma, but I'd get in big trouble if I told you."

She is someone who is constantly seeking a connection to faith. She actively seeks holiness, always searching for answers to life's most challenging questions. Her life is one guided by a Greater Being, and a person like that, I'm finding more and more, is someone I like to spend time with.

Grandma Martin, or Lee as she wants me to call her, is like a kid in a candy store once we arrive at the biblical archaeology exhibit. Oversized crates stamped with "Made in Israel" in block lettering dot every corner of every room. There's nothing actually in the crates. They're just here to add some archaeological ambience. I imagine it's what the *Indiana Jones* prop room looks like.

I bump into some fake sheep and their fake shepherd as we stroll through the bazaar, also known as an excuse for shameless marketing tie-ins disguised as ancient goods and sold in makeshift cloth booths. One was selling Judaica items. Another was selling Bible-themed DVDs (which I'm sure were very prevalent back in ancient marketplaces). One was even offering a "heritage affinity" credit card with a 5.6 percent introductory rate.

Once inside the exhibit itself, we walk by a fifteen-foot stone replica of the Ten Commandments. I offhandedly remark how cool it would be to have these in my living room. "No, not in your house," Grandma Martin tells me. "They should be in all the courts of justice."

Later, we pass by a large curtain with Hebrew writing from the Old Testament. The docent speaking in our rented headphones says it's from Deuteronomy, but I tell Grandma Martin it's actually from Genesis. Other patrons hear me, and I start to read and translate each verse for those gathered around us. As we peruse other mislabeled Hebrew artifacts, including a Torah scroll from fifteenth-century Germany, I regale the growing crowd with my bilingual abilities. Here, amid senior citizens and evangelicals, I am a rabbinic rock star. Finally, my dad would be so proud.

THE *HASHKAMA* HIGH Holiday service takes place in a small classroom in the synagogue building. Including Elizabeth and myself, there are fewer than twenty people here—a vast and welcome difference from the hundreds gathered in the nearby main sanctuary. The intimacy and overall lack of pomp and circumstance remind me of the synagogue of my youth, the small sanctuary my dad had built onto the side of our home, the one where I first (and ever too briefly) encountered God through prayer.

Sitting on a metal folding chair in the corner of the classroom, I feel all alone—and that's a good thing. Too often during the High Holidays I feel as if there's a spotlight shining on me and the hundreds of people congregated are all staring at me. I myself have always pictured conversing with the Almighty as a one-on-one endeavor. What this small *hashkama* service has figured out is a way to bring the conversation with the divine back down to the personal level, and it is refreshing.

Our tradition teaches that Rosh Hashanah is the Jewish holiday when God determines who will live and who will die during the coming year. That's pretty serious. As the liturgy eloquently states, "Who will die at his predestined time and who before his time; who by water and who by fire, who by sword, who by beast, who by famine, who by thirst, who by storm, who by plague, who by strangulation, and who by stoning." It's like a menu at a macabre take-out joint, a laundry list of divine retribution that would scare even the most devout atheists.

And it continues: "Who will rest and who will wander, who will live in harmony and who will be harried, who will enjoy tranquility and who will suffer, who will be impoverished and who will be enriched, who will be degraded and who will be exalted." These words always got to me. Even as a kid, I remember connecting with these simple, yet profound, sentences during the service. Among pages of Hebrew text about high-minded topics like benevolence and kingship, these sentences were the proverbial bottom line. The Cliff Notes to what the entire Day of Judgment was all about.

Praying to God doesn't have to be this awkward and deeply existential experience. It can be about the very things that matter most—living a life of harmony and tranquility, not one filled with suffering and tragedy. Forget the sacrifices, ancient Israel, agrarian needs, and all the other obscure topics usually discussed in our daily Jewish prayers. As hard as I tried, I was never going to be able to relate to those. I was not a farmer offering up a lamb on an altar in Jerusalem. That stuff made as much sense to me as IRS tax codes.

As we do on each Sabbath and holiday, the congregation takes the Torah scroll from the ark and places it on a table to read in the middle of the service. It's like a brief intermission, and today is no different. On Rosh Hashanah, synagogues read from Genesis, the episode of Abraham attempting to sacrifice his son Isaac. At first glance, this seems like an odd section to read. What relevance does it have for us on this Day of Judgment?

I once read a book by Rabbi Reuven Bulka, a noted psychologist and Bible scholar, who answered this question by pointing to the end of the incident, the part where Abraham miraculously finds a ram to sacrifice in place of his son. It's a good thing for Isaac, but what sometimes gets forgotten is a short phrase in that verse. As it says in Genesis 22:13, "And Abraham raised his eyes and saw—behold, a ram!—afterwards, caught in the thicket, by its horns; so Abraham went and took the ram and offered it up as an offering instead of his son."

What point is the Bible trying to make by adding the phrase "caught in the thicket"? What significant detail is added by relaying to readers that the ram was stuck by his horns?

Picture the scene. Abraham notices a ram approaching him. The ram gets caught in some nearby hedges. If it hadn't gotten stuck, we could naturally assume that the ram was headed directly for the biblical patriarch. It would have been easy for Abraham to take this ram—which had fallen into his lap so conveniently—and sacrifice it to God. But that's not how it went down. The ram gets stuck by its horns in the hedges. Now Abraham is forced to expend his own energy, untangle the horns from the hedges, and then sacrifice the animal.

By the minor addition of this phrase, Rabbi Bulka explains, the Bible is teaching us a profound lesson. We cannot sit idly by and wait for faith to nonchalantly come strolling up to us. We cannot expect that it will come and simply tap us on the shoulder. If only it were that easy. No, instead, we need to take that important first step and make an effort to run after faith.

As the Torah scroll is brought back to the ark, I recall Abraham's zealousness and look to it for an inspiration. In years past, I had become the grinch who stole Rosh Hashanah. I looked forward to this Jewish holiday season with the same enthusiasm as a guy being wheeled in for open-heart surgery. But now, this year, I am beginning to see it in a new light. God is not just judging us today; he's actually giving us the opportunity to grab life by the horns, so to speak, and make something special out of it. Faith, after all, is not a spectator sport.

I hadn't fallen off a religious path. I had merely sat down on the path and taken a break. My religious observance had been a stagnant pool, a quagmire in which I attempted to wade around, barely moving at all. And year after year of fruitless wading was tiring.

So this is the challenge before me. After I leave the high of the High Holidays and reenter a predictable day-to-day existence, I need to somehow find a way to carry this feeling of religious vigor with me as I continue on my journey. I need to look to my ancestor Abraham. His early-to-rise attitude, his active untangling of the ram from the thicket—these are the actions of a go-getter, someone who doesn't sit idly by waiting for moments of faith to come to him. For that matter, I need to look toward a more recent ancestor as well—Grandma Martin. She, in her own unique way, is zealous in her constant and active search for spiritual meaning in her life. Like Abraham, she has taught me the importance of not standing still. And that is a model I hope to follow on the path to meaningful growth.

Yes, the High Holidays may be over, but I hope their message will stick with me. Perhaps it is a shame, as the clever gurus of Starbucks eloquently point out, that the holidays only happen once a year.

EIGHT

Any Given Sunday

The king asked, "Is there no one still left of the house of Saul to whom I can show God's kindness?" Ziba answered the king, "There is still a son of Jonathan; he is crippled in both feet."
—*2 Samuel 9:3*

OF ALL THE types of Christian churches I know, evangelical churches seem to be the most exciting, the most fantastical, and the most entertaining. I wholly admit that this notion is based on nothing more than multiple viewings of the 1992 Steve Martin comedy *Leap of Faith,* about a crooked preacher who inspires the downtrodden at elaborate Holy Roller tent revival services. So, Steve Martin notwithstanding, I really am not sure what to expect.

I arrive about a half hour early at the Milestone Church in Norcross, Georgia, just in time for church-sponsored breakfast before the service. Kids are running wild around the social hall, some old men are socializing at one table, and there is a group of women gossiping in the corner.

The scene reminds me a bit of Saturday morning at synagogue. After the service, we have *kiddush,* which is basically a Hebrew term for refreshments in the social hall. *Kiddush* actually means "to sanctify" and refers specifically to the special blessing we recite beforehand over a glass of wine, but this *kiddush* has nothing to do with sanctity. It has to do with eating and socializing.

I've been going to church for a few months now, but I still feel uncomfortable breaking bread with those of another faith. And since I keep kosher (and, for that matter, shouldn't really be enjoying eggs benedict and oatmeal at Jesus' house), I steer clear of the cafeteria line here at Milestone and just plop down in a folding chair directly underneath a display of world flags on the wall. Israel is up there. I'm hoping people don't put two and two together.

In an effort to get a good seat in the sanctuary (and, at this point, feeling a tad nauseous from the overpowering stench of bacon), I walk next door to the other building. No sooner do I open the door than a woman who looks like a librarian in a jean jumper and shoulder pads unexpectedly leans in and kisses me on the cheek.

"Welcome to Milestone!" she says a bit too cheerfully.

I'm not a fan of kissing strangers or, for that matter, of women who look like librarians in jean jumpers. Or jean jumpers in general. But the kissing, that's an invasion of my private space and definitely not the way I'm used to being greeted when walking into worship services.

The Milestone Church sanctuary has kind of a rustic feel to it, like a really large lodge living room. I half expect to see Fred Flintstone and his bowling buddies. There are enough seats for about three hundred people, and by the end of the service, they are all filled with blue-collar types (perhaps some of whom may have actually been bowlers).

The menorah on the wall, an absurdly placed Judaic symbol, creeps me out. I guess I've always known that many Christians are fascinated with Jewish artifacts. Every time I see Elizabeth's evangelical grandmother she asks my opinion on the latest archaeological find in the Holy Land. I tell her I let my subscription to *Biblical Archaeological Review* lapse, so I'm not up on the latest dig.

Like many evangelicals here at the Milestone Church, Grandma Martin is what's known as a Christian Zionist. She believes that the Jewish return to Israel is part of biblical prophecy and, on some level, is a necessary precursor to the Apocalypse. In lay terms that means that the Second Coming of Jesus won't happen until all Jews are safe and sound in Israel. That being said, these Christians are Israel's new best friends and are often on the front lines, hand in hand with their Jewish compatriots, in the fight for peace in the Middle East. In this era of constant war in Israel, the Christian Zionists are still coming en masse, pumping much needed money into Israel's battered tourist economy.

San Antonio's Pastor John Hagee is one of the leaders spearheading this movement. In 2006, he created Christians United for Israel, a quasi-lobbyist group in support of the Holy Land. At an event one night he donated more than $7 million to Israel and to the Jews of Texas. This is a guy who once said, "Anyone who makes the life of Jewish people difficult or grievous, as did the Pharaoh, as did Hitler, will be cursed by God."

Although some Jewish leaders have been reluctant to embrace this Christian help with open arms, there is a growing cottage industry of Jewish groups who are taking advantage of this newfound financially beneficial friendship. One is an interfaith group called Toward Tradition, created by Rabbi Daniel Lapin. To give you some idea of how far he's willing to go out on a limb, he was one of the only rabbis in America to give two thumbs-up to Mel Gibson's *The Passion of the Christ.* Talk about your leap of faith. Then there's Rabbi Yechiel Eckstein, who founded the International Fellowship of Christians and Jews and has raised a quarter of a billion dollars by speaking at megachurches on behalf of Israel. Eckstein has Pat Robertson on speed dial and has the ear of America's other leading evangelical leaders. In the enlightening book on the relationship between Christian Zionists and Jews called *A Match Made in Heaven,* Zev Chafets writes of Eckstein: "No rabbi since Jesus has commanded this kind of gentile following." Now that's a ringing endorsement.

The truth is, Christianity has its roots in Judaism, so I guess it's not so far-fetched for Christians to be supporters of Israel and of my religion in general. But when Christian support for Israel turns into curiosity about Jewish religious symbols and traditions, I'll be honest—it freaks me out a little. For example, the Holyland Experience, a Bible-based Christian theme park just up the road from Disney World, sells Jewish books and knick-knacks in its gift shop. As the religion columnist for the *Orlando Sentinel,* Mark Pinsky has made more than two dozen trips to the park. In his book *A Jew Among the Evangelicals,* Pinsky writes of the Holyland Experience's Old Scroll Gift Shop, "It was filled with skullcaps, prayer shawls, shofars, mezuzahs, menorahs, braided Havdalah candles, and Passover plates." Among the books for sale, Pinsky "spotted *The Diary of Anne Frank* next to a biography of the Apostle Paul, and Chaim Potok's popular novel *The Chosen* opposite such evangelical materials as *What Every Jewish Person Should Ask,* promoting conversion to Christianity." He also notes that the hottest-selling piece of jewelry in the store is a Star of David with a cross in its center.

•   •   •

ON THE STAGE, erected in front of a huge fireplace, a band is setting up
its equipment. The church, which encourages early comers, is showing a
Christian music video on two flat panel televisions. Two dozen people, who
look like normal folk you would encounter on a daily basis, are swaying to
the music, hands raised to the heavens.

As for me, people keep coming up to me as if I'm running for political office. Within a few minutes, I count six people (including the senior
pastor) who shake my hand, pat me on the back, and welcome me to the
church. All I need is a baby and a photographer and my poll numbers
would spike ten points.

There's a wide array of parishioners: old, young, black, white. Of all the
churches I've prayed at so far, Milestone has the least homogenous crowd.
Perhaps it's because, of all the types of churches, evangelical Christianity
works in overdrive to promote the Good Book and spread the gospel. Its
open-door policy, for better or worse, attracts all kinds.

The service gets under way with a few songs by the house band. A di-
verse crowd of all ages is boogying to the music. Even the ten-year-old next
to me is high on the Spirit and, like most everyone, sporting a disturbingly
wide cultlike smile. There's a real palpable lack of cynicism here that is
new to me even as a regular synagogue-goer. I'm used to making fun of the
choir, not getting jiggy with it.

The music ends, and four preschool children line up next to a small pool
of water. It's their big day. They're being baptized. Before dunking, they all
"accept Jesus" to the cheers of everyone present. It's a strange sight, for sure,
but what's more strange to me is that these young kids are making such a
lifelong decision. The closest thing we have to this in Judaism is a bar mitzvah, which takes place when a boy is thirteen. For girls, who apparently
mature faster than boys, it's called a bat mitzvah and takes place at the
age of twelve. But even on this important day, Jewish kids are not given a
choice to accept Judaism or not. It's our obligatory rite of passage into adulthood more than anything else. We are now responsible for our own actions.
Indeed, at the ceremony, our parents recite a special blessing that basically
says, "Hey, this kid's not our problem anymore. He's on his own now." Because, if there's anything Judaism is good at, it's making us feel guilty. And,
as you can see, we don't mind starting that process at an early age.

The baptism comparison may work better for kids who want to *convert* to Judaism. Most rabbis will have them see a shrink first (seriously). And then, if they still want to be discriminated against for the rest of their lives, the rabbi will usually ask them to wait until they're at least eighteen, so they can be old enough to make such a serious lifelong decision. But here little children are giving their lives over to Christ. I don't know whether to be shocked or awed.

Just as I start to mentally compare the ritual waters of the *mikvah* to the baptismal bath, a fifty-something construction worker from the audience walks up to the front and gives what he calls a "praise update." He'd been in an accident five months ago and wants to say he's doing better now, thanks to the prayers of the congregation and the good grace of God. A few "Hallelujahs" fly out from the row behind me and linger in the air for a while.

The lead singer in the band, a seventeen-year-old girl, introduces the next prayer. She says she chose this verse because it spoke to her. At synagogue if a verse starts speaking to someone, we kindly escort them to Dr. Steinberg, the resident synagogue psychologist. It's a bit odd to see the church's prayer choices being dictated by a girl who's not even legally allowed to vote.

Our prayers were instituted centuries ago and haven't changed much at all over the years. I never understood this. How can we be inspired by a call to prayer that we recite exactly the same way, three times a day, twenty-one times a week? This spicing things up that I'm witnessing here may not be such a bad idea. Maybe Christians are on to something.

Congregants are invited to the altar, where a hundred or so people get on bended knee for personal prayer requests. I consider praying for something—perhaps asking if I could take that menorah off the wall—but think better of it. "Team leaders" assist the people who are crying by offering hugs. When the tears subside and people can now see clearly into their wallets, the collection basket is passed around, followed by a tiny shot of grape juice and bread. The series of disconnected activities is jarring to me, a veritable game of spiritual spin the bottle.

As I take the bread and pretend to eat it, an African American woman makes her way to the stage. "The doctor told me I only had 15 percent of my heart left," she says, clearly revealing more about her medical history than I care to know. "Isn't it marvelous how they don't know anything? But

God is *goooooood*. God knows everything." And then, totally unexpectedly, she breaks into an operatic song. "I'm going to let God take control," she belts out. In the last few minutes, we've somehow spiraled from Holy Communion to an *American Idol* audition.

"Is this a great place or what?" the pastor asks as he dives into his sermon. "You ain't seen nothing yet. Amen?"

"Amen," the crowd roars back.

He speaks about Exodus 3:7, the verse in which God talks to Moses from the burning bush, but he somehow makes a transatlantic leap to how God talks to everyone, especially children. Moses, Shmoses.

As Jews, we are taught that when God gave the Ten Commandments at Mt. Sinai, He first started speaking to the entire Jewish population gathered there. But His voice was so "powerful" that whenever He spoke, the people simply fainted. They just couldn't handle direct conversations with the Almighty. So God gave the rest of the commandments to Moses, who, in turn, passed them down to everyone else.

Although in Jewish tradition we can speak to God through prayer and supplication, we don't believe that God converses directly with mere mortals. Throughout biblical history, Moses was the only human to ever actually speak with God. (Talmudic sages explain that although God did talk with other prophets—Isaiah, Samuel, and Ezra, for example—it was not on the same "friendly" level as with Moses.) The bottom line, we were taught, was if you think God is speaking to you, go clean out your ears.

To hear this Christian preacher take this traditional Jewish text and explain that it means God speaks to everyone puts a knot in my stomach. This preacher was skewing the classical Jewish interpretation to fit his religion's beliefs. It's like someone moving into your house and playing with all your remote controls. You wouldn't be too happy.

Jewish versions of the Old Testament come with long commentaries surrounding the text on the page. The main biblical commentator is known as Rashi, who was an eleventh-century French rabbi. Others are also centuries old. We take this tradition very seriously.

I guess Christians would just say that I'm spiritually oppressed. When Jesus debated with the rabbis of old, that's precisely what they disagreed upon—tradition. Part of Jesus' original philosophy was to free his fellow Jews from the shackles of their religious tradition.

Maybe Christ was on to something, but to hear what this modern-day preacher does with what I know as sacred makes me itch. The sermon pokes at me, at a part of my soul that I didn't realize even cared about such things. *Hey, pastor, I don't go near your Testament. Stay away from mine.*

I feel uncomfortable and start to get fidgety. I came here today in a show of good interfaith understanding, to see what I can learn from Christians to make me a better Jew. So far, all of my Christian experiences on this journey have been pleasant at worst and inspiring at best. But this . . . this was something else altogether.

"Oh, praise God!" a woman yells from the audience.

I know deep down inside that I have no justifiable reason to feel this way. I recognize the humanity of the congregants here at Milestone. There are obviously kernels of genuine faith present here. These are people who, like me, are stumbling their way toward a more spiritual life. I know I shouldn't knock their service. Yet I am still unable to feel comfortable here.

I can take the chaotic potpourri of prayer, baptisms, and musical hijinks, but the biblical revisionism is just too much to handle. Feeling uneasy, I quietly leave the sanctuary. I notice a sign above the exit: "You are now entering the mission field." For me, my mind numbed by the whirlwind service I just witnessed, my mission is unclear.

THE MILESTONE CHURCH left a bad taste in my mouth (and, no, it wasn't the bacon). But I don't want one negative experience to throw me off track and derail my yearlong quest to live among and learn from my Christian neighbors. So I decide my next stop will be a more traditional church, one where ritual takes precedence over showmanship. Perhaps this more conventional prayer environment will sit better with a Jew like me.

Elizabeth tells me that if ritual is what I'm looking for, I should try an Episcopal church. And, as luck would have it, we live right across the street from one, St. Bartholomew's Episcopal Church. I can actually see inside the sanctuary from my bedroom window. So I do what any religiously bi-curious Jew would do who lives across the street from a church. I decide to go in.

I've come to the early service, which starts at 8 A.M. and obviously brings out a more devout crowd. I find myself, as on many Sabbath mornings, lazily dragging myself out of bed.

The church is literally a stone's throw from our home, so I walk over there. The problem is I live in a densely populated Jewish neighborhood. Within one square mile, more than 50 percent of the homes belong to

Jewish families. And they all know me. Not as Benyamin Cohen, but as the rabbi's son. Even in the few minutes it would take for me to walk over there, I'm sure I'd be spotted by someone I know.

I look both ways before crossing the street. But it isn't cars I'm trying to avoid. It's my community.

I pretend I'm just taking a walk, although being dressed in a suit on a Sunday morning kind of blows my cover. I think I spot someone I know, so I pass by the church driveway and keep walking. As soon as the car drives by and is out of sight, I backtrack and quickly run up the grassy hill to the church. I step in dog poo.

This is either pure coincidence or God's way of mocking me. After all, even if I can outrun my fellow Jews, outrunning the Lord above is a lot harder. I feel like Cain in Genesis 4:9, when God asks him about Abel. God knows what Cain did, just as He knows where I'm headed.

Dog poo aside, St. Bartholomew's seems like some holy digs. I'm not quite sure why. Maybe it's the ornate robes the reverends are wearing. Maybe it's the bells ringing a call to prayer. Maybe it's just the way the light shines through the glass section of the ceiling and directly onto the altar like rays from heaven.

As I find a seat, I notice the Hebrew word *Shalom* on a sign. It's as if the Episcopalians have been expecting me. The service starts with a thundering organ, a nice touch actually. It sounds like a movie score and adds to the drama of the moment.

Episcopalians in America—numbering five million (including, surprisingly, more than a quarter of U.S. presidents)—really know how to make a Jew feel comfortable. Unlike the light shows of New Birth and the cacophony of activities at Milestone, a peaceful solitude pervades the sanctuary here. We're right by a major street, but a small forest of trees serves as a natural barrier, providing a protected inner sanctum for those of us nestled inside.

As for the service itself, it's all very ritualistic. That's what I'm used to. So much of what I had witnessed at other churches was completely foreign to me, especially the prayers themselves. Instead of asking for specifics (sustenance, peace in Israel, Uncle Mort's successful gallbladder surgery) as we do in Judaism, those at the services at other churches seemed to pray for one thing and one thing only—to have a relationship with Jesus. Accept Jesus into your life and everything will be okay. That's all, folks.

For someone not brought up in a religion focused solely on our love for one man and what he did for us, this seemed vague and made little sense to me. But here at St. Bart's they were reciting an ancient liturgy, reading Psalms, and performing traditional rituals. This is the first time since I started this trip that I feel a connection to what Christians are doing during the service.

In a certain sense, the scattered activities that took place at Milestone Church are very all-American. Foremost is the power of the individual, the mantra of "I'm going to worship God the way I want." That translates into opera singing, praise updates, and having a teenager with a guitar decide which prayers to recite. For Jews, however, worship is a collective experience. We are only allowed to pray in the presence of a quorum of ten. The set prayers we recite each day are starting to make more sense to me. And I have St. Bart's to thank for that.

Here I am trying to run away from the strictures and monotony of Jewish prayers only to stumble upon and appreciate their Christian counterpart in the traditional Episcopal service. Everyone reaches the divine differently. My relationship to God, I'm beginning to realize, is through an ancient tradition. I knew this all along, but spending Sunday morning at St. Bart's was like a breath of fresh air.

Back at St. Bart's, about five different church leaders are now on the dais, all in Crusade-era robes, preparing for Communion with an elaborate wine-pouring ceremony using shiny silver vessels over a large table. All of them are facing the middle one, a slight reference to the Last Supper I suppose, in this moving ecclesial ritual.

The service at St. Bart's concludes as it had begun—on a dramatic note. The organ comes to a crescendo, and the congregants file to the front for their wafer and blessing. I watch silently from the back.

I once heard that it used to be if you weren't a Christian, you'd have to actually leave the church during this part of the service, the Eucharist. It's like an exclusive secret club, and we Jews are not invited. This intrigues me for two reasons. One, I'm curious to know which non-Christians before me spent so much time in church that a law barring them had to be enacted. And, two, this reminds me of the Jewish prayer known as the Yizkor. It's a prayer we recite during certain holidays in memory of loved ones who have passed on. If your immediate family is still alive, you don't recite this prayer and you're asked to actually leave the synagogue for a few minutes while the mourners pray.

As an elementary-school kid, I was pushed outside into the lobby with all the other nonmourners. But I always wondered what went on in the sanctuary after we left. My childish mind actually thought the ghosts of those who had died came back, ever so briefly, to visit their still-living relatives. This childish notion was shattered when I was just thirteen and my mom passed away.

After her death, I eagerly awaited the first holiday that rolled around on the calendar. Passover came about three months after she died. I got to synagogue early. It came time for the recitation of the Yizkor and more than half the congregants shuffled outside. With nervous trepidation, I remained in my seat.

That first Passover I recited the Yizkor, I looked around the room at my fellow mourners, this new category that now included me, unwittingly, as its youngest member. We all recited the prayer, and I was the first to finish. I stood there waiting for something magical to happen. There were no ghosts. There was no update from God telling us our loved ones were in heaven and doing well. At the very least, I half expected a gust of wind to blow through the synagogue popping open the doors to the ark.

Ten minutes went by, and it was all over. There was no visit from my mom. There was no Jewish Casper the Friendly Ghost to be seen. Maybe I hadn't prayed the Yizkor correctly, I wondered.

I've since read up on the true meaning of the Yizkor. More than being a mere form of emotional release for the relatives who are left behind on this earth, the prayer is supposed to remind us of a central tenet of Judaism—that the living can redeem the dead. Through our prayers and Torah study, we have the ability to sanctify those who have passed on. The merit of the children has the ability to help those who have passed. This is the truest legacy of the deceased. My mom no longer had the opportunity to fulfill God's commandments, but through her children and our pious acts here on earth we are able to elevate her soul in her stead. This is supposed to be one of the most selfless acts we can do.

So now, standing in the back of a church, I begin to feel guilty. I shouldn't be in here. What kind of merit is this for my mother? Is her soul being downgraded to a lower plane of heaven because of my selfish crusade to be a better Jew by gallivanting through Bible Belt churches?

• • •

I SLOWLY TRUDGE outside and leave St. Bart's less quickly than when I had dashed up the hill on the way in. I see a man in a wheelchair waiting at the bus stop in front of the church parking lot. I noticed him inside during the service rolling up the aisle to receive his Communion wafer. Instead of crossing the street to go back home, I walk over to the bus stop to introduce myself.

He tells me his name is Ron Peterson and he's thirty-eight years old. For the last several years he's been making his way to the early service at St. Bart's. Which must be extremely hard considering he's confined to a wheelchair and living by himself several miles away.

He has dystonia, a rare neurological muscle disorder that causes him to twist into abnormal poses. His contorted body gives him the appearance of a younger Stephen Hawking. The disease has already ravaged his body and reduced him to slow and stilted speech. It's a progressive disease, so it's only getting worse for Ron. Yet here he is. Week in and week out. Taking public transportation from his home to the church and back again.

The truth is I had actually seen Ron before. Every Sunday morning as I walked my two dogs, I'd seen Ron rolling his way from the church to the bus stop. I wondered what would compel a man such as him to believe in a merciful God. Ron had every right to turn his face from the Almighty for inflicting him with this disease. If this wasn't a case of the age-old question "Why do bad things happen to good people?" then I didn't know what was.

I begin to feel indignant. Ron doesn't deserve to be punished like this. He's a religious man. He's a man of God. So why would the Almighty strike him with such a debilitating disease? Just as the thought crosses my mind, I already know the answer. That's just it—he's a religious man. He's a man of God. Not only can he handle his fate in life, but he looks at his lot in life as a blessing. He tells me this is what God intended for him. Ron has simply accepted it and moved on.

Thank God, I don't have a chronic illness or a physical handicap, because I don't think I could handle it with the same grace and courage as Ron. I would become an angry young man and, my guess is, it would make me less religious. But not Ron. Becoming practically paralyzed has transformed him into a man of deep faith.

"God plays a major role in my life," he confides to me as traffic whizzes by in front of us. "I think I would be lost without the church."

It's not just church. Ron is an overachiever when it comes to just about everything. He has two master's degrees and just graduated from the Emory School of Public Health. He now works for the Centers for Disease Control in its data department. This guy, confined to a wheelchair, is more active than I am—even on a good day.

The bus is running late, so I have some time to chat with Ron about my own spiritual journey. I'm hoping some of his unfiltered enthusiasm for life and faith will rub off on me. As if I was an old friend, he immediately opens up and tells me that going to St. Bart's is the one thing that makes him feel like a complete human being again. Inside the walls of the church, no one looks at him as a gimp or a handicap. They look at him as their fellow parishioner and treat him as one of their own. It's this incredible sense of fellowship and brotherhood that brings him back each week. The disease may have terrorized his body, but it hasn't gone near his spirit.

Perched on the corner of the sun-dappled sidewalk, we are two men in our thirties, each on a totally different path in life. One of us is disgruntled with religion, while the other can't roll his wheelchair fast enough for a faith fix. Yet we have both converged on this one spot at this one point in time in each of our spiritual journeys. I feel woefully inadequate.

Seeing how other people worship, how other people relate to God, is starting to have an effect on me. I still didn't totally "get it," but at least I knew that the joy Christians had about religion, the joy I had anticipated at the beginning of this journey, was indeed genuine.

I ask Ron what advice he would give to those who don't frequent a house of worship. "I would get them to try it out once," he says. "Once they're there, show them how enjoyable it is." Then, without flinching, he adds, "And get them to come again."

The bus arrives and lowers its handicap ramp, and Ron rolls inside. A moment later I am left alone on the sidewalk. Spending time with the parishioners of St. Bart's was a truly inspirational way to start my week. Spending time with Ron was even better. I scrape the remaining dog poo off my sole. It's my soul, however, that is already starting to be cleansed.

NINE

The Prince and I

Are not you Israelites the same to me as the Cushites?
—Amos 9:7

AT THIS PRECISE moment in time, I find myself sitting wedged between two princes of the African Hebrew Israelite community in the backseat of a brand-new white Cadillac DeVille winding its way through southwest Atlanta. It's a chilly November day, and smoke from the exhaust pipe billows out the back as we wait at a red light by some dusty train tracks and what appears to be an abandoned crack house. As the light turns green, I ask Prince Asiel, the royal fellow to my left, if he has any children. He tells me he has fifteen, which is actually not such an astonishing number once you hear what he tells me next.

"Well, you know, from four wives."

Admitting you're polygamous is not normally preceded by the casual southern California phrase "you know," but then again nothing I had experienced today could be described as normal.

He explains to me the benefits of polygamy, including having more people around to help take care of all the children. "Also," he says looking me straight in the eye, "when one of them is a *niddah,* you have other wives you can be with." *Niddah* is the Hebrew term for the Jewish law that requires a man and wife to abstain from marital relations while she is menstruating.

Here I am sitting next to a guy who's polygamous, yet versed in the laws of the Torah. And oh, yes, he's black. And a prince. Of what I wasn't yet sure.

•   •   •

ALLOW ME TO back up. It's Thanksgiving. As usual, Elizabeth and I
are spending the day with her extended family—aunts, uncles, cousins,
cousins' new girlfriends—the usual coterie of non-Jews in my life. Not
having grown up celebrating Thanksgiving in any meaningful way, I
looked forward to our annual pilgrimage to the outskirts of Atlanta to
participate in the celebration of Elizabeth's All-American Christian Family
Thanksgiving.

Each year, I try to prepare myself for the occasion. The first time
Elizabeth brought me, I came dressed in a suit and tie (which is what I
would wear to a Jewish festival meal with my family). I quickly realized
a nice casual sweater would have worked better for this crowd. The next
year, I read the sports scores before we went, so I could pretend to have
typical guy conversations with all of Elizabeth's uncles (one of whom is a
high-school football referee). But even then I could never quite grasp the
gist of the conversation.

Hunting is also a popular sport among Elizabeth's family. Last year, at
Christmas, her youngest cousin got a gun. At his age, I was lucky if I got
a water pistol. This morning, one of the teenage cousins actually shot and
killed a deer nearby, and part of it is now on the grill in the backyard. Moments later, Elizabeth's aunt offers us some barbecued venison, most certainly not slaughtered according to the myriad kosher laws. And, as if that
isn't enough, she hands the meat to me wrapped in a piece of bacon.

The food, scrumptious as it looks, is the least of my concerns today. This
afternoon I will be interviewing a polygamous prince of a cult known for
being a hybrid of Judaism, Christianity, and some made-up religion; so I'm
a tad distracted. I had been trying for nearly a year to get in touch with
him—or anyone from the cloistered communities dispersed in various
cities across the United States. But to no avail. My calls were not returned.
And, to be perfectly honest, it was no surprise. The group has been (for
lack of a better word) crucified in the press since its inception in 1968.
Rumors of cultlike behavior and criminal activity have surrounded much
of the mainstream press given to the African Israelites, known to many
simply as the Black Hebrews.

Like reports of many supposed cults, I had heard bad things about
them. I read wild claims on the Internet of murders of ex-members who

had fled the group, FBI warrants, and charges of wire fraud and cashing forged checks to the tune of millions of dollars. In 1985, the U.S. government arrested twenty-seven members of the group—including the prince I was meeting today—for running a complex credit-card and passport fraud ring. The convictions were ultimately overturned, and when prosecutors sought a retrial, the prince pleaded to a lesser charge.

It's no wonder they didn't want to be interviewed. They were fugitives.

So it was quite a surprise when my phone rang not too long ago, and it was a woman, the secretary of the highest-ranking member of the sect in America, Prince Asiel. "The prince will speak to you now," she said in a very businesslike manner.

Moments later, a bombastic voice. "Mr. Cohen, so nice to speak with you." It was the prince. He seemed nice, genuine, and told me he'd be coming to town in a week's time to visit the Atlanta community on Thanksgiving. He said I could come and spend the afternoon with him at the group's headquarters. I had planned on a day of watching the Macy's parade and family time but, hey, the prince was coming. You don't want to mess with royalty.

So despite offers of deer enveloped in pig, I have to leave the family celebration with my in-laws. "Sorry, guys. The food looks delicious, and I hate to eat and run, but I've got to go interview a polygamous cult leader who, apparently, doesn't celebrate Thanksgiving."

They look at me oddly and offer to pray for my safety. I exit stage left.

I venture downtown to meet the Chicago-based American leader of the African Hebrew Israelites of Jerusalem. Yes, I know, it's a mouthful.

It's about 2 p.m. when my photographer, Alex, and I drive up to the block of stores that are owned by the local contingency of the Black Hebrews. As I help Alex, a South American Catholic, unload his equipment, I notice he's wearing a rather large belt buckle with "Jesus" emblazoned across it. I could only pray his sartorial decision wouldn't offend.

We walk past the barbershop and welcome center and into a third store, a vegan restaurant called Soul Vegetarian. We're the only nonblacks in the entire place, and everyone is wearing African garb and various head-dresses. I hear people speaking Hebrew at one table. A poster on the wall touts "The Genesis Forum: Adamic Man vs. Evolution."

A waitress greets us, and I tell her we're here to see Prince Asiel. She runs to the back and returns with Sister Yafah, a woman in her forties dressed in an orange African outfit and sporting a necklace with the Hebrew words *Chai Yah* ("God Is Alive").

She introduces herself and leads us down a hallway and into a back room. The term "back room" really doesn't begin to do this justice. This isn't Tony Soprano's boys club in the back of the Bada Bing. It looks more like a hotel ballroom. The dim lights add ambience; the regal table is set with fancy silverware and dishes atop black and gold tablecloths. Tribal art lines the walls.

The room is a sea of excitement. A few bodyguards line the room. Several young women are bustling back and forth putting drinks down on the table and covering them with napkins (a custom that I would later learn was so the germaphobic Black Hebrews could keep dust out of their drinks). Sister Yafah grabs a seat next to Daniella, the prince's personal secretary. It all seems like a carefully choreographed dance.

Prince Asiel, a towering man at well over six feet tall, bounds forward to greet me. With his salt-and-pepper beard, he reminds me a bit of Afghan president Hamid Karzai. Maybe it's because he's wearing one of those hats that African politicians wear. Think Eddie Murphy and Arsenio Hall in *Coming to America*.

Next to him is Prince Rahm, the local Atlanta leader of the group. The African Hebrew Israelites have twelve princes, each corresponding to one of the twelve tribes. Asiel is the highest-ranking prince in America and the second in command to the group's leader in Israel.

They offer me something to drink—tea, juice, even one of their no-sugar smoothies. I opt for water. I can't quite bring myself yet to drink from the proverbial Kool-Aid.

After we sit down and exchange pleasantries, I turn my tape recorder on and begin. I don't want the first thing out of my mouth to be "I hear you're a convicted criminal," so I opt for a safer query about the group's origin.

Asiel launches into a thirty-minute meandering history lesson, trying to prove that there must have been black Jews in biblical times. He explains that when the Romans destroyed the Second Temple in 70 c.e., many Jews fled to Africa.

"I bring all this up to show you that this wasn't just something that grew out of the 1960s," he says with a laugh, obviously making that comment because he knows most articles about the group make exactly that point. In the aftermath of the civil rights movement, blacks were trying to find a reenergized identity. Some chose the black power movements or Louis Farrakhan's Nation of Islam. And some followed a man named Ben Carter.

Carter, a factory worker from Chicago, claims that in February 1966 the angel Gabriel appeared to him in a vision and told him to lead African Americans (who he believed were from the lost tribe of Judah) back home to the promised land. Carter promptly changed his name to Ben Ammi (Hebrew for "Son of My People") and began hosting classes to spread his new message.

Ben Ammi told his followers that before they could return to Israel, they would have to cleanse themselves of Western culture during a layover in Africa. So in May 1967, Ben Ammi and a couple hundred followers landed in Liberia, where they spent two and a half years "detoxing" themselves from what Prince Asiel dubs the "mentality that America had super-imposed upon us in terms of its culture. Then we reconnected with our Jewish roots," he says.

In July 1969, the first family left Liberia, went to Israel, and eventually settled in the desert community of Dimona, about thirty kilometers south of Be'er Sheva, the biblical city of Abraham. The town, which happens to house Israel's little-known nuclear research facility, was pretty much deserted before they got there. As soon as he mentions Dimona, I'm re-minded of news reports from a few years back about Whitney Houston and Bobby Brown making a pilgrimage there. It couldn't hurt to ask. In fact, the prince smiles when I bring it up.

"I met Whitney about six or seven years ago," he says. "She heard about the African Americans who lived in Israel and wanted to visit. Her and Bobby and the family came over and spent a week there. It was a fantastic trip for us as well."

There are now about three thousand African Hebrew Israelites living in Dimona, and another twenty thousand in American cities such as Chicago, Atlanta, Cleveland, St. Louis, Los Angeles, Houston, Dallas, Philadelphia, and Detroit.

And, despite public opinion to the contrary, the Black Hebrews all consider themselves Jewish. It's why I've been trying so hard to interview them. Mainstream American Jewry looks at them, at best, as a circus act and, at worst, as a cult. Regardless, they claim to be my biblical brothers, so I wanted to hear them out.

The prince, who rarely grants interviews, was actually intrigued by my upbringing. Since I'm an Orthodox rabbi's son who married a minister's daughter, the prince thought that made me an open-minded Jewish journalist who could look past the peculiarity (and the decades of poor PR) of the Black Hebrews. It does, to a certain extent, but nothing I had ever been exposed to had prepared me for the bizarre traditions of this group.

"As most Jews who have been scattered, we picked up many of the habits of the African countries that we were in as well as the African American community," the prince, who grew up in Chicago and nowhere near Africa, tells me. "But I think the common thread that we maintain, like all Jews, is next year in Jerusalem, the Torah is the basis of our fundamental belief in the God of Israel, a kosher diet, a clean diet, the recognition of the Sabbath as the holy day—these were the things that we maintained."

He goes on to explain that their goal is to follow everything in the written law (i.e., the Five Books of Moses), but not the oral law (i.e., the Mishnah and the Talmud). So they celebrate biblical holidays like Sukkot and Passover, but stay away from the Jewish holidays of Chanukah and Purim, which weren't instituted until later on in history. They believe in the "biblical diet," so they are strict vegans, don't eat any processed food, canned goods, or anything with sugar in it. They are so obsessed with their health that they also abstain from all alcohol, caffeine, and even most pharmaceutical drugs.

"Most of the European Jews took the traditions of the Mishnah and the Talmud and the writings of the sages," he says. "Most of us maintained that because we didn't have access to those writings, the Tanach was the fundamental document that we stayed closely aligned with."

Asiel's use of the word "Tanach," Hebrew for the Old Testament, catches me off guard. Indeed, throughout our day together he peppers his speech with mentions of the Rambam (an obtuse nickname for Maimonides) and other Jewish phrases. It is clear he is well versed in *halacha* (Hebrew for "Jewish law"—and another word he uses frequently). Indeed, he sounds strangely rabbinic.

The prince goes on and on. And somehow his monologue evolves into a meditation on how black performers have brought jazz and soul back to the Middle East. I wasn't aware that (a) there actually was a jazz renaissance going on somewhere in the underground dives of Jerusalem and (b) that it was the African Hebrew Israelites who were carrying said burden on their broad shoulders. Indeed, I have no idea what any of this means, and I'm waiting for Prince Asiel to explain it to me.

"I see us enriching Judaism in a very special way," he says, as he leans back in his chair. "Because in our genes, remember, what we brought back to Israel is Miles Davis, Johnny Coltrane, Martin Luther King. We brought the richness of the best of the African American experience to the Holy Land. We have brought soul back to Israel."

I'm still not sure where he's going with this. At first glance, Coltrane wouldn't appear to be the very epitome of African American culture to use for this example. After all, wasn't he born a Christian and didn't he marry a Muslim, only to end up singing about Hinduism in his seminal 1965 recording "Om"?

But like the religiously curious Coltrane, Asiel's group is a holy hybrid of many cultures, a veritable amalgam of the best Jews and blacks had to offer. At least that's what I think he was saying.

ABOUT AN HOUR after I arrive, Asiel and his entourage give me a tour of the facilities. He leads me through the winding hallways of the nineteen-thousand-square-foot compound, barely any of which is visible from the main road. On the front of each door is a sign. Except for the actual words displayed, they are all pretty much identical. Same size, same typeface. One says "Ginger Root Production." Another, "Wisdom Hut" (a bookstore). And yet another, "Braids Unlimited." I poke my head in and see several women braiding each other's hair. When they notice the prince behind me, they all sheepishly smile and say, *"Shalom, nasi. Baruch habah"*—Hebrew for "Hello, prince. Blessed is your coming."

Another door says "Boutique Afrika"; behind it they're selling tribal garb. And across from that is a spa where, at the moment, a woman is getting a manicure. The prince tells me that, as part of their biblical health regime, the women receive reflexology treatments and are required to get monthly massages. Around the corner is another barbershop and spa—these are for the men. A sign on the wall says it was voted best barbershop in Atlanta by a local newspaper. I feel as though I'm getting a tour of the Wonka factory.

We walk through the kitchen of the restaurant and through another labyrinth of hallways lined with photographs of Ben Ammi in gold frames and into a large auditorium. "This is our royal banquet hall," Asiel says, spreading his arms wide for added effect. People are setting up rows and rows of chairs facing a podium atop a stage. Hundreds of people are expected here in a couple of hours from as far away as St. Louis to hear the prince's remarks.

Off to the side is a closed door that, when opened, leads to a winery where they bottle their own fermented nonalcoholic fruit drink. Inside, Sister Yafah serves as the vintner. "Here, take," the prince says grabbing a bottle. "It's kosher wine."

I assume this is the end of the grand tour, but I can't be more wrong. They proceed to take me down a dark staircase with no exits in sight. To say that I was scared is an understatement.

The stairs lead us into a basement. To the right is an office with dated computers and furniture. "This is our travel agency," the prince nonchalantly tells me, as if it's normal for religious compounds to have fully functional travel agencies in their basement.

"And over here is our architecture firm," the prince says, pointing to another area, again very casually. It has its own waiting room and mock entrance as if it's a stand-alone storefront—yet it's just facing the travel agency across the room. I feel as if I'm in a warehouse of sets from television shows. I peek inside and see a man sitting behind a drafting table. Of all the shops and businesses in this building, this one actually makes some sense. Many of the community's members are in the construction industry. After all, it was they who constructed this compound and all the stores in it.

We turn a corner, and another room reveals a toilet and a massage table. "This is where we come to get colonics," the prince says. He pats me on my stomach and, laughing, suggests maybe I need one.

We round another corner and come face-to-face with what appears to be the inside of a state-of-the-art video production facility. There are screens all around the room. The prince tells me this is where they make infomercials and educational DVDs, many of which are sold in the bookshop upstairs. As well, the group boasts the Kingdom News Network, which includes a twenty-four/seven Internet radio station and, of course, the official KNN blog.

Outside that room are cubicles filled with computers. Each desktop wallpaper features a picture of Ben Ammi. "This is our Internet café," he says. There's practically a whole underground civilization down here that no one knows about. None of this is advertised from the street level. I snap a mental picture in my head. Nobody is going to believe this.

Back upstairs and outside, the sun is beginning to set as more people are driving in from various cities to see the prince. As we stand on the sidewalk across the street from the raw food market, which the group also owns, people approach the prince with hugs and high-fives.

A group of teenage boys with skullcaps and *tzitzit* (Jewish fringes) are chatting with the prince in Hebrew. He hugs each, smiling. To many, some of whom come from broken homes, the prince is somewhat of a father figure.

Suddenly, almost out of nowhere, a white Cadillac DeVille pulls up to the curb and the prince grabs my arm. "Come, let's go for a ride. I want to show you our preschool." One of the bodyguards is driving the vehicle. My photographer, Alex, sits in the front, and I squeeze into the middle of the backseat between Prince Asiel and Prince Rahm. The crowd on the sidewalk looks on as we speed off. It's all too surreal.

And it's now, as we drive to a place where children play, that the good prince informs me of his polygamous ways. Fifteen kids. Four wives. I turn to Prince Rahm and ask him the same question. Turns out he has twelve kids, five grandkids, and a number of wives. Asiel informs me the ideal in their tradition is to have seven wives.

We pull up to the Genesis Early Learning Center. Before the African Hebrew Israelites came along, this property was an abandoned crack house. Now I'm staring at a beautiful building, carefully constructed by the members of its community. It's a few years old, but it still smells brand-new.

They may not celebrate Thanksgiving, but the place is still closed for the day. The bodyguard unlocks the front door, and we walk in. I feel as if I'm standing in the lobby of a typical Jewish school. Hebrew letters surround children's festive Sukkot artwork on a bulletin board.

The first classroom has a dozen cribs in it; the school starts with kids just a few weeks old and goes up until first grade. The place is filled to capacity with more than a hundred students, and they have plans to build an adjoining elementary school within the next two years. As we walk through the other classrooms, I notice Jewish names on the cubbies: Esther, Adina ... Muhammad? Apparently, this kindergarten is so highly regarded in the community, many of the people who live in the area send their children here. And it certainly doesn't hurt that it only costs a hundred and twenty-five dollars a week—and that includes the vegan meals catered by the nearby Soul Vegetarian restaurant.

As we leave the preschool, the prince points to a row of homes. "You see those three houses? Those are owned by the community. Come, let me show you."

The bodyguard walks in front of us to knock on the door of the first house. I feel terrible. What if the residents aren't prepared to welcome the prince into their home? I protest and say we don't need to see the homes.

"No, no, I want to show you. This way you'll know that we didn't prepare this just for you," he says. Well, he has a point.

When the bodyguard knocks on the first door, an attractive young black woman answers. She sees the prince and bows her head. "*Shalom, nasi.*"

"*Hakol bseder* (Everything well)?" he asks her.

"*Ken, ken* (Yes, yes)."

They've lit some kind of incense, and the place smells wonderful. In a strange way, this reminds me of a Jewish home. A big dining-room table with candlesticks, a traditional couch, and on the wall Hebrew artwork hangs alongside photos of Ben Ammi.

As we walk down a corridor, beautiful young black women poke their heads out of bedrooms. They all bow their heads and say, "*Shalom, nasi,*" as we pass.

THE BLACK HEBREWS consider themselves Jewish and, although the ones living in America may not have daily or even weekly synagogue services, they do have some sort of communal prayers. It's called the Institute of Divine Understanding. Yes, it sounds a little like Scientology, something Tom Cruise would promote while jumping on Oprah's couch, but I figure if I'm spending a year going to various houses of worship, I should probably check this out.

It's held each Sunday afternoon in the royal banquet hall. When I enter, there are already about forty people—men, women, and children—there, but the crowd will balloon to well over two hundred before this is all over.

There are two men on the stage. One is preaching about something from Psalms, and anytime he wants to quote from the text, he points to the second guy, who reads from the text. Only in their translation the word

"Ben Ammi" is substituted for the word "God." "And we will dwell in the house of Ben Ammi forever," the reader calls out to the crowd. I feel like asking a question, but the two bodyguards at each end of the stage make me think twice.

After the speech, another man is called up to tell us the Divine Current Events. It sounds like a bad parody of *Saturday Night Live*'s news-update segment, but it's not—this is real. Wearing a tan African outfit and a purple skullcap, the man recites a Hebrew formula. I caught a few of the words. *Rabeinu hamashiach* ("Our master the messiah") . . . *Kol hakavod* ("He should be honored") . . . Hallelujah. Throughout the next three hours there are many speakers. And they all start off their speeches with this same Hebrew blessing. It's their own homemade gospel, their own Lord's Prayer.

Mr. Black Hebrew Cronkite begins a dissertation on heaven and hell. "Strip clubs would not exist in the Kingdom of Yah, but since we live in hell we have to navigate around them." He speaks of "social constructs," and in addition to quoting from the *Atlanta Journal-Constitution,* he cites the Old Testament and a Bible-like book written by Ben Ammi.

The more I listen, the more I get the feeling these are a peaceful people stuck in an evil world of anti-Yahs. They may look strange on the outside, but inside they are a conservative, family-values-oriented community just trying to get by like the rest of us.

The news-update fellow finishes, and then a woman in a headdress comes to the stage to give the weekly Divine Health Update. Afterward, she finishes her health speech by making an announcement about their self-imposed "National Sugarless Week," which, she says, starts on *Yom Shishi* (Friday) and ends a week later on *Motzei Shabbat* (after the Sabbath). As with any Jewish custom, she rattles off a list of laws regarding what's permitted and what's not.

Just as she's finishing, someone on the side of the room shouts at the top of his lungs, "All rise in the presence of the great Prince Rahm!" Everyone jumps up and shouts back, "Hallelujah! Hallelujah!" repeatedly with arms raised in the air. "*Yah Chai!*" they continue, Hebrew for "God is alive," over and over.

It all feels a little cultish, but who am I to judge? As an observant Jew, I do weird things too. I walk in the rain, sans umbrella, on the Sabbath. So these people welcome their leader with great dignity and lots of shouting. It could be worse.

Prince Rahm, dressed in a gray robe with gold lacings, ascends the pulpit. He recites the Hebrew prayer each speaker has invoked and then launches into a tirade about the AIDS crisis in South Africa. "This is Deuteronomy 28 coming into effect," he says referring to the biblical curses decreed by God. Rahm reads from an article with the headline: "South Africa approves gay marriage." There's an audible gasp from the audience.

"Teach, *nasi,* teach," some in the crowd shout back, as if they were at a church tent revival—only spoken in perfect Hebrew.

Their commitment to their beliefs is actually pretty inspiring. It's more than just blind faith, more than merely following the wild teachings of a charismatic teacher. These people, all of them in this room, have made sacrifices. They no longer eat certain foods, they no longer dress the way most people do, they no longer drink beer with their buddies while watching the football game on Sunday afternoon. Nope, they decided to come here instead. They chose a godly life, a holy endeavor, and, to be perfectly honest, I've got to respect them for that.

FLASH BACK A few days, and my tour of the compound, the preschool, and the three community homes ends as the Cadillac DeVille drops me off in front of the vegan restaurant where my journey first started. It had been just a few hours, but it felt much longer. For a brief moment in time, I was given entrée into a whole other universe.

As we exit the car back onto the sidewalk, it's nearly night. The prince stares off thoughtfully into the distance. Ahead of him, as far as the eye can see, are mountains of time. Decades of telling the story of the African Hebrew Israelites and trying to convince those who are not familiar with them that they are a people of peace. A people of God.

Time has already begun to heal some wounds. When the Black Hebrews first arrived on the shores of Israel in the late 1960s and expected to be welcomed with open arms under the law of return, they were told they were not Jewish and could not be automatic citizens of Israel. Over the years, the Israeli government has slowly started to recognize Ben Ammi and his community, first as temporary workers and now as permanent residents. Indeed, one of Asiel's sons is currently serving in the Israeli army.

I bid the prince farewell, wish him good luck on his speech, and thank him for welcoming me into his community. As I lean in to shake his hand, he grabs me by my shoulder and offers me a warm embrace. We promise to stay in touch (he actually invites me to join him on an upcoming trip to Israel), and no sooner had we met than our encounter was over. Kind of like summer camp.

WHILE IN THE back room where we first met, the prince had showed me an infomercial he made about the tiny West African town of Benin. People from Asiel's community had come to the town and breathed new life into it. They set up clean running water, built an auditorium seating a thousand, and even constructed a tofu factory so the town could be financially independent. They established an organic agriculture program, planted fourteen thousand fruit trees, and taught the townspeople how to farm the land. The residents have become self-sufficient, even exporting their fruit to European countries for a profit. Not surprisingly, other nearby villages have invited the Black Hebrews to come to their towns as well.

When I asked Asiel if, like Christian missionaries in Third World countries, he was trying to proselytize and get the villagers to convert to his religion, he looked at me, puzzled. Judaism is not a proselytizing religion, he reminded me. "We don't say die and go to heaven, but have heaven on earth," he explains. "The children of Israel need to be a light unto the nations." At this moment, Prince Asiel was not a stranger, but my fellow Jew.

Like most people, I had walked into the interview with preconceived notions. Yes, the Black Hebrews do weird things. For people who have never met them or whose only interaction with them has been on the six o'clock news, it's easy to dismiss them as nothing more than a weird cult with weird customs. They embrace polygamy and shy away from modern medicine. But these are not the sum total of who they are. At their core, they are a people of faith.

And people of faith sometimes do what seem like weird things. When I started this journey, my gut reaction was to mock what I did not know— the religious customs that seemed foreign to me. Why do Christians hunt eggs on Easter? Why do Muslims kneel on carpets? Why do Mormons abstain from drinking coffee? Why do the Black Hebrews only follow half of the Jewish laws that I do?

But I'm coming to realize that people of faith come in all shapes and sizes. Even all Jews aren't the same. Some of us grew up with rabbis for dads, and some did not. Some are tall and some are short. Some are liberal, and some are conservative. Some are black, and some are white.

Despite our skin color, our feelings about steak, and our number of wives, the prince and I are both pretty much the same. We are followers of God and, as such, are governed by a sense of morality. Nothing could be more black and white.

TEN

Christmas at the Cohens'

So they hurried off and found Mary and Joseph, and the baby, who was lying in the manger.

—*Luke 2:16*

HAVING NEVER CELEBRATED Christmas before, I figured I would go all out for my one shot at achieving full Christmastime potential. But armed with little knowledge of proper December etiquette, I do what any clueless person would. I open my Web browser and head straight for Google.

I type "holiday spirit" into the world's leading search engine and the number-one site listed is an unsuspecting page on eHow.com titled "How to Get into the Christmas Spirit." Perfect. One click later and I am staring at this introduction: "Christmas is supposed to be a time of peace, love, and goodwill to all. But with all the stress and commotion of the season, many of us end up feeling more like Mr. Scrooge than Santa Claus."

As it does throughout its site when imparting wisdom on how to do things (like transfer music onto an iPhone or make artichoke barigoule), the page contains a list of instructions along with a difficulty rating. "Holiday spirit" was categorized as moderately easy. (By comparison, the entries for "How to Gain Weight" and "How to Grow African American Hair" were rated moderate and easy, respectively—although both entries are entirely disturbing.)

The site goes on to list eleven steps for getting into the holiday spirit. Step number one? "Shop early." Step three? "Drop spare coins in the Salvation Army collection buckets." Step seven? "Play Christmas music." Step eleven? "Don't spend more money than you have. Anxiety over after-Christmas bills can ruin your holiday." These sounded more like helpful tips from Dr. Phil than the spiritually infused steps to a more meaningful holiday that I expected to read.

I was starting to think this "holiday spirit" concept had nothing to do with the holiday at all. Step four, I should've mentioned, was "Offer to babysit for a friend." Unless the kid's name was Baby Jesus, I wasn't sure of the Christmas connection. Not one step mentioned anything about going to houses of worship, praying, or fulfilling specific God-mandated tasks on the holiday—you know, like what we do during Jewish festivals.

But I wasn't going to let a Web page ruin my premeditated fun. Christmastime is the ultimate in pomp and circumstance for a needy Jew. I'm not the first to notice this religious discrepancy. In *The Hebrew Hammer,* a 2003 comedy with a devilish premise, Santa's evil son Damien tries to make Christmas the only December holiday. His evil plan's modus operandi? Distributing bootlegged copies of *It's a Wonderful Life* to Jewish children to get them hooked on the holiday (Curtis Mayfield's drug-themed song "I'm Your Pusher" plays in the background). As for me, I didn't need the whiff of a bootlegged narcotic to become a Christmas junkie. Religious envy was already my drug of choice, Christmas merely its syringe.

Christmas is all-encompassing in the Bible Belt. And this year, with the equivalent of a doctor's note from a very understanding rabbi, I would be able to experience it for myself. Finally.

So when Elizabeth nonchalantly asked if I wanted to attend a performance of *The Nutcracker* starring her sister as one of the many dream fairies, she assumed I would rebuff her generous offer to be bored by two hours of ballet. Normally, she would have been absolutely correct. I am not a ballet guy. But this year things were different. Ballet was finally going to get its chance to impress me.

The brochure I was given as I entered the theater told me that Tchaikovsky conceived this ballet in the 1890s and, believe it or not, thought it was one of his lesser works. That Tchaikovsky, he was so humble. First performed a week before Christmas in 1892 at a Russian theater, the story of a girl and her beloved Christmas present was imported to the United States in 1944. A later 1954 version, with updated choreography of course, sealed its position as a favorite pastime for families during the Christmas season. I had no clue what I was watching, but I loved the ballet anyway—a sweet confectionary Eden filled with dancing candy canes. While the rest of my

Jewish friends were out doing Jewish activities, I had crossed over into Christendom and was fully embracing the Christmas spirit.

The pageantry continued when I attended the tree-lighting service at a nearby Presbyterian church. After a few opening songs, we broke up into small groups and hung wreaths and garlands and tinsel (oh my). They had baked cookies (nonkosher, of course), which were served in a Fellowship Hall. I wanted a Fellowship Hall. They were wearing sweaters, despite the unseasonably balmy seventy degrees outside. Inside the church, it was so toasty, so warm, so inviting, so non-Jewish, so forbidden.

Oh sweet Noel, I would celebrate all twelve nights. With Dasher. With Dancer. With Prancer and Vixen. I would watch *Home Alone. National Lampoon's Christmas Vacation. Miracle on 34th Street.* Ben Affleck in *Surviving Christmas.* Ben Affleck in *Dogma.* Ben Affleck in *Reindeer Games.* Unlike veterans of Christmas past, I would celebrate Christmas as if it were going out of style.

I bought some eggnog (kosher, of course) and drank it while walking around the house wearing my bathrobe and some new fleece pajamas. I drove through a local "Celebration of Lights," a dizzying display of outdoor Christmas decorations. I jammed out to holiday music. (Okay, I'll admit I now regret purchasing the Hanson brothers yuletide album. But I still enjoy "White Christmas," which, for the record, was penned by the very Jewish lyricist Irving Berlin.)

I, like millions of Americans, meandered through the mall looking for gifts (in my case, for my non-Jewish in-laws). Braving the crowds and the children waiting in line to sit on Santa's lap, I felt in good company. Indeed, in 2006, Americans spent $455 billion during the holidays.

But one man is trying to curb our country's shopping addiction. On a recent trip to New York, I popped into a tent revival service featuring Reverend Billy, who leads the Church of Stop Shopping. Reverend Billy, I should point out, is not really a reverend and his organization is not really a church. He's an actor-activist who, along with his street-theater troupe dressed as gospel singers, brings a cheery message of anticonsumerism. He's on a crusade to drive the demons out of America's cash registers. He calls it the Shopocalypse. Sporting a white suit and a matching bleach-blond pompadour, Reverend Billy whips the crowd into a tizzy, wiping his sweaty brow at every turn.

He sings parody songs like "Are You My Lover or My Logo?" The performance I attended was inside the Spiegel Tent at Lower Manhattan's

South Street Seaport, just steps away from big-box chain stores like J. Crew, the Gap, and Victoria's Secret. I'm sure they appreciated Billy's ranting. In a scene from the 2007 documentary *What Would Jesus Buy?* Reverend Billy is seen, with gospel choir in tow, performing an exorcism on a Wal-Mart.

To me, Billy seemed like the grinch who was trying to steal my Christmas thunder. And Elizabeth was hopping on that bandwagon. Noticing my overzealous glee at immersing myself completely into this one particular Christian holiday, Elizabeth stepped in and put the kibosh on a Christmas tree I tried to drag into our home under the guise of my interfaith education. She knew there was more to Christianity than Christmastime. But as I was growing up, a Jew, that's all I thought about when I imagined the good life as a Christian.

"What about a wreath?" I asked hopefully.

"No," she responded curtly.

"What about a Chanukah wreath?"

"What's a Chanukah wreath?"

"Um . . ."

"No," she responded before I could fudge an answer.

"A wreath isn't inherently Christian," I tried to explain. "It's just *seasonal*."

But I was out of luck. In her mind, wreaths *were* inherently Christian. She was hijacking my holiday mojo.

But celebrate the holiday I would. No one could stop me from having my Christmas cake and eating it too. I could get in the spirit without the tree. I didn't need the wreath. I didn't need all the hoopla of the holiday season.

But, of course, that was just a bunch of lies. I *did* in fact need all those things. Those were the things I had coveted—not the church service recalling the birth of a Savior in a manger. This was the one time this year I actually didn't need a church service. At this precise moment on my journey, I needed the regal trappings of the season itself. Those are what had been denied me all these years—a holiday season with pomposity, an entire month of living among my fellow Americans in a society that celebrated the sheer joy of the month of December. I wanted a Charlie Brown Christmas. I wanted green-and-red sweaters. I wanted an endless loop of Santa music on the radio. Yes, Christmas was the one holiday I didn't want to spend in a church. But I went anyway.

• • •

'TWAS THE NIGHT before Christmas when all through my house, not a creature was stirring, not even my wife.

Elizabeth was already asleep as I tiptoed out of the house and went to midnight Mass at St. Bart's Episcopal Church across the street. The service was awe-inspiring. Everything was stepped up a notch from a normal Sunday. Candles were lit and placed in every window, their warm amber glow reflecting throughout the sanctuary. There was a full choir with booming orchestral voices singing "Silent Night" and ringing large bells. Various children and clergy walked around in a rather elaborate flag ceremony. It all kind of reminded me of the myriad nations entering the stadium at the opening ceremonies of the Olympics.

Since it's right across the street from our home, I've spent many Sundays at this church, yet I was seeing so many new faces at this service. I could tell I wasn't the only lost soul who had sought spiritual shelter here tonight. I watched in envy as the congregants walked down the center aisle to receive Communion. For the past few weeks I had immersed myself in all that this holiday had to offer, so I hesitated for a moment, as part of me actually wanted to partake of this wafer. But I thought better of it and stayed back.

The choir concluded the service with a powerful and rousing rendition of "Joy to the World." For the first time in a while, I actually felt God's presence.

With the requisite church service now out of the way, Christmas morning couldn't come soon enough. Although Elizabeth and I hadn't gotten gifts for each other, we did spend a lot of time (and money) purchasing presents for all the members of her family during the preceding weeks. We packed up our car with the gifts and our two dogs (how Americana of us) and drove to Elizabeth's family home to help set up for the extended clan that would be gathering for Christmas dinner.

By late afternoon, everything was in place. The food smelled delicious. Elizabeth even precooked some kosher dishes and desserts that we brought along so we could break bread with the family and enjoy the time together. Gift-giving time came. Wrapping paper littered the floor. The dogs barked by the fireplace. The room was full of merriment. Everything was Norman Rockwell picture-perfect.

My parents never gave us Chanukah presents when we were growing up because they felt the custom was too similar to Christmas. But now I was getting iPods and designer socks from my wife's family. Elizabeth's mom and grandmother even banded together and bought me an expensive Talmud set they knew I wanted. A Talmud for Christmas—how cool was that?

Unlike our festivals, which usually mark some morbid anniversary on the Jewish calendar, it was refreshing to finally have a holiday that was just about having fun. Not unlike the girl in *The Nutcracker*, I was having a dream come true.

AND YET HERE I am, slouched on my couch the morning after with a half-drunk cup of eggnog in one hand and a kosher gingerbread cookie in the other. I'm suffering from a Christmas hangover.

It seems I may have extended myself a little too much. I think I may have gone overboard, and now my tummy hurts. And my head. And my spirit. I feel dizzy.

I had come with all ye faithful, even went way down in the manger with the little boy Jesus, but all I returned with was an empty feeling. My head ached, my spirit was deflated. My house has become cavernous in this post-Christmas malaise. *Hi, my name is Benyamin, and I'm a Christmas crackhead.*

I need detox or rehab or both. I had done all of the things that Christians do at this time of year. I had gone through all the motions, yet I was left feeling incredibly unfulfilled inside. Save for the beautiful midnight service I attended, the bulk of my Christmas experience seemed to be nothing more than prepackaged kitsch.

Christmas, marketing gurus will explain, is popular in modern society because it plays perfectly to two vast, but distinct, audiences: religious and nonreligious Christians. For religious Christians, it celebrates nothing less than the birth of the Savior and is one of the holiest nights on the entire calendar. For the nonobservant, Christmas provides a monthlong overdose of mass-marketed consumption. I had celebrated the latter. Hence the holy hangover. "A perpetual holiday," George Bernard Shaw once said, "is a good working definition of hell."

Many Americans opt for a Christmas bereft of any real religious influence like the one I had. In its stead is a new religion—one based on charity, goodwill toward men, and, as I discovered on eHow.com, babysitting. This time of year possesses its own spirit, its own seasonal ambience that permeates and pervades our culture. It has little to do with the birth of Jesus. It's Christmas lite.

On the plus side, I guess it's good that the population of Jews in America (only 2 percent) is so small. We are not a serious target for mass-marketing efforts. There will never be, much to the chagrin of teenage Jewish girls everywhere, a Ben Affleck Chanukah heist movie called *Maccabee Games*. Wal-Mart's one lonesome Chanukah shelf—flimsily filled with cheap plastic decorations and random Jewish-themed magnets—is merely David to the Goliath that is the multiple aisles of Christmas items the store stocks. It's a wonder Chanukah ever got its own postage stamp.

On the contrary, Jewish holidays are meant to take us *away* from pop culture, to remove us from anything remotely related to the modern world. As such, on Jewish holidays we are forbidden to shop, use the telephone, check e-mail, even use electricity altogether. Instead, we are asked to immerse ourselves completely in the holy rituals of the day.

With all the sugarplums dancing in my head, this December had not been a religious experience; it had been a cultural one. One I'm happy I had the opportunity to embrace this one time. But I can't fool myself. Celebrating this mock version of Christmas gave me no religious insight—except that real religion comes from real observance. Not from what sweater I put on. Not from what movies I watch. And not from a tree.

For me, all the tangible things I had associated with Christmas were just that—things. They were not representative of the inherent nature of the holiday itself. Indeed, I will never know what it feels like to celebrate Christmas like a religious Christian.

A holiday is like a little rest stop along the highway of the year when we are given the opportunity to pull over and catch our breath. It's a time to focus on nature, to reflect on where we've been and where we're going. More important, it's a time to reconnect with God.

In biblical and Talmudic times, the Jewish people would make pilgrimages to Jerusalem to celebrate the three major festivals each year—Sukkot, Passover, and Shavuot. Sukkot was originally only seven days long but, the Torah teaches, God added an extra day. Everyone had made the long trek to the holy city and had spent the festival busy in prayer and worship. But before the Israelites rushed back home to their regular lives, God was asking them to just relax and spend one more day with Him.

This eighth day, known as *Shemini Atzeret* in Hebrew, is the one Jewish holiday in the entire year that does not have any special commandments associated with it. We are no longer required to live in the hut. We don't light a seven-branched candelabra. We don't eat special foods. This holiday is simply a time for God and humans to enjoy each other's company. It's His paternal way of saying to His children, *Don't go yet.*

This year on that day, Elizabeth and I had lunch at the home of our synagogue's rabbi. At the meal, he explained it as follows. Picture Sukkot as one weeklong party hosted by the Big Man Upstairs. *Stick around after everyone else leaves,* God says. *That's when I'm breaking out the good stuff.*

And so we stay. For one more day. With no special requirements, it is a day completely and solely about our relationship with the Almighty. This is a beautiful insight about the observance of holidays, one that was right in front of me the entire time. I just needed a December drunk with yuletide cheer to wake me from my spiritual stupor.

Judaism, sometimes to a fault, is a very intellectually focused religion. In Orthodox Jewish homes, role models are those who spend the most time studying the ancient texts. I crack open one of the Talmud volumes that my in-laws gave me for Christmas and scan a line or two of its Aramaic text. Without knowing it, they had given me the gift I needed—a reminder of my roots, a reminder not to stray too far from whence I came.

Closing the Talmud, I hop in the car to attend the nightly synagogue service. Afterward, I decide to stick around for a little alone time with God. I wait until everyone leaves and stay seated on the pew, left by myself in the sanctuary. I look around—at the ark, at the Jewish symbols on the wall, at the prayer book on my lap. This is where I belong. Wait long enough and God will eventually bring out the good stuff.

ELEVEN

Wrestling with God

So Jacob was left alone, and a man wrestled with him till daybreak.
—Genesis 32:24

I'VE HEARD OF people doing some crazy things in the name of the Lord—martyrdom and murdering infidels come immediately to mind—but never in all my travels through religious houses of worship have I seen this—Christian wrestling. And we're not talking about just any Christian wrestling. This is Ultimate Christian Wrestling.

It's a frosty winter night at the Harvest Church just outside Athens, Georgia. Down a rural dirt road, this is the Bethlehem of Ultimate Christian Wrestling. It says as much on its Web page. And when I had stumbled across the site while aimlessly surfing the Internet a few days earlier, my first reaction was of utter disbelief. Could this be real?

The drive to the event is long and dark. Night set early on this winter's eve, and the road to Athens is long and littered with little of interest. But I know I'm entering Jesus country. After all, a lone billboard states so. Another billboard, miles later, asks rhetorically, "What part of 'thou shalt not' don't you understand?"

It's Saturday night, only hours after the conclusion of the Jewish Sabbath, and I had hastily rushed out of synagogue to get on the road. For the moment, at least, I had ditched my own faith in favor of watching half-naked men wrestle in the name of their faith.

After getting lost in the vastness that is the back country of rural Georgia, I finally arrive at the church, which is situated in a large open field.

My liberal-leaning leather-seated black Toyota Camry sits in a sea of dusty pickup trucks with "Bush Country" bumper stickers on them.

My stomach starts to churn. All of the churches I had been to until now were in major metropolitan areas. If necessary, I was always able to make a quick exit and hightail it back to my Chassidic hood. But here I was, a lone Jew in Jesusville and miles from nowhere. If I took off my skullcap, would I blend right in? At the very least, people would see me for the hypocrite that I am—an observant Jew watching Christian wrestling.

The moment I push the door open and enter the church gymnasium, I see hundreds of people's heads bowed in prayer. I'm guessing by the stage and curtains this also doubles as an auditorium. About two hundred people are here, and I'm one of the few not wearing jeans. Heck, some are even in overalls. A sign declares "Souled Out for Christ."

At one end of the gym, near a draped American flag, is a makeshift concession stand selling hot dogs and nachos under a banner that somewhat cryptically reads, "Sow a seed, reap a harvest." I'm not sure if it refers to something religious or something the concession stand is actually selling. Across the room, atop another folding table, is the propaganda area. It's covered in Ultimate Christian Wrestling T-shirts, "I heart Jesus" bookmarks, assorted key chains, action figures, and Confederate flag bandanas.

As I settle into a seat toward the back, I notice many people are on dates or have come with their families. I'm probably the only one here traveling solo, and I begin to wonder how much I stand out. A burly blond man with a mustache who looks like a security guard slowly approaches me. Do I have a target in the shape of a Star of David on my back?

"Can I help you?" he asks.

I tell him I'd like to meet Rob Adonis, the ringleader and mastermind behind Ultimate Christian Wrestling (UCW). I had contacted Rob a few days earlier to get the lowdown and told him I might be coming to tonight's event. As soon as I mention Rob's name, it is as if I have been given the keys to the kingdom. A smile comes over the guard's face, and he slaps me on the back as he leads me backstage.

My newfound comfort doesn't last long after I'm led into a small room where I'm the only man with clothes on. Everyone else is wearing spandex. And they all have facial hair—every variety you can possibly imagine: mustaches, goatees, Elvis-style sideburns, all three of those together. They're all stretching and waiting for their respective matches to begin. The guard points Rob out, and I introduce myself. A little uncomfortably the 290-pound Adonis gives me a bear hug, his beefy arms enveloping me. He's wearing a blue-and-white spandex wrestling getup. It's what you would expect any typical wrestler to wear—except his pant legs have huge crosses taped on them.

Ultimate Christian Wrestling is the brainchild of the thirty-year-old Adonis. He founded it in the summer of 2003, after he received a "calling" from on high. "I had a vision that I could combine two of my passions, professional wrestling and evangelism," he tells me as sweat drips down his face.

Adonis had been a wrestler for years, competing in more than four hundred matches all across the eastern seaboard. Hanging around backstage at these events, he was exposed to more than a few ungodlike heathens. "Drugs, alcohol, and sex were just some of the things that haunted the sport I so dearly loved," he recalls. "All the while, when I talked about Christ there would be just a couple of guys at every show who even had a clue who I was talking about. I sat and saw my friends and foes destroy themselves."

Unsure what God wanted him to do, he did nothing. Until his twenty-seventh birthday, that is, when Adonis believes God revealed His true desires. And what did God want? Apparently, a ministry–slash–sports entertainment company. "I started to piece together a show that would serve the purpose of entertaining, educating, and, most important, ministering to the world."

Yes, the *world*. Just about everything connected with UCW is referred to on a grand scale. Titles like "World Heavyweight Champion" are bestowed upon its athletes, and the matches are ambitiously called "crusades." Giving such bold names to these seemingly mundane matches is just one of the many reasons Adonis is so successful. If this were *just* wrestling, it wouldn't be so vital. But those in attendance at tonight's event really feel they are watching soldiers of God on a mission. A battle between good and evil, a veritable Passion play for the hillbilly set.

Even Adonis, who during the day is a middle-school special-education teacher, admits that the idea of wrestling for God is a bit strange. "When I get to heaven, the first thing I'm going to ask God is, 'Where in the world did you come up with that idea?'" There may be many of us asking that very same question. As far as Adonis is concerned, there is a minister for every ministry, and this, well, this just happens to be his calling.

At the moment, Adonis is choosing songs from iTunes to play over the loudspeaker. Before I get a chance to see the play list, he tells me it's almost game time and ushers me out the door.

•   •   •

TONIGHT, INCREDIBLY, WAS not the first time I had met a religious wrestler. My Jewish auto mechanic had a previous career as a professional wrestler. When I found out I'd be coming to the UCW event tonight, I stopped by his shop to brush up on things like body slams and half nelsons.

When you walk into the A Plus Auto Shop a block away from the courthouse in downtown Decatur, Georgia, the incongruity practically smacks you in the face. By no stretch of the imagination is this your typical mechanic's garage. A Hebrew Beavis and Butthead poster shares wall space with a car-parts calendar. A photo of the saintly Lubavitcher Rebbe hangs alongside one of pro wrestler Brutus "The Barber" Beefcake. It's a purposely dichotic mood set by the twisted mind of Greg Herman, the shop's forty-year-old owner.

He may look like any other of a dozen auto mechanics you've come across over the years of strange brake noises and broken Johnson rods. You know, the tattered baseball cap, the scruffy facial hair, the weathered hands covered with smudges of black grease that make you think twice before shaking hands. The sweat-stained and leathery machismo that can only come from keeping your head under a hood for twelve hours a day.

So far, so typical. But then he says something so utterly at odds with who he appears to be that you actually have to stop and sit for a moment on one of the many random battered car parts that litter the four-bay garage. "I hope all my children become rabbis," he says with a straight face. Yeah, he's not your typical mechanic. And since we're already breaking down stereotypes, I might as well let you in on one more secret. Herman's pro wrestling name used to be Demon "The Madman from Miami" Hellstorm.

Make no mistake. You don't want to mess with this guy. If you look at him closely, you realize Herman could be a ticking time bomb. If you were to cross him, he looks as if he might grab you by the collar and shake the living daylights out of you.

Yet, astonishingly, there is another, softer side. He is a man full of pathos and compassion, with a tender heart.

"I don't let my kids watch wrestling," he says. "It's too violent." This coming from a man who, when sporting a mohawk and face paint, was once ranked number 241 in the world for his unique ability to smash the head of another grown man with a metal folding chair. In fact, only his oldest son (of three kids) is even aware of his previous incarnation.

Indeed, Herman keeps his past life boxed up (literally) in several cardboard storage bins in a closet off the back room of his auto shop. Open one chest and you'll see newspaper clippings from Demon Hellstorm's heyday, photos of Herman and Hulk Hogan, videos of his classic bouts, and the *pièce de résistance*, his old wrestling costume.

For Herman, it's like opening up a time capsule from a bygone era. "I don't even remember that time anymore," he says, although a tiny but discernable glint in his eyes says otherwise. "It was so long ago."

Well, not exactly. Herman's last professional match took place just a week prior to 9/11. But a seemingly unquenchable thirst for religious growth had already been leading Herman away from the sordid world of professional wrestling for almost a decade.

When Herman was living in one of the many nondescript towns that dot the South Florida peninsula, his life was a lonely one. Under contract with the now defunct International Wrestling Union (IWU) and with no matches to fight, Herman was basically being paid to sit at home. It was this period of inactivity that opened Hellstorm's eyes to his Jewish faith. "I had all this time and nothing to do. So I started reading." In fact, for his thirtieth birthday, he asked his mother to get him a Bible. "She almost had a heart attack," Herman recalls of his mother's response.

But for Herman it was no laughing matter. "I wanted to learn who I was. I had spent sixteen years on the road with born-again Christians who had tattoos and wanted me to believe in Jesus. And none of that ever happened."

Even now, years after shedding his demonic alter ego, Herman takes pride in his Jewish heritage wherever he can. He points to a beat-up station wagon currently being worked on by one of his mechanics. "That's the rabbi's car."

Perhaps for nostalgic reasons, Herman still has a thing for wrestling. Although he claims to be "way out of shape," the burly 210-pound, five-foot-eleven Herman is still a force to be reckoned with, and when he has time he works out on the weight sets in an abandoned area of his auto shop. In fact, up until recently, Herman actually had a wrestling ring in the extra garage, where he and some of the guys would joke around for old time's sake. "People think wrestling is this big glamorous life," he says, as he munches on some greasy chicken fingers. "It really isn't. After six months, it was just a job."

That monotony and his newfound focus on Judaism brought him out of the religious wasteland he had been wandering in. His children now attend a local Jewish elementary school, and Herman, in his new career as an auto mechanic, finds ways to infuse their lives with a sense of uniqueness. In the back of his garage, amid the valuable antique cars that Herman fixes up, lies one of his most treasured items: a large menorah he made for his son out of scrap metal and spark plugs.

Greg Herman may be many things—a father, a friend, an existential mechanic—but one thing he isn't is regretful. Unlike many professional athletes who find themselves retired by forty with nothing to do but watch the highlight reels from the glory days of their youth, Herman can barely sit through a tape from one of his old matches.

Instead, he focuses on his future—his new business, his children, and his religion. "It's a slow process," he admits, looking off into the setting sun. But a journey he's more than happy to take.

As the show starts, I snap out of my reverie. Half-naked in his wrestling regalia, Rob Adonis leads the audience in a prayer service. Days earlier, a fellow wrestler died in a car accident, and they're giving him a tribute tonight. Adonis, a large man with a tough-guy exterior, closes his eyes and begins to well up. In the background, amid total silence, a ten-bell salute is sounded in memory of the fallen comrade. To me it seems overly dramatic. It seems more like a somber funeral processional than a wrestling match. This is just the first of many times tonight that people will act out of context.

The crowd shouts a glory-filled, collective "Amen!" as the prayer comes to a close.

Adonis waves to the crowd and darts back to the control room, where he mans the sound and light equipment, pumping out mood-appropriate tunes from his laptop. Right now it's Kenny Loggins's "Danger Zone" from *Top Gun*. This is the point in the evening when the histrionics and poor man's light show begin. Plumes of smoke and rays from a half dozen flashing strobes emanate from the stage as two wrestlers come through a shiny silver curtain. They swagger across a makeshift bridge between the gymnasium's stage and wrestling ring.

As they begin to fight, it becomes glaringly obvious which one we're all supposed to be rooting for. One, dressed in white, is a well-groomed man who's more Ward Cleaver than Hulk Hogan. The other, dressed in all black, comes across as boozy and egotistical. It's a modern-day version of David and Goliath. The audience, comprising both children and adults, is going wild. A few of the teenagers have crosses painted on their cheeks.

I spot an elderly man hooked up to wires and dragging along an oxygen tank on wheels. I guess I'm not the only one without a date. I assist him in finding a seat and ask why he came out tonight. After all, it's certainly easier for him to just stay at home, in the comfort of his living room, and watch some good old-fashioned wrestling on television. But instead, he has geared up and come out in the cold to witness this spectacle firsthand.

"This gives me strength," he says matter-of-factly. "This is a boost of energy I can't get from the TV or anywhere else. God is here tonight, and I want to be here with Him."

A sincere thought, but one I personally find hard to grasp as I watch the white-spandex guy (good) being pummeled to the floor by black-spandex guy (evil). But that's when I see it. I'm watching a biblical metaphor played out in front of me. The good guy has been bruised and beaten for our sins. But with the power of the crowd clapping in unison, white-spandex guy is resurrected. He flips the black-spandex guy on his back for the "One, two, three!" and the people let out a cheer. The match is called in favor of the good guy, and both wrestlers run off stage, one pumping his fists and the other doing the walk of shame.

Before the next set of wrestlers emerges from behind the curtain, Pastor Curtis (the founder of Harvest Church) gives a mini-sermon. He explains that these fighters are soldiers of God and we should support them in their worthy mission. As he says this, a collection basket is being passed around. All I have is a five-dollar bill, so I throw it in.

Those in the crowd bow their heads as the pastor offers a prayer on behalf of the mighty wrestlers. "Bless them, bless their lives, and bless their ministry. Amen." The crowd responds and takes a moment for reverence before returning to the hooting and hollering that is par for the course at any sporting event.

Like mainstream wrestling, UCW has story lines. Bad people, perhaps in reference to Judas, are often referred to as double-crossers. When I first came across UCW's Web site, it promoted tonight's event with the following verbiage: "Colt Derringer turned his back on God and UCW, but maintained the World Heavyweight Title. What's in store for this tortured soul?"

After a ten-minute intermission, the next match begins with the thumping sound of "Sweet Home Alabama" blaring over the loudspeakers as a wrestler dressed in a janitor's outfit and drinking beer out of a plunger saunters up to the ring. He's the Custodial Crippler. Seriously. And the guy he's about to do battle with is Lucifer. I know this because someone in the crowd shouts out to him: "Lucifer! You sold out!" So in case you're keeping score at home, the janitor drinking beer out of a plunger? He's the good guy.

This routine—a wrestling match followed by some words from the pastor—continues for the next two hours.

Adonis performs in the grand finale of the night against one of the bad guys and ends up losing. Not just losing, but actually dying. At least, for the purposes of dramatic effect, Adonis is lying on the mat pretending to be dead. But the kids gathered here tonight, some of whom are now teary-eyed, don't know the difference. They believe their hero has just perished as the other wrestlers cover Adonis's still body with a black cloth.

I should point out here that this type of thing never happened at the Jewish youth group activities I participated in back during the Reagan era. Nobody ever died at one of our events. At least none that I'm aware of. The feeble Jewish male body is genetically constructed to avoid dangerous physical activity at all costs. We studied the Torah. On good days, we had pizza parties. The closest thing that came to a sport was the day we went bowling. We didn't have wrestling matches that led (even metaphorically) to somebody's death. The worst thing that ever happened was that one of our group leaders accidentally showed us the *Return of the Jedi* video. Our parents (at least mine) disapproved because we weren't supposed to see Princess Leia in her famous golden metal bikini slave outfit at Jabba's palace, her beautiful auburn hair braided into a long and lustrous ponytail. Not that I was paying attention.

On the large screen above the ring, a prepackaged video tribute to Rob's career highlights is being shown. He's seen wrestling, being interviewed on various newscasts about his ministry, and baptizing dozens of children—all while a sad Christian pop song hums in the background. Suddenly, the deep, booming voice of God is heard: "Arise for the Lord, Rob Adonis. I'm not finished with you yet."

Rob's lifeless body begins to move, and the kids cheer. Apparently not dead at all, he gets up from the mat and grabs the microphone. "It's time for all Christians to stand up and fight!" It sounds like a battle cry. The crowd goes wild; kids jump up and down in their seats.

"Selling Girl Scout cookies and helping old ladies cross the street won't get you into heaven," he explains to the little tykes. "Only through salvation will you get into heaven." The smiles and cheering come to a screeching halt. Suddenly silence fills the room. The kids have puzzled looks on their cherubic faces.

Adonis veers off and talks about lust and gluttony and funerals and deaths. This is getting very dark very fast. The children seem scared straight. *Is this what resurrected heroes talk about? We liked him better before he died.*

Ever since I started going to church, I've been troubled by this fascination with all things death. Mentions of the crucifixion were commonplace. Images of a bloodied Jesus upon the cross were everywhere. I never considered what this kind of horror did to the psyche of children.

Earlier this year I saw the documentary *Jesus Camp,* about young evangelical children who were being indoctrinated into an army of God. The counselors weren't teaching the campers to have good morals or to be nice to their neighbors. It was all accept Christ or die—all so black and white. Obviously, I understand that the very basis of evangelical Christianity is that one must accept Christ as one's Savior, but the camp seemed to be so fundamentalist in its "us versus them," socially isolated theology. It seems all of this was taught at the expense of what I would consider good Christian morals and values like charity, grace, and goodwill toward others.

It seems Adonis was stating a similar sentiment, that there is apparently no redeeming quality to helping an old lady cross the street. That is worthless. What really matters is giving your life to Christ. Yes, giving your life over to Christ should mean that you will do acts of love and kindness and help old ladies cross the street, but these things are never mentioned. Moreover, talking about lust and gluttony and death, in my opinion, only scares kids into believing while failing to show them the beauty of what religion truly has to offer.

By no means does the Christian community have a monopoly on this fear-driven teaching method. Jewish author Shalom Auslander, in his wickedly funny memoir *Foreskin's Lament,* details the black-and-white, all-or-nothing way his rabbis scared him into observance. He was taught that doing the commandments would keep a God quick to anger at bay, a vengeful deity content. Not doing them would literally unleash the wrath of an Almighty hell-bent on bringing famine, disease, and death down onto this world. Sounds inspiring.

Faith and fear may go hand in hand, but that can't be the standard way to get kids excited about their religion. Children raised that way will never be religious because they *want* to, but only because they *have* to. Scare tactics may work initially, but they will only foster the development of religiously dysfunctional adults who are too crippled to cope with the many shades of gray that accompany true faith. Is that what God desires?

Somebody's cell phone rings and interrupts the dark drama of Adonis's speech. He passes the microphone to a fellow wrestler, one who didn't just pretend to die and be resurrected.

"My wife is not a believer," this second wrestler confesses to the crowd. "She doesn't believe in UCW. She doesn't believe this is a ministry. But that doesn't matter. I'm the man of the house." His wife seems like someone I would get along with.

There's a "Bless your soul!" and a few "Hallelujahs" from the audience.

Eerily echoing President Bush talking about terrorists, the wrestler intones about God: "You're either for Him or against Him. That's the way it is. That's the facts." The wrestler peppers his speech with Gumpisms. "Gratitude is an attitude." "A dusty mind is a dirty life." "You've got to be in control of your soul."

We rise as the wrestler leads us in prayer and asks if any of us would like to accept Jesus in our lives. "Step away from your old lifestyle," he says in a loud Southern drawl. A sappy love song pulls at the heartstrings as it plays over the loudspeaker. To my surprise, several people actually approach the ring. A middle-aged bald guy begins to bawl. A college coed embraces her friend as she cries her way to the front. And a handful of children, each no more than ten years old, lean on the ropes.

The woman selling nachos tells me that more than thirty children have given themselves over to Christ in the last month after these matches. Since its inception, UCW has inspired hundreds to be saved.

Throughout the night, my innate cynicism bars me from taking any of this too seriously, but the folks here couldn't be more serious. This is real to them. While I had been doodling in my notepad, they had actually just had a reverent religious experience.

I understand how children get caught up in this holy hullabaloo and look at these wrestlers as heroes the same way they revere Spider-Man or the Teenage Mutant Ninja Turtles. But what surprises me most is how much the adults in the audience are moved by this experience, looking to the wrestlers as true warriors in the proverbial battle of good versus evil.

It wasn't as though we had just witnessed a wheelchair-bound grandmother miraculously walk or any other awe-inspiring act of God. I saw nothing more than overweight men in tights participate in a fake wrestling match. How could such an objectively absurd act to me be so inspiring to others? Was I the shallow one? Was I missing something?

Before coming here tonight, I had e-mailed religious historian Randall Balmer, who's written several books on America's evangelical subculture. I asked him how people can get so excited over something as basic as wrestling. "I think the genius of American evangelicalism is the ability of the evangelist to speak the language of the people," he wrote back. "My guess is that it would be some combination of niche evangelism and muscular Christianity. These initiatives generally draw on one of two New Testament metaphors (or both): militarism ('the full armor of God') or athleticism ('running the race'). Evangelicals, especially in America, have been extraordinarily adept at speaking the idiom of the culture no matter where they find themselves."

Echoing those anti-intellectualist notions, evangelist Billy Sunday famously stated, "When the word of God says one thing and scholarship says another, scholarship can go to hell."

These thoughts swirl through my head as I exit the gym, pull out of the parking lot, and embark on the long drive home.

The wrestling reminds me of another form of Christian worship Elizabeth told me about. There's a group called the Power Team, which visited her middle school. The bulky, beefy "soldiers of God" use feats of strength like breaking baseball bats, bending steel bars, crushing concrete walls, and ripping phone books in half to show how much they love Jesus.

The Dallas-based group travels the country and has conducted more than fifteen thousand school assemblies since its inception more than thirty years ago. The organization claims that 60 percent of its audience (made up mostly of students and a handful of teachers and parents) is "unchurched" and that, by the end of the assembly, 20 percent of those in attendance choose to take a leap of faith.

Yes, this is crazy. Objectively. But taken in the sincere spirit of religious rejuvenation, this was the real deal. Truth be told, upon closer examination wrestling is actually more religious than you think.

The Talmudic sages teach us that Jacob and Esau wrestled while still in their mother's belly. The fighting between them continued throughout their childhood as each jockeyed for the birthright blessing from their father. Jacob ultimately received it and quickly hightailed it out of town before Esau could seek revenge.

Years later, Jacob was about to have a fateful reunion with his twin. Jacob hadn't seen his brother since receiving their father's blessing, and assumed reconnecting with Esau could only mean bad things ahead. Despite heavenly assurances that everything would turn out just fine, Jacob was still petrified. He was so sure of impending doom and failure that he divided his family into two camps, so one would survive if attacked.

The night before the reunion with Esau, Jacob was left all alone in the dark. Anyone who's even remotely familiar with the horror-movie genre can tell you that being left alone in the dark never leads to anything good. It usually leads to something violent like a chainsaw massacre or the ghost of an evil fisherman exacting revenge on the teenagers who killed him last summer. But for Jacob there were no zombies or vampires that night. There was, instead, a wrestling match. For the bookworm Jacob, this physical altercation was as scary as any horror flick.

What's more, the Bible states Jacob wrestled with a man, but most rabbinic commentators explain it was actually with a supernatural being, an angel, specifically the angel of Esau. And God spoke, *Let's get ready to rumble!*

This seems like a bizarre episode even by biblical standards. A wrestling match? Hulk Hogan and half nelsons don't usually come to mind when you think of the Old Testament. Which is why it's no surprise that many Jewish scholars have debated these very verses. Was this an actual wrestling match, they ask, or was this Jacob metaphorically wrestling with his own inner demons? The fact that this debate even exists is itself interesting. Wrestling, it seems, can have two different connotations—it can mean an external struggle as well as an internal one. Jacob experiences both; he leaves the altercation wounded, limping, but he also leaves with a reinvigorated appreciation for God.

Before the wrestling match Jacob was suffering from a lack of faith. He was so sure of impending doom before the upcoming reunion with Esau that he divided his family into two camps. But after the wrestling match, Jacob arose with a newfound confidence to deal with Esau.

The wrestling match—whether physical or spiritual—was an essential step for the restoration of Jacob's faith. He had to first conquer his inner demons before he could conquer his physical fear of Esau. Success against external adversaries is only possible if you first have success over your internal ones. Only when we are equipped with a strong foundation of faith can we better attack the physical challenges that lie before us.

The rabbis debate whether Jacob's wrestling match was real or metaphoric, but tonight's wrestling event had certainly encompassed aspects of both. It seems wrestling with faith is a very critical part of any religion. We all have our internal struggles with God. Jacob's spiritual struggle foreshadows the physical encounter he will have with Esau the next day. One begets the other.

When you think about it, each of us in our own way is a wrestler. We all confront our fears and grapple with personal struggles, belief in a Higher Power, or whatever particular inner demon ails us at the current moment. We're all wrestlers. Just not all of us wear spandex.

Indeed, the more I think about it, the more I realize I have in common with the wrestling audience at Harvest Church.

For starters, there are more than enough things that observant Jews do to attain some sense of spiritual nourishment that would look utterly bizarre to an outsider. Waiting six hours between eating steak and Munster cheese comes to mind. As does our fear of leavened food on Passover—we go so far as to avoid even entering a room where leavened food might be. In the heat of every summer, we observe three weeks of mourning when we don't get haircuts or shave. Every Saturday night, we wave at a braided multiwicked candle. And these examples are just the tip of the iceberg. Judaism, I'll be the first to admit, is replete with seemingly ridiculous rituals.

But, obviously, the rituals mean something. Going through the motions, adhering to God's commandments (as odd as they sometimes may seem), is a religious experience in and of itself. So who am I to judge others when you can catch me wrapping myself in leather straps every day for morning prayers?

Put simply, we do all these things because God told us to. Yes, perhaps Judaism's dictates come across to the average reader as ancient prescriptions while sticking a cross onto your wrestling spandex with electrical tape seems spiritually improvisational at best. But take a step back. These are merely variations on the path to sincere religious observance.

God wants us, we all assume, to be good human beings. And being a good Benyamin Cohen is, at times, markedly different from being a good Rob Adonis. Yes, we both try not to steal, cheat, and lie. Beyond that, our "goodness" differs. He wrestles. I eat latkes. But we're both adhering to our own religion as we meet up on the collective road to faith. Yes, we are all wrestlers.

And suspend cynical reasoning for just another moment. Adonis, like many prophets and religious leaders before him, claims a heavenly calling plucked him from his mundane existence in rural Georgia and dropped him into a world of worship. He didn't have a choice. Even he agrees the idea of UCW is a tad peculiar.

But this idea of a magical "calling" is not as foreign to Judaism as I once thought. There's a denomination within Orthodox Judaism known as Chabad. Its adherents believe it is their mission to proselytize (to Jews) around the world about the benefits of leading a more spiritual life. By any indication, they're doing a remarkable job. In far-off cities that have zero signs of Jewish presence, there's a lone Chabad emissary there doing the work of God. In Bangkok, Azerbaijan, Nepal, Costa Rica, and even Nebraska. In total, there are hundreds of "Chabad Houses" throughout the world.

I was recently chatting with Rabbi Yossi New, the director of Chabad of Georgia, which has six centers spread throughout the state. When I asked how he came to choose his path in life, he simply said, "I felt a calling."

Throughout Jewish circles, Chabad is known as a movement that will stop at nothing to spread the word of God. In full Chassidic garb, its members wait at airports like Hare Krishnas. They stop traffic when they parade through Main Street America with their Chanukah candelabras on the hood of their cars. But they are successful. They are doing more to stop the tide of Jewish assimilation and intermarriage than any Jewish organization on the planet. Admittedly, it's an odd motif coming from a religion that frowns on proselytizing.

Although Ultimate Christian Wrestling isn't as widespread as Chabad (Adonis says that besides Georgia they have only performed in Kentucky and Virginia), I wouldn't be surprised if they wrestled in Azerbaijan someday soon.

As I drive deeper into the moonless dark night down I-85, I realize that there's a sweet charm to the way this community just outside Athens, Georgia, practices its religion. And for that I am eternally grateful to Adonis, the crowd, and, I guess, to God Himself. After all, gratitude is an attitude.

TWELVE

Gut Check

The Lord will sustain him on his sickbed and restore him from his bed of illness.

—Psalm 41:3

JANUARY AND I have never gotten along. Its reputation for dreariness proves true. This is the month each year that I become the biblical Job, experiencing bad luck at every turn.

Our house got broken into this January. Almost every girl I ever dated dumped me in January. I got braces in January—twice. Once in fourth grade and then again in seventh. Tenth grade brought with it a January retainer. As a kid, this month was nothing more than one long nightmare of gingiva, orthodontia gone wild.

For the last few years I've been suffering from chronic insomnia. My neuroses, my constant calculating, my religious unfulfillment—something has been keeping me up at night. This January, in an attempt to get off all the sleep meds to which I've become addicted, I started to see a cognitive sleep therapist. Her methods are sinister. It's basically sleep deprivation. She keeps me to a strict regimen of going to bed at 2 A.M. and waking up at 6 A.M. This way, when nighttime arrives, instead of worrying how I'm going to fall asleep, the challenge now becomes how I'm going to keep myself awake. I'm playing voodoo mind games with myself. This is January. It's mostly a blur.

But nothing marks January as my least favorite month as much as what happened eighteen years ago this month. My mother passed away. Ever since, I've held a vendetta against these thirty-one winter days. They've never been good to me.

She suffered a sudden brain aneurism on Tuesday. By Thursday I had become an unwitting member of the Dead Parent Club. It was mere months after my bar mitzvah and immediately threw my proper transition into Jewish adulthood off course. I felt helpless. My life had imploded at a moment's notice. My religious growth, tracked along the path of a stable Jewish family, diverted into treacherous territory.

They say when a parent dies, a kid learns to grow up quickly. That is certainly true on some level; after my mother's passing I quickly took over many of the household chores including laundry duty and making everyone's lunch to take to school. But on a much more raw level, a parental death stunts the very trajectory of maturity. Losing a parent causes a child to curl up and retreat into the fetal position. This was me. This was my adolescence.

Each year, as is Jewish custom, relatives recall loved ones who have died by the Hebrew lunar date of their death. This is known as a *yahrzeit*. For my mom, this was the sixth day of the month of Shevat. On that date every year since her passing, my siblings and I lead services at synagogue for my mother's merit, with the hopes that our prayers will help elevate her soul in heaven.

This year is no different. I put church aside momentarily and attend synagogue to lead the services. I feel like a fraud. Just the day before I had attended a Catholic Mass. Now I am leading a congregation of Jews in prayer. Even if those in attendance don't know it, my mother certainly has been keeping score from her heavenly plane. What can she be thinking looking down at me? *Was that Benyamin getting shpritzed with holy water by the priest?*

Leading the prayer service is something a Jew does for the entire year following a relative's death. But for me, it went beyond that. Throughout high school, with a dad as a rabbi and a synagogue in my home, I led the services weekly, if not daily. I did it flawlessly, all the while daydreaming about a television show or how stupid I looked in braces. I could do it by heart, with my eyes closed. Leading services was second nature for me.

So, despite my Christian excursions as of late, I slip right back into the prayer leader groove. I remove the Torah scroll from its ark. As I carry it around the synagogue, those gathered lean in to kiss the holy scroll in reverence. I place the scroll on its specially designated table and, during a momentary lapse in attention, I exert too much pressure. It's too late. The

Torah's wooden handle breaks off, its sudden snap waking me to attention. In my three decades of attending synagogue I have never seen anyone do this. I'm an idiot. This must be God's twisted sense of humor. An ironic practical joke on a Jew with wandering eyes.

The congregants look at me in horror. This January was going to be no different from the previous ones.

TODAY IS JANUARY 23. Only eight more days to go, but month's end can't come quick enough. At the doctor's office today, I was informed that I have Crohn's disease. This can't be good.

For quite some time, I've been feeling a pain in my gut. Unfortunately, I don't mean that as a metaphor. I was—and still am—having tummy trouble. On bad days, I find myself dashing to the bathroom nearly twenty times a day. It's gotten to the point that, when I'm running errands, I can tell you the exact location of the nearest public restroom.

When I go to the movies now, I scope out the bathroom nearest to our theater. Two hours of sitting still isn't likely, and I'll need an exit plan. How is this going to affect my church habits if I have to keep getting up out of my seat? *Pardon me, pastor, but your sermon is making me queasy.* Like an actuary of crime and punishment, I begin to wonder about the effect of my Christian activities. Maybe this is God's way of telling me to stop looking outside my religion and to steer clear of Christianity. And bam, as if to prove His point, I'm smitten with Crohn's disease. As I said, this can't be good.

The obvious irony is that, although doctors have absolutely no clue what actually causes someone to get the intestinal disorder known as Crohn's, they do know this one tidbit of information: Jews are much more likely to get it than the rest of known civilization. I guess it's the Jewish inbreeding, but our genetic makeup makes us susceptible to all sorts of chronic diseases. Considering that most of those other Jewish diseases all lead to a very early death, I guess I got off easy with a little bowel discomfort.

I went to a gastroenterologist. After asking me a series of embarrassing questions, he said he thought I had Crohn's. "But to be sure," he explained, "I'll need to conduct a colonoscopy"—which is, coincidentally, the absolute worst sentence anyone can utter in the entire English language. For a moment, I half considered opting out of the exam. Do I really need to know if I have Crohn's? Maybe all this stomach pain will just magically disappear. Yep, feeling better already. There's no need for me to be anally probed.

But common sense got the better of me, so I scheduled the colonoscopy for the following week. Looking back, I realize this is a common procedure, but I built it up into something much grander than it actually was. Because I'm a neurotic Jew, and that's what we do. I tried to take care of any unfinished business before the arrival of that fateful day. I showed Elizabeth where the key to our safe deposit box was and, in the event that something happened to me, I gave her permission to remarry—assuming, of course, she first spends years and years mourning my horribly unfortunate death in the name of gastroenterological research.

I don't remember much from the actual procedure itself. They gave me some pretty good sedatives and, before I could count backward from ten, I was knocked out, blissfully dreaming of a man sticking a camera up my tush. The next thing I knew, I was in a busy recovery room with other drugged-out patients. A nurse told me to go to the bathroom to try to release the extra air that was blown into my rectum. This was embarrassing. I did as I was told. Walking out of the bathroom, I bumped into a girl from my synagogue. This was also embarrassing.

My doctor entered the recovery room, showed me some pictures he took of my intestine, and said he didn't find anything. I wasn't sure whether to scream or strangle the guy. I did neither.

A week later, in his office and with the advantage of now having clothes on, I asked the doc what my other options were. He told me about an Israeli company that had invented a jelly bean–sized pill that contains a tiny camera. When swallowed, it takes a seven-hour video of the upper intestine, and you don't even feel it swimming around in your body. I wondered why the doctor didn't inform me of this painless option before the colonoscopy. Once again, I wasn't sure whether to scream or strangle the guy. I did neither.

It's true, you really don't feel the camera when it's inside you. You can actually go to work and go about your normal day-to-day business while the camera floats innocently around in your innards. The brochure they gave me shows an attractive young woman in business attire with a cell phone in one hand and a latte in the other. The reality, however, is somewhat different. The camera is constantly sending a signal to a tiny computer that is attached to you by a belt so big that it's hard to walk around without a stiff back and robotic arms. I felt like Frankenstein in a workmen's belt. Also, and this is the part they should really advertise, anyone who sees you will instantly think you're a suicide bomber.

The camera did its job and ended up finding eight ulcers. That sounded like a lot and even my doctor seemed, to my chagrin, surprised. "I've never seen anything like this," the doctor said, alarmingly bewildered, as we watched the video together. Remember Dennis Quaid floating around Martin Short's intestines in the movie *Innerspace?* Just add eight ulcers, and that's what this video looked like.

This is when the doctor kindly informed me I have Crohn's.

Why couldn't I be afflicted with a cooler disease? I don't know of any Hollywood actor who has Crohn's. To my knowledge, there's no annual Crohn's Telethon or Crohn's Three-Day Walks. The best thing we've got is the image of Katie Couric having a colonoscopy on national television. But that wasn't even for Crohn's awareness. That was to help promote early detection of colon cancer. Cancer; it's always cancer. Crohn's is like the bastard stepchild of cancer. For God's sake, we have an apostrophe in our name. How cool can that be?

The doctor, sensing my frustration with my new lot in life, told me to log on to a Web site that offers advice and puts me in touch with others out there who have Crohn's. I didn't want to be in touch with others. I wanted to suffer alone, in the privacy of my own bathroom. But curiosity got the guy who has Crohn's, and so I logged on to the site. I couldn't believe I was going to one of these support-group sites. Weren't they for people with chronic illnesses? Was that me now? Had I become, overnight, one of them?

At first I couldn't even find the site because I kept spelling Crohn's with a "K," as in Krohn's. The typo led me to pages having nothing to do with poop problems, pages instead littered with info on Michael Krohn (lead singer of the Norwegian band Raga Rockers), Lisa Krohn (a postmodern industrial designer), and Juan María Fernández Krohn (a former Catholic priest who tried unsuccessfully to assassinate Pope John Paul II). The concept of being struck with a lifelong illness was so foreign to me that I didn't even know how to spell it properly.

Once I reached the site, I found out I'm not alone. Apparently, half a million Americans suffer from the same embarrassing bathroom issues as I do. Including, I learned, Pearl Jam guitarist Mike McCready. The site says that in 2002, McCready "made public" his twenty-year battle with Crohn's disease. Made public? Oy, how bad is this disease going to get?

The site has video testimonials of people from all walks of life living with Crohn's. Most have happy music in the background as patients smile and talk about all the humiliation of having accidents in public. (Accidents in public?) There's a video from Ben Morrison, a Jewish comedian, that caught my attention. He also suffers from Crohn's and has a whole series of videos titled, appropriately enough, *Pain in the Ass*.

He's a Scottish Jewish comedian, so his classic one-liner is: "If you're looking for a castle, I can get you a good deal." In one of his videos he tells the story of having a colonoscopy and how his insurance company did not want to pay for it because, as they put it, it's an *elective* procedure. "What, did they think I was just sitting around really bored one day? You know, I haven't seen the inside of my own ass in a while. Let's go get probed."

I clicked around the site some more and read about Alley's Law, which is supposed to give anyone with Crohn's access to any restroom even if it's not designated for public use. First of all, I feel bad for Alley, the fourteen-year-old Chicago girl the law is named after. Something tells me she's not going to be the most popular girl at school anymore. Second of all, stop reading this book (just for a moment) and ask anyone in the room if they've heard of Alley's Law. What boggles my mind is that nobody knows about this law, thus negating its effectiveness. How can a bouncer at the front of a hip nightclub let you in to use a private restroom if he's never even heard of Alley's Law? And even if he has, am I going to receive some kind of Crohn's VIP card to let me past the velvet rope? Ah, yes, membership has its privileges.

While doing more research, I kept coming across the same line: There is currently no known cure for Crohn's. This was constantly being repeated as a statement of fact, and it made me feel completely helpless. I have a disease—nobody knows what causes it and nobody has any clue how to cure it. Why would God do this to me?

There are obviously worse things that can happen than getting Crohn's. I'm reminded of a friend of mine who woke up one morning in college and realized he had gone blind overnight. This is, quite possibly, the scariest scenario I can imagine and, incidentally, would make a great story line for a horror movie. The doctors said he had a rare medical disorder and would most likely never be able to see again. It's been about a decade since everything went black for him, yet he has persevered and made the best of his bad situation. He is living a full life—he even took (and passed) the bar exam and is now a successful attorney. He does this because, despite his disabilities, he has a profound sense of what it means to just be alive.

As for me, I can't say I'd deal with a disability the same way. If I woke up blind one morning, I'm not sure I'd be the guy grabbing life by the horns. I think I'm missing the courage gene. I'd be the "Woe is me" guy, most likely conjuring clever ways to commit suicide.

A few years ago I read *Lucky Man,* Michael J. Fox's autobiography, in which he discusses his struggle with Parkinson's. He's one of my favorite actors—*Family Ties* is my favorite sitcom, and *Back to the Future* is my favorite movie. But after reading his book, I'm not so sure I'm still a fan.

This guy is bionic, remarkably superhuman, to the point where the lessons he's trying to impart are on such a high plane that we mortals will never be able to comprehend, much less practice them. The entire premise of the book can be summed up like this: *Hi, I'm celebrated actor Michael J. Fox. You may remember me from a movie with a time-traveling DeLorean in it. But I'm here to tell you that I have Parkinson's. It's killing me. And it's a gift from God. It's a blessing. Hope you enjoy my book.*

He makes it all sound so easy. He will likely never meet his grandchildren, and he's dying a slow and agonizingly painful death. And yet he wholeheartedly and truly feels that being struck with Parkinson's was the best thing that could happen to him. (Hence, the title of the book.) I guess I'm just not as evolved as Michael J. Fox.

I know plenty of people in my community who have been struck by unbearable tragedy. The family who lost a baby to an incurable disease. The husband whose wife of thirty-five years was killed by a drunk driver as she was walking home from the Sabbath service.

Suffering is not my cup of tea. I don't do well with illness. I know nobody does, but when it comes to pain, I'm not the guy you want protecting state secrets in a torture chamber. I'd cave in a second. When it comes to being sick, I'm a horrible patient. God knows all this about me, yet He must have other plans. Apparently, I'm supposed to be the writer with Crohn's.

God must think I'm strong enough to deal with it. Although I'd beg to differ with Him. Just as soon as I finish using the restroom.

•   •   •

JANUARY IS JUST about over. My sister Chanie called me today. We speak often, so this was not out of the ordinary. But what she said to me was. As of late, she had been experiencing odd feelings of numbness, to the point where she sometimes couldn't move her leg. She had gone to the doctor several times in recent weeks and even had an MRI. My Crohn's diagnosis was nothing compared to what the doctors had to inform her of. They think she has multiple sclerosis. She's only twenty-six.

She told me the news with such calmness I didn't even know how to respond. It was as though she skipped right over the diagnosis, flew past anger at the Almighty, and went right to the resignation that this would be her life from now on. And it was only a few hours ago that she received the awful news.

I had figured, and bear with me on this discourse, that after our mom died when we were just kids (I was thirteen, Chanie was only eight), we would be free from future ills. I know it's a naïve notion, but I thought that in some sick way we were getting off the hook, dodging future tragedy by bearing the brunt of God's wrath while we were still children. We had rolled the dice and played a divine version of *Let's Make a Deal*. Behind curtain number three was a lifetime without a maternal figure, no mom to watch us grow up, to see what we had become, to meet her grandchildren. We had lost, but at least we wouldn't be called to be contestants again for a long time hence. I was secure in the blissful knowledge that after God had tallied up the divine pluses and minuses, He would just leave us alone.

I guess Chanie, like me, is no longer immune from God's abacus. It had become glaringly apparent that our eighteen-year free pass, bestowed upon us at the moment of our mom's death, had officially expired. Our good luck had come to an end. God was cashing in His chips. January was rearing its ugly head.

I like to think I'm a down-to-earth kind of guy. But once in a while I find myself turning into a dime-store philosopher, pretending to be deeply existential. I like that Benyamin. He seems to have his act more together than I do.

That version of me comes out of hiding each January. Amid the torrent of unusually bad luck I seem to experience during this dreadful month, I often find myself asking that question of all questions: Why do bad things happen to good people? The dime-store philosopher version of me is, of course, not the first person to ask said question. There's a famous book, written back in 1981, called *When Bad Things Happen to Good People,* by Rabbi Harold Kushner. But as the author himself points out in both the book and his public lectures, there are limits to his discussion. He is only dealing with *when* bad things happen to good people, not *why.*

For the answer to that more complex quandary, I turn to another book, one written by a mentor of mine, called *If God Is Good, Why Is the World So Bad?* The book, written by Rabbi Benjamin Blech, picks up where Kushner left off. It's actually based on a twelve-hour lecture series I once heard Blech give that elucidates the various responses he offers to the age-old question.

Rereading Blech's book this January, one particular response to this proverbial question sparked a special resonance with me. He explains that one of the psychological coping mechanisms for dealing with suffering and tragedy is derived from an Old Testament passage in which Moses asks God to reveal Himself. It seems like a fair request, but God shuts Moses down by responding, "You cannot see My presence and live" (Exodus 33:20).

"What in the world does this mean?" Blech asks. "Moses wants to 'see' God, to understand God's ways. But God tells Moses, 'As long as you are alive you will never fully 'see.' The entire picture is not visible from our limited perspective in the world."

Too often we seek to understand, in human terms, why God decides to do the things He does. Why does He mete out punishment to seemingly innocent people? Why is there suffering in this world? Why do babies die? As we see from God's response to Moses, we are in no position to judge. *You cannot see My presence and live.* As mere mortals, we cannot begin to fathom God's master plan. All we are seeing is the blip that is our lives or a particular tragedy that we suffer from. We are not all-knowing, despite what our egos think. We are not privy to the entire picture.

As Blech further writes: "Imagine yourself with your nose pressed to an impressionistic painting. In one place you see splotches of the most breathtaking royal blue, in another there is a big splotch of black, in another a splotch of white. It is not until you step a good dozen feet away that you see what the painting depicts—it is Van Gogh's *Irises.*"

The biblical verses of Moses and God's "Hey, can I see you?" conversation go a step further in explaining this "big picture" insight. God informs

Moses, "When My glory passes by, I will put you in a cleft of the rock and I will cover you with My hand until I pass by. Then I will remove My hand and you will see My back, but My face shall not be seen" (Exodus 33:22–23).

Moses will get to see God's presence, but only from the back. In essence, as Blech points out, "God is saying that it will be impossible for Moses to understand the events as they are happening. But later, in retrospect, it might be possible to make sense of what occurred. While you are confronting a crisis, while you are in the eye of the storm, you will not be able to understand God's purpose or logic. But once the crisis has passed, then, looking backwards in time, it will be possible to begin to understand God's ways."

Here's the classic Philosophy 101 example. Think of a businessman who misses an important flight. He's annoyed and cursing God for his bad luck. Missing this flight means missing meetings and losing money. Then, later, he finds out the plane crashed, and everyone aboard died in a blazing inferno. The formerly irate traveler can now be seen thanking the Almighty for this good fortune. He's happy to be alive. At the moment he was "suffering," he couldn't see why God had made him miss the flight. But now, in retrospect, it was all clear.

This is the beauty of perspective. *You will see My back.* In hindsight, God is telling Moses, these things will make sense. And it may not even be in our own lifetime. We should just know that there is a divine purpose for tragedy, even if our simple human mind can't make heads or tails of it.

This is the challenge I face each January. When bad things strike, and they most certainly will, I need to breathe. I need to realize that, difficult as it may seem, this too is for the best. Even Crohn's. Even my sister's MS. Even my mother's passing.

On the anniversary of my mother's death, my siblings and I (like all Jewish mourners) recite the millennia-old Kaddish, a majestic and poetic Aramaic prayer that honors the Almighty for His infinite wisdom. This seems like an odd time for us to be praising God. A close relative just died—why are we spending this time blessing God and not, instead, reciting a sad prayer about life and death?

Viewing the question through the prism of Blech's explanation, I begin to realize why we recite this laudatory prayer to God. It is at this exact moment, when we are stricken with the tragedy of losing a loved one, that we need to be cognizant that God indeed has infinite wisdom. He has a reason for this tragedy. There is purpose to this suffering. We may not see it now, but this is certainly part of God's master vision. This too, somehow, is for the best.

It's been eighteen long years since my mother passed away. In Hebrew the number eighteen and the word for "life" are the exact same word, *chai*. I consider this for a moment. This is a propitious year for me, an opportune time for me to take tragedy and turn it on its head. Grow from it. Use it for something positive. Live life. Find meaning. Praise the Lord.

These thoughts provide me peace while contemplating my mom's death. Now, as the hand of God is once again clearly present in my life, these thoughts also give me comfort. For my Crohn's and my sister's MS. Maybe one day she'll write a book called *Lucky Woman* explaining why being struck with this illness was her life's greatest blessing.

As for me, well, I'm just not that evolved. But I'm working on it.

THIRTEEN

G.I. Jew

Experienced soldiers prepared for battle with every type of weapon, to help David with undivided loyalty.

—*1 Chronicles 12:33*

EACH SABBATH FOR the past few months, I've been finding myself praying next to a guy who had a lobotomy. I mention this not because I feel superior (I don't) or because it's a bad thing (it's not). I actually enjoy praying to God in the company of a guy who had a lobotomy. And, as of late, I've actually been enjoying praying altogether.

Don't get too excited. I haven't earned my wings just yet. But I have unearthed, at the very least, the beginnings of a renewed appreciation for my prayers.

It all dates back to the High Holiday *hashkama* early service that Elizabeth and I attended. You'll recall that was the small service during which I was able to tap into the purity of prayer the way I had once did as a child. I had a good time—well, about as much of a good time as you can have on the somber Day of Judgment when your life hangs in the balance. But it was a good time nonetheless. It was something I hadn't experienced in a synagogue in far too long. And something I didn't want to have to wait for the next High Holiday season to experience again.

It seems enough of the people gathered that day enjoyed it too; we were able to convince the synagogue to let us keep this alternative service going during the rest of the year. So on the weekly Sabbath, before the long and drawn-out main service takes place from 9 A.M. until noon, our group meets from 7:15 to 8:45. (We start and end so early so we can get out of the sanctuary before the main service starts.) Bereft of a long sermon or copious amounts of singing, we complete our prayers in half the time. Think of us as the drive-thru of Jewish prayers. *Do you want some fries with that plea for mercy?*

It's not just the shorter length of the service that seems to work for some people; it's also our start time. Considering the fact that observant Jews usually have Friday night Sabbath dinners that regularly end well past midnight, it's no wonder we get an odd array of congregants who decide to cut their Sabbath sleep short to wake up before sunrise and walk over to our service. The guy with the lobotomy is, not surprisingly, par for the course.

What's particularly nice about this service is its intimacy. On a typical Saturday morning we only get about fifteen people. Elizabeth has the entire women's section all to herself. That's compared to the hundreds who show up for the main service. And because it's so small, each one of us gets to be a part of the service. Lobotomy Guy is the perennial ark opener anytime the service calls for the ark to be opened. Another person is the one who always sets up the post-service refreshments. As for me, I've become one of the *gabbais*. A *gabbai,* just in case you're wondering, is basically the maître d' of a Jewish prayer service. Among other things, he chooses who will lead the service, calls up congregants by their Hebrew names to the Torah scroll for special blessings, and makes the announcements at the service's conclusion. As part of my *gabbai* duties I've also been sending out weekly e-mails reminding people to show up to our service along with a riddle of the week. (Recent entry: What Jewish holiday can be found on every New York City subway map?)

Most of this comes naturally for me because it reminds me so much of the synagogue I had in my house growing up. I was also the *gabbai* there, straightening up the chairs before services and putting the prayer books away afterward. I guess somewhere amid my Crohn's and allergies, there's a *gabbai* gene lurking inside my DNA, its double helix twisting around my soul.

Since we have to skedaddle out of the sanctuary before the main service starts, we often have to pray the last section at an extra-quick pace. I'm often asked to be the prayer leader of this final homestretch. I guess the others know I like doing it quickly, and, because I'm a rabbi's son, they know I can deliver. I feel like a relief pitcher, brought in as a closer at the end of the baseball game to finish things off for the team.

I've got to admit it feels good, real good, to be involved hands-on with prayers again. No longer am I sitting on the sidelines. The coach has brought me in to play and pray with this merry band of misfits.

IN ADDITION TO Lobotomy Guy, a military chaplain also comes to our service. I guess the army has prepared him for waking up before dawn. Chaplain Horovitz is no ordinary American military chaplain. For starters, he's not even American. Born in Britain, he always felt it was his duty and his honor to serve in the U.S. military for, as he put it, "America invented freedom of religion. It was the first country to be hospitable to Jews."

One Sabbath morning at the *hashkama* service, Chaplain Horovitz let me in on a little secret. The largest Jewish prayer service on any U.S. military base in the world happens where he's stationed—at Fort Benning, just a few hours south of Atlanta. At first, I brushed off the staggering statistic. This was the year of *church* field trips. Jewish prayer services, no matter how odd, were just not on the itinerary. The chaplain seemed like a nice guy, but I couldn't waste a Sunday at the world's largest Jewish military service unless I'd be guaranteed a Jesus sighting. Or could I? Maybe the change of pace would do me good. I had spent the past months immersing myself in all things Christian. I guess the least I could do was spend a Sunday with my own religion.

Before I caved in to his request, I should've considered the details. The chaplain pulls into my driveway shortly before 3 A.M. on Sunday morning. Apparently, a group of infantry cadets is graduating at a ceremony that starts at 5 A.M., so we've got to hightail it there in time for the chaplain to recite a blessing and say some inspiring remarks in front of a ridiculously large bonfire. I had never left for church at this ungodly hour. Coffee in hand, I hop into his car and he zooms off way above the speed limit, confident in the fact that because he's dressed in his army uniform no cop will bother to stop us.

Horovitz proves to be a fascinating conversationalist for the next two hours as we blaze down the highway in the pitch-black night. He's forty-six years old, has six kids, and is already a grandfather. He grew up on the outskirts of London, moved to Israel, and then to New York, where he signed up for chaplaincy school. Although there are thousands of chaplains in the U.S. military, he is one of only a few Jews.

His position ministering to those in need has taken him to the far reaches of the globe—to Afghanistan, Iraq, and Korea (where he was part of what he dubbed "Seoul's soul community"). At each of these places, he has taken a special interest in cataloging places of religious archaeological import. In the small Iraqi town of Kifel, he visited the supposed tomb of the prophet Ezekiel. He's visited the purported ruins of the Tower of Babel and the palace of Nebuchadnezzar. He was a rabbinically ordained Indiana Jones.

Before I know it, we arrive at the army base. I had never been to a fort before except for the ones of the blanket-and-chair variety I had built as a kid. Fort Benning is a little larger than those of my youth—it's home to more than a hundred thousand people and covers nearly two hundred thousand acres.

Two soldiers rise to attention as the chaplain and I enter an administration building. I feel unworthy of entering in on his coattails. I'm getting the respect without all the work.

We stop off at his office so he can check his e-mail before the service begins. Jewish soldiers stationed across the globe e-mail him with all sorts of religious quandaries, and he responds daily. On his computer screen, he shows me a picture of him with President Bush taken during the commander-in-chief's recent visit. On his desk is a copy of the *Fort Benning Bayonet,* the "town" newspaper. On his bookshelf are boxes of kosher military meals, which he delivers to Jewish soldiers.

The prayer service is held in one of the many chapels on this base. Sunday at Fort Benning is like a United Nations parade of religions. Besides the Jewish prayers, there are a myriad of Christian services (e.g., Lutheran, Catholic, Mormon) as well as Wiccan and Muslim services. Had I known about this earlier, I could've spent my entire church-hopping year on this one base.

About 150 soldiers dressed in camouflage uniforms with matching camouflage-colored skullcaps jump off barrack trucks at the front of the chapel. Inside, all of the crosses have been covered. One lone picture of Jesus remains near the exit. The Son of God's eyes seem, like the Mona Lisa's, to follow me wherever I go. He's making me feel uneasy. *Um, Benyamin, how come you're not at church today?*

The chaplain shows a few of the soldiers how to properly don the *talit,* the Jewish prayer shawl. As the service begins, they go through each blessing. One soldier reads it aloud, and the chaplain then discusses it. At one point, Horovitz takes the Torah scroll out of its ark and shows it to the soldiers. "Our country was founded on these Judeo-Christian values," he says. I can't say I've ever heard that declared in a synagogue before. They recite a prayer in Hebrew for the U.S. government.

The stained-glass window shows a soldier on bended knee praying and holding a gun. More soldiers continue to stream through the entrance. So many people show up that the prayer books actually run out, forcing people to share.

Holding a microphone so everyone can hear him, Horovitz declares, "When you say the prayer about healing, think about all the soldiers, that God should heal them." During the Kaddish prayer, usually recited only by mourners, many of the soldiers mouth the Hebrew words in memory of fallen comrades in Iraq.

In the back of the room, I strike up a conversation with two older men, army vets, it turns out, who live nearby and help Chaplain Horovitz run the service. I ask them why they get such a crowd. "They're nominally Jewish, but they rediscover Judaism here," one of them says, mentioning the old adage that there are no atheists in a foxhole. "Soldiers find the spirituality with the mortality."

At the end of the service, one of the old army vets leads the soldiers in a rendition of "God Bless America" and then announces, "We're going to do battle this week to get more prayer books." It must be a slow week.

Horovitz strikes up an Israeli song and leads a dance around the perimeter of the room. For the first time this morning, the soldiers let loose and join the circle, their camouflage skullcaps bouncing off their heads. We dance our way to the parking lot for the post-service refreshments set up on a few folding tables. There are bagels, lox, cream cheese, cookies, and donuts. I'm told none of the other religious denominations at the base offer this cornucopia of refreshments at their services. I begin to wonder if that's what draws the crowd. I've got to believe a bagel and lox taste better than army rations.

But maybe it's not all about the nosh. It seems a different kind of soul food is what's drawing in the crowds. I ask a soldier named Gilbert from California why he comes to the service. "It's a way to reconnect to my Judaism," he tells me. He says before he signed up for the military, he never thought twice about his religion. But being introduced to the caring Horovitz has sparked a new interest in his faith.

When you think of the army, you think of conformity. Boot camp is all about stripping you of your identity. From the uniforms to the haircuts, everyone is treated just the same. There is no place to express yourself. But here, at Sunday services, the soldiers have found a fascinating way to carve out an identity for themselves. Here they can be Jewish. Or Catholic. Or Wiccan.

This gets me thinking about my own Jewish identity and what it means to me. Despite my spiritual vertigo, I am positive that even if I weren't religious, a Jewish identity would still be a strong part of my very being. Being Jewish is something unique and special for me, yet so many American Jews try to escape it by assimilating into society. All the seemingly obscure rules and prayers may be difficult for me, but I've never actually struggled with the identity part of the equation.

I speak to more soldiers as they wolf down donuts and Entenmann's cookies. And this is when I find out something I never expected—most of them are Christian, a fact confirmed to me later by the chaplain. More than 50 percent of those who attended this Jewish prayer service are non-Jews.

They were reverse-engineering my yearlong experiment—here was a group of Christians who believed Jewish prayers were more enjoyable than those of their own faith. An artillery soldier named Private Peebles, whose dad is actually a Baptist minister, tells me he's been coming to the Jewish services since he arrived at the base. "I was always curious about the Jews," he explains. "At my dad's church, we studied the Old Testament, but now I have access to a rabbi who makes it authentic." These soldiers are looking to Judaism as the ancient source of their own religion, give or take a Jesus Christ.

Peebles is one of about forty soldiers who stick around after the refreshments for an hour-long class on Judaism taught by the chaplain. Horovitz is used to this kind of thing. While stationed in Seoul, he taught a weekly Talmud class to more than a hundred non-Jewish Koreans.

Of all places, the army is teaching me the beauty of interfaith dialogue. The chaplain is its prime example. He's in the trenches ministering to those who need it most. It doesn't make any difference what faith they are. Just that faith will help.

What's more, this interfaith outreach was having a surprising boomerang effect. His Jewish prayer service, the largest on any U.S. military base, comprised mostly non-Jews. What did they see in my own religion that I could not see?

I guess it shouldn't surprise me that it takes a bunch of soldiers in boot camp to appreciate Judaism. After all, isn't that the way I felt all the time—in the boot camp that is Jewish ritual life? My religion dictates when to pray, where to pray, and what to pray among a whole host of other restrictions. Like the army, my religion tells me how to cut my hair, what to wear, and what I can eat. In a way, my life was just as regimented as theirs. It's no wonder Judaism struck a chord with them.

But it's much more than that. After all, they were only getting a glimpse of Judaism at the Sunday service. They weren't experiencing what I endearingly refer to as "Judaism's dark side," all the labyrinthine laws that encompass daily life. They experienced a view of Judaism untainted by my cynical point of view. And what they experienced moved them. If only I could somehow tap into that same feeling.

At the end of the day, all of us are blessed with curiosity. They about Judaism, and me about Christianity. We all seem to think the grass is greener at the house of worship across the street. Perhaps it is. Perhaps it isn't. What's important is that we're crossing the street and taking a look. We are seekers looking for something more. Some may be seeking Old Testament insight, some may be seeking bagels and lox, and some, like me, may be seeking a little salvation.

FOURTEEN

Upon This Rock 'n' Roll

Then Moses and the Israelites sang this song to the Lord.
—Exodus 15:1

I AM NOT a concert kind of a guy. I don't like smoky joints, loud music, or—to be perfectly honest—any activity involving long periods of standing. And since we're on the topic, I don't dance either. The only concerts I attended were the kitschy ones performed at Jewish summer camps. I recall watching Uncle Moishy and his Mitzvah Men perform. Let's just say they were not exactly the Rolling Stones or the Dave Matthews Band. They were more like the Jewish equivalent of the Wiggles, only not nearly as popular or color-coordinated.

That they were one of my only live music memories is a woefully sad portrait of the extent of my remarkably nebbish childhood. I did actually attend an outdoor rock festival during high school sponsored by a local radio station. C & C Music Factory and Wilson Phillips were the headliners. I went with my friend Josh, who proceeded to embarrass me and the entire Jewish nation by dancing and twirling his *tzitzit* (religious fringes) to "Everybody Dance Now." His anachronistic Chassidic horah should've waited for the Factory's only other popular song, "Things That Make You Go Hmmm."

But since this is the year that I'm reexamining faith (both my own and others'), I figured I should suck it up and get jiggy with Jesus. So when I found out that Winter Jam, one of the country's largest Christian rock festivals, was going to be nearby, I knew I had no choice but to don my dancing shoes.

"Nearby" is a relative term, I'm finding out, as I drive the three hours to Augusta to the concert. Ironically, the last time I was in Augusta was also for a religious experience, although one of a completely different nature. And a completely different religion for that matter.

During the summer months, when my dad's schedule as a Jewish school principal was less hectic, he would take on some extra work by performing kosher supervision at various food-processing plants throughout the Southeast. Kosher supervision, contrary to popular belief, doesn't simply mean a rabbi reciting a Hebrew blessing as the food whizzes by on the conveyor belt. It means, among other things, examining all the ingredients to ensure they're kosher (no traces of gelatin or pork, for example). Oftentimes I would tag along with him, pretending to be a little rabbi in training. As I got older and went on these trips, my dad would actually introduce me as his rabbinical student. This was most likely wishful thinking on his part.

We went to the Honey Nut Cheerios plant. The Breakstone sour cream factory. The Nature Valley granola bar manufacturer. We even went to a Styrofoam cup company (which, for the record, doesn't actually require kosher certification, but wanted it anyway since they thought it would provide an edge in the marketplace).

Once a year we drove east to Augusta to the place where NutraSweet is created. There's one basic difference between this place and the other factories we visited on our kosher tours. They don't actually make food here. They make chemicals. Just to remind you, my dad's a rabbi, not a chemist. My dad would just stare at the large tanks of aspartame, and then we would turn around and drive back home. We were in the factory for only a few minutes. We actually spent more time at the manager's office donning protective suits and signing confidentiality agreements that we wouldn't reveal the secret formula.

Now here I am two decades later coming back to Augusta for one of America's largest Christian rock concerts, an event I highly doubt would garner my dad's kosher seal of approval.

Before this year, I never would've imagined Christians and rock concerts going hand in hand. Using the 1984 film *Footloose* as my only barometer for this logic, I just assumed that all reverends (a) looked like John Lithgow and (b) prohibited dancing and rocking as antithetical to Jesus' teachings. This is what I'm thinking as I enter the James Brown Arena to rock out to Jesus. The locale seems a bit odd considering Brown grew up not too far from here in a house of ill repute. But then again isn't Christianity all about forgiveness and redemption?

I step in some gum as I enter the pitch-black arena, only catching a glimpse of the thousands gathered here in the beams of roving strobe lights. The shouting and screaming of pimply teens and tweens is deafening. There are some introductory contests to get the crowd riled up. One sponsor is giving away an iPod. Another, Tennessee Temple University, is giving away a full scholarship. iPods and scholarships seem a bit pricey. The last Jewish event I went to was only giving away T-shirts. And not even humorous or ironic ones. Ones that simply declared, "With support to our Jewish friends from the local branch of Wachovia Bank." With prizes like that, accepting Jesus becomes all the more tempting.

In between the corporate sponsor giveaways, a band performs a song or two, much to the audience's delight. At the end of one song, a preview is shown on the large screens for a movie called *Amazing Grace,* about abolitionist William Wilberforce and his crusade to end the slave trade in eighteenth-century Britain. It's not *Shrek* or any other youth-friendly flick. Maybe if Wilberforce's girlfriend was played by Hannah Montana or someone from the cast of *High School Musical,* but this looks more like a Merchant-Ivory period piece.

Turns out Wilberforce experienced a midlife conversion to Christianity, and this movie was produced by Walden Media. I know this because after the preview a young woman named Laurie grabs the microphone and says to the confused audience, "I'm from Walden Media." Pause. "We're the people who brought you *The Chronicles of Narnia.*" The James Brown Arena erupts in shouts of joy and adulation.

Narnia, coproduced with mainstream Disney, was released in 2005 as the Christian equivalent of a *Lord of the Rings* fantasy film. Its box office success (it grossed nearly $1 billion) cemented a growing belief in Hollywood that there's actually money to be made in religious cinema (a trend that first started with some movie by Mel Gibson that wasn't even in English). *Narnia*'s actual religious imagery is a little less obvious than that in Gibson's *The Passion of the Christ,* but much of its success is attributed to the groundswell of promotion from churches and Christian events like this.

Trying to make the film seem relevant, Laurie shouts into the mike, "Slavery is at an all-time high this year!" The audience, not sure how to respond to this political declaration, does what it's been doing all night when the various bands take the stage—they cheer. I can't help but think that a concert promoting the abolition of slavery, held here in the heart of the former Confederacy, would make Abe Lincoln proud.

The antislavery hurrahs blend into the cheers for the next act. Sanctus Real, a Toledo-based band, starts performing. I vaguely recognize the song, which doesn't surprise me since this year I've set all my car-radio buttons to Christian stations. But this wasn't a Christian song. It sounded familiar because it was a cover of the popular U2 song "Beautiful Day."

I'm not exactly sure what it is about U2 that makes them such an inspiration to spiritual seekers. Perhaps it's the scriptural-sounding lyrics, or maybe it's Bono's God complex. I recently read about Reverend Paige Blair of York Harbor, Maine, who incorporated U2's songs—like "Mysterious Ways" and, of course, "Yaweh"—into her Episcopal service. She called it the "U2charist." It caught on and is now performed as a prepackaged PowerPoint presentation in more than three hundred churches from Omaha to Hong Kong. When asked by the media if she was looking for U2's blessing, Blair responded, "Although I respect him and I'm grateful for the gift he has given us, this is not about meeting Bono," she said. "This is about meeting Jesus."

As for Sanctus Real, not all of its music is copped from Irish rock bands. Its songs are typical Christian pop-rock fare, and by that I mean they substitute lyrics about love of God for those about love of a girl. All Christian pop songs can basically be split into three categories: I love Jesus; Jesus loves me; or I'm not worthy of his love. Some of these songs attempt, with varying degrees of success, to cover all three permutations.

All of these songs blend together and ultimately start to sound the same after a while. And that's a good thing, I suppose, in that their vanilla music encourages adoration of Jesus and not the band's front man. Imagine if Nirvana had been a Christian rock band. Maybe Cobain would still be alive. At the very least, he'd be filthy rich. In an industry with plummeting sales, Christian music has a big halo around it with $700 million in sales in 2005 compared to $381 million in 1995.

The traveling road pastor, Tony Nolan, bounds onto the stage after Sanctus Real finishes its set. He's in his early forties, but with his spiked hair and distressed jeans you can tell he tries hard to relate to the audience. Nolan, like all good youth ministers, has a tale of loss and redemption to tell. His biological mother was a mentally insane woman who sold him, at the age of three, to a dysfunctional foster family for a couple hundred bucks. His new parents beat him up, threw him down staircases, and burned him with cigarettes. In drunken rages, Nolan tells the audience, his dad would exclaim, "Is this all my two hundred bucks got me? I wish I'd never bought you."

Nolan says his teenage years were a downward spiral into drug addiction and thoughts of suicide. But then, on February 24, 1989, at the age of twenty-four, Jesus Christ rescued his soul. (It seems born-agains always have exact dates for their salvation. Think of it as a new birthday for them.) "God said, 'Tony, I have never regretted purchasing you with the blood of my son, Jesus Christ.'"

I can't help but think how incredibly harsh this tale of drug abuse and parental neglect must come across to the kids gathered here tonight. And this is not the first time I've heard such rags-to-riches salvation stories. I almost wonder if a bad beginning is necessary for a happy ending in a Christian life. As if a life of sin is a prerequisite, maybe even a blessing.

It's an awfully fine line for Christian educators to walk. It seems as if children of religious parents who themselves grow up to be religious are failures in the eyes of Christianity. I know this can't be true, but that's the impression I'm getting. What if religious kids in attendance tonight think they need to sin so that Jesus will love them? So that they can become a road pastor with a good redemption story to tell? What if they purposely go astray only to create an opening for return? What if they never return? I'm not sure I would, if given the choice.

ALTHOUGH JUDAISM DOESN'T have a notion of being "saved," we do have something somewhat similar. It's a concept called *baal teshuvah* in Hebrew, and it basically means to return to faith.

Many American Jews are assimilated, have intermarried, and have no connection to Judaism. And of those who do, many are only marginally observant—not keeping kosher, barely attending synagogue, and woefully uneducated about their faith. In the communal Jewish world, they call this a crisis.

So there's a large swath of Jews who, to put it in the parlance, need saving. Unlike Christianity, which is a proselytizing religion and emphasizes missionizing to those outside the faith, Judaism doesn't seek converts, but it does work just as hard to proselytize to its own.

As I had witnessed at the Ultimate Christian Wrestling event, people can accept Christ into their lives and become "saved" in an instant. In Judaism, however, the process of connecting with one's faith doesn't happen instantly, but occurs over months or even years of effort. This is simply because there's no magic "accept God" statement; instead, there's a long list of rules to learn and incorporate into your life. Those "returning to the faith" usually start the process after they experience a jolt of Judaism in the form of a meaningful synagogue moment, a trip to Israel, or time spent with a more observant family over Friday night dinner. These events serve as conduits to an untapped part of their soul and rekindle the fire within.

My mom and dad, who themselves had not grown up religious, experienced this sort of religious discovery when they were young adults. Recognizing the power of religion to inspire, they returned the favor and invited nonobservant Jews to our home each week for the Friday night Sabbath dinner. My parents hoped that being exposed to the beautiful religious traditions and family values of this meal would serve as a sort of soul food for the uninitiated. The highlight of the evening was when my siblings and I would spontaneously break into Hebrew a cappella songs to the delight of our dinner guests. We were like a Jewish Partridge Family.

Growing up, I was the only one of the siblings who didn't play a musical instrument. My mother played classical piano. My dad, when he wasn't being a principal or doing the kosher supervision of NutraSweet, played the drums in a band called Matzah, a nod to the 1970s rock group Bread. Its Jewish music, whether performed in our home or for a friend's bar mitzvah celebration, inspired people to come closer to their religion.

But my parents were not working in a bubble. There's a wealth of Jewish organizations whose sole purpose is to get nonobservant Jews more actively involved in Judaism. Birthright Israel, for example, is a group formed in the winter of 2000 that gives away free trips to Israel to college-aged Jews who've never been to the Holy Land. To date, they've sent more than a hundred and fifty thousand Jewish kids from fifty-one countries to Israel. The Manhattan Jewish Experience, where my rabbinic brother Ezra works, is an outreach institute geared toward nonmarried Jews in their twenties and thirties. It offers everything from beginner's services and educational classes to Jewish parties and singles-themed ski retreats. In my hometown, there's the Atlanta Scholars Kollel, which employs more than a dozen rabbis (unaffiliated with a synagogue pulpit) whose only job is to teach Judaism to any Jewish adult who wants to learn. One of its popular programs is called "Lunch 'n' Learn," in which the rabbis fan out across the city each day teaching classes at places like law firms and college campuses.

I often wonder what my life would have been like had I been brought up Jewish, but not religious. Would I have become a *baal teshuvah*? Would I even have cared about finding faith or would I have remained comfortable in my religious stagnation?

These "what if" questions swirl through my mind as the youth pastor wraps up his story of personal salvation. "We all have this infection, and it's called sin. You will spend eternity in hell," Nolan tells the children, nearly scaring them, as the Ultimate Christian Wrestlers had. "But whoever believes in Him shall not perish!" Everyone shouts as if on cue. He ends with a prayer and a call for donations for Christ. The lights are turned on so we can properly sift through our wallets for cash.

While the buckets are being passed around, Nolan asks if anyone wants to be saved tonight, noting that "we've already seen thirteen thousand decisions this year," which is actually a pretty staggering number considering this concert tour only started two weeks ago. Since the crowd is too big to have individuals who wish to be saved approach the stage, Nolan asks us to fill out a decision card, which is readily available in tonight's program, and drop it in the bucket along with our donation. The card also directs us to the tour's Web site, which has a downloadable pamphlet to guide us in the first steps to a life filled with the love of Christ.

A five-minute video from Holt International, a Christian adoption agency, plays on the large screens as the stage is being set up for the next band, Hawk Nelson. I take the opportunity to roam the arena's halls and notice something very strange. There's no beer being served at this concert. All the taps are turned off tonight. It's a kids' event, sure, but more important, this is God's house, so there's no alcohol for sale. James Brown, at times a raging alcoholic, is probably rolling over in his grave.

John Morgan, a President Bush impersonator, is hanging out in the corridors signing autographs for the mainly red-state crowd. For eight bucks, people are taking pictures with him in front of a faux White House rose garden while three actors playing secret service agents look on.

I see some kids wearing flashing red-and-blue cross necklaces, which look pretty cool in the darkness of the arena, and I ask where they got them. They point me to a booth, and I buy one as a reminder of my time here. It was only two dollars, but add that to the ten I paid for the ticket to get in and the five bucks I threw into the collection bucket, and I'm helping support the industrial Christian entertainment complex. My job here is done.

ONE OF THE concert's sponsors was the Gospel Music Channel, which makes perfect sense since the television station, founded in 2004, is the Christian equivalent of MTV. The channel is slickly produced and not your run-of-the-mill religious ministry that sermonizes and asks for donations. Its income comes from advertisers, from blue-chip companies like Ford, Kraft, and Allstate.

Don't let the Gospel Music Channel's name fool you either. It's more than just African American gospel–style music videos. It highlights the myriad faces of Jesus rock: contemporary Christian, country, soul, and even heavy metal—a genre the network promotes during *Metalhead,* a Saturday night block of programming that features two hours of the loudest and hardest gospel metal your virgin ears have ever heard. To paraphrase Keanu Reeves from *Bill and Ted's Excellent Adventure* (who said it way before Harold and Kumar were old enough to even drive to White Castle), "That's righteous, dude."

And, like MTV and VH1, the network goes beyond the usual music video fare by offering shows like *Faith and Fame,* a Christian version of *Behind the Music.* The only difference here is that the part of the narrative arc when the musicians get addicted to drugs and go into a downward spiral happens *before* they become famous. They accept Christ, get saved, and—bam!—they get a recording contract. Yes, the Lord works in mysterious ways. GMC also made headlines with its *American Idol*–style talent show called *Gospel Dream,* in which Simon Cowell was replaced by a friendlier, Christ-loving judge.

The station is the brainchild of two very disparate people. The first is Charley Humbard, the son of a preacher man. And not just any preacher, but one of America's first television ministers. Rex Humbard's show, *Cathedral of Tomorrow,* was broadcast on more than six hundred stations at the height of its popularity in the 1960s and 1970s. Along with his siblings, Charley was part of the Humbard Family Singers. When I visit the Gospel Music Channel's headquarters, Charley shows me a framed album cover from when he was a kid; the group looks strikingly like a Christian version of the Monkees, moppy hairdos and all. So mixing television and faith was a natural part of his life.

As intriguing a character as Charley is, it's his business partner who catches my attention for one simple reason—he's a Jew. Brad Siegel, a former president of Turner Broadcasting's entertainment networks with multiple Emmys to his name, left his cushy mainstream gig to dare do what his fellow Jewish television executives have never done: spread the gospel of Jesus.

Dressed in an untucked, button-down shirt, jeans, no socks, and loafers, Siegel invites me into his office with friendly camaraderie, as if we've known each other for years. Maybe it's the fact we're the only Semites on this floor. Before I even ask the obvious question, he does it for me. "You want to know, am I doing the right thing?

"I feel totally good about it," he tells me. "I believe in this as a business and even though I'm not of this faith, what can be wrong with taking something that is so inherently good and bringing it into people's living rooms?"

He's got a point, and even Siegel's spiritual adviser agrees. Hanging above his desk is a framed letter from his rabbi, sent when the channel first began broadcasting. It's one of Siegel's most prized possessions. At the conclusion of the long letter comes this line: "If anyone questions the appropriateness of a nice Jewish boy running a gospel network, tell them to speak to your rabbi."

Siegel hopes this will be his television legacy. The way he sees it, at least he's doing something positive by offering family-friendly fare that will touch viewers on a more meaningful level than, say, the products of his previous gig, where he worked on shows like *The Powerpuff Girls* and *Frisky Dingo* for the Cartoon Network.

"My journey is being a television executive because that's really what I am," he says matter-of-factly. "And because our audience is so passionate and so faithful, it makes our job a little easier."

Just then, Charley pokes his head into the office, interrupting our conversation. "Good news," he announces. "We just got Comcast in Jacksonville." That new partnership will now bring thousands of new viewers to this multimedia piece of God's pop-culture empire. It's no wonder it's growing at such a breakneck speed. In an AP/AOL survey, Jesus was the number-two hero of 2006 (albeit he was tied with Oprah; number one went to George W. Bush—who, coincidentally, also topped the list of biggest villains that same year). On Jesus' MySpace page (yes, he has one)—which lists his hobbies as carpentry, beard care, and extreme water-skiing—the Son of God adds an average of a dozen friends a day.

After spending some time in churches and being inspired by their music, I ask the one Jew I know besides me who can tell the difference between Hawk Nelson and Family Force Five (two Christian punk bands) why it is that music plays such an important role in religion. "Singing does something to you spiritually," Siegel explains. "It's a release. That's why I think contemporary Christian music is doing so well. It's using music so effectively to lift people's spirits, to inspire them, and in doing that it's connecting them to Jesus Christ. Music can move you in a way that nothing else can move you."

Of course, this is not an inherently Christian concept. In the times of the Jewish Temple, the Levites were highly regarded for the joyful music that would accompany the ancient services. But Siegel feels, and I've got to agree with him, that Judaism is missing the boat when it comes to marrying worship with music. "Jews are missing the modernity," he says, leaning back in his chair. "Synagogues think contemporary is a folk song. Why are we, as Jews, stuck in history? We have such a hard time moving into the modern world. Jews are great songwriters. It's not as if we have a gene that prevents us from doing it. Why can't that be translated en masse to the religious world? Jews don't have a great experience at synagogue, so they only come twice a year. I'm just as guilty."

Siegel, like the majority of American Jews, only attends synagogue for the High Holidays—Rosh Hashanah and Yom Kippur. And it gets me thinking. What is so wrong with our service that we can't jazz it up enough to get even mildly religious people interested in stepping foot into synagogue? Dragging Jews through the synagogue's doors is nothing short of a miracle from heaven.

Even without the accompaniment of musical instruments, there's no excuse for not having meaningful music during the service. Case in point. One of my most spiritually uplifting Friday night services came a few years back when the Sydenham Men's Choir from Johannesburg, South Africa, came to lead the services at my synagogue for one weekend.

What's interesting is that in Johannesburg many of the synagogues have similar types of choirs, and Friday night attendance is markedly higher in their country even among nonobservant Jews. What's more intriguing is that on Saturday morning, the main Sabbath service, the choir is absent and attendance drops accordingly. My South African friend Bradley told me he sees more Jews at the mall on Saturday than he does at synagogue.

Their performance was sans instruments, completely a cappella, and it was truly invigorating. Not because there were fifteen overweight men harmonizing Psalms, but because it was the first time I saw people happy to be reciting our prayers. I know it sounds ridiculous, but it's true. I had been brought up viewing our thrice-daily prayers as just another item to rush through in between doing more important things in our life. Perhaps it's because Judaism requires so much of us that's not prayer-related (wearing a yarmulke, the ritual laws of family purity, not eating ham) that the prayers themselves often take a backseat in our religion. Or, better put, the *enjoyment* of those prayers takes a backseat.

I'm not even sure why some churches have seats, because most people spend the entirety of the service standing, dancing, *enjoying* the moment. I've been to churches where people are holding placards with the words "Preach Preacher," as if they're at a political rally. You just don't see that in synagogue.

And the lack of inspiring music is a big part of that. As for Siegel, in a quieter moment he reveals to me that spreading the musical gospel has actually helped him reconnect with his own Judaism. "It has made me get closer to my religion in a wanting kind of way. It brings you closer to your faith."

Here's a guy who's thanking Jesus for making him a better Jew. Now that's a notion I could get on board with.

To be fair, I actually came across someone else who fits squarely into that category as well. And his name is Moses. And, at the moment, I'm having falafel with him.

Moses Staimez looks nothing like his biblical namesake. For starters he's twenty-eight and clean shaven and dresses like a rapper complete with baggy shirt, shorts that almost reach his ankles, and an oversized Atlanta Braves cap turned to the side. As I said, he's currently munching on some falafel. But in between bites of this Mediterranean delicacy he keeps talking about Jesus. About how the Christian Messiah, of all people, is making him a better Jew.

And also unlike his namesake, this Moses actually stepped foot into the Holy Land. In fact, he grew up in the biblical town of Be'er Sheva in Israel, the very same place where Abraham made a pact with King Abimelech. A perfect hometown for this interfaith rapper wannabe.

Moses wasn't always a Jesus freak. He's an Israeli Jew who moved to America in the hopes of making his music career take off. And, by all accounts, it did.

Soon after arriving on these shores, he performed as a session musician on various records including an India Arie album. For steadier work, he joined up with a band named New Edition. If that group sounds the least bit familiar—it was huge in the 1980s—it's primarily because it was fronted by Whitney Houston's ex-husband, Bobby Brown, who, Moses tells me, still tours with them occasionally. That's his nice way of saying they only get to see their ringleader when he's not in jail or otherwise predisposed with his various legal embroilments. But when Moses is not performing songs like "It's My Prerogative" and the oh-so-eloquent "Do Me," he's at his best gig yet: playing in the house of God (just not his own).

A few weeks back I drove an hour to the Ray of Hope Baptist Church on a typical Sunday morning to watch Moses in action. I sat with his girlfriend, Lisa, in the balcony section so we could get a bird's-eye view of about a thousand people who had gathered here to dance in the mosh pit of Moses's music.

And he delivered. This was, by far, one of the best bands I had witnessed during my church visits. And I'm not just saying that because I'm friendly with a guy in the band or because I fancy myself an expert in all things church rock. I don't, and even if I did, my criteria for something like that would be all screwed up. I just know what I felt. For me, this band was the most inspirational.

They ended their first set with a song called "Days of Elijah," which is just about the worst name for this song. I mean no disrespect to days or Elijah. It's just that the highlight of this particular piece of music is the refrain "There's no God like Jehovah," which is recited over and over again toward the end of the song. Moses's rendition lasted more than twenty minutes, and the more the choir and congregation repeated that line, the louder it got. *There's no God like Jehovah.* It became a mantra for those of us assembled.

There was just something about the phrase and the way they were singing it that totally mesmerized me. I'm not sure why. In Judaism, Jehovah is a name for our God as well. As a matter of fact, it's such a special name of God, we were taught as kids not to even utter it. And here I was listening to a thousand people repeat it until they were blue in the face.

"There's no God like Jehovah" also reminded me of that popular party anthem by the Isley Brothers called "Shout," in which the lead singer keeps repeating the phrase, "A little bit louder now, a little bit louder now," and we keep raising our voices with each stanza. It's a logical jump, since the Motown group started out as church gospel singers in 1954. For days afterward I found myself humming the tune to the Jehovah phrase at the most random of times—at the gas station, at the grocery store, even in synagogue.

More to the point, I don't believe "Days of Elijah" is a good name because it took me nearly a month to find the song on iTunes. I kept searching for "There's No God Like Jehovah" and got nothing. I've since downloaded three different versions of the song, originally made popular by gospel superstar Donnie McClurkin. They're all phenomenal, but none strikes the same chord as when I heard it live, from the strumming guitar of Moses.

Repeating a phrase over and over, getting louder each time, reminded me of a prayer called Kol Nidrei, which we recite on Yom Kippur. It's the first thing we say as we begin the twenty-five-hour fast on Judaism's holiest day. It's recited three times, the first in almost a whisper and the last in a rousing rendition. I never understood why we do it that way. The sages of yore probably instituted this tradition for a whole host of reasons, but I bet none of them had a gospel choir in mind.

Repeating something, engraining it in our minds, is a way to make it stick with us. *There's no God like Jehovah.* Not only is it the one thing I remember from that morning at church, but its haunting tune has stayed with me for months afterward. That's powerful. The Kol Nidrei, likewise, has made it into the pantheon of popular prayers among even the least observant of Jews.

(The song overshadowed what could've been an entire chapter devoted to this church's charismatic female minister, who had some of the best one-liners: "Get so close to Jesus you know what kind of cologne he's wearing" and "We baptized 85 people last week. That's 12,750 pounds of souls we saved.")

Back at the falafel stand, I ask Moses about the song. Turns out it's one of his favorites too. "You cannot *not* react," he tells me in his Israeli accent.

"You have to have emotions about what's going on. These people are not acting. They're worshiping."

That really hit home for Moses once when he was playing a guitar solo during another prayer. "It hit me then," he recalls of the time he sat center stage, all alone in front of the entire church. "Your art is touching people's hearts. It makes them feel closer to God, what they call the Holy Spirit. And I felt good about that."

Coming from Israel to America's Bible Belt has given Moses a strange connection with his Christian counterparts. "You have so many varieties in this country. I think it's beautiful to make friends with other types of people. And these people in church are people who believe they should be good because of God. I can get on board with that," he explains. "It's hard for me to believe that Jesus Christ is God. Other than that, I totally agree with everything."

What's more, Jesus is actually helping Moses become a more devout Jew. "In the beginning, I thought that it's only a gig," he says. "But soon after, I realized it's real. It makes me feel more spiritual. It makes me feel closer to God, my God.

"Playing in church, it's really changed my whole perspective about religion in general and Judaism in particular. Judaism, for me, is my identity." An identity this Israeli is embracing more and more in America.

BELIEVE IT OR not, there's actually a small, but growing, cottage industry of Jewish gospel music. Yes, this is about as odd as Dolly Parton rapping hip-hop, but stranger things have happened. Legendary Jewish tunesmith Shlomo Carlebach, who looked like the long-lost twin of the Grateful Dead's Jerry Garcia, is single-handedly credited for invigorating Jewish prayers with soulful tunes. He passed away in 1994, but his daughter Neshama is continuing the family legacy by becoming one of the only living musicians who is writing tunes that are sung in synagogues the world over. Most recently, she's been singing her Jewish songs at a Baptist church in New York with a full gospel choir backing her up.

"Their voices are exquisite, so soulful," she tells me. "I feel as though the world is full of light when these people are singing. The world is too broken, and we have too much to fix to be walking around and judging." Together with the choir, she's beginning to perform at synagogues across America.

I suspect this trend stems from a scene in the 2000 comedy *Keeping the Faith,* starring Ben Stiller and Ed Norton as a rabbi and a priest who are best friends. In one particularly clever sequence, Rabbi Stiller invites a Christian gospel choir to his synagogue in the hopes of rejuvenating the bored and apathetic crowd. The choir unleashes a whirling-dervish rendition of a Jewish prayer called Ayn Keloheinu, and the congregants dance as they've never danced before. (I should point out that Jews, in general, are not known for dancing.) Throughout Jewish circles, this scene became something of a running joke, something we all dreamed would happen to liven up our often staid services, but a joke nonetheless, something that would never end up in reality.

That's what I thought. That's what we all thought. Until I met Joshua Nelson, the self-proclaimed prince of kosher gospel.

The Brooklyn native was in Atlanta earlier this year for a concert performance at the Temple, one of the oldest synagogues in town and famous for two things. One, it was bombed by white supremacists in 1958, and, two, it was the synagogue used in several scenes in the Oscar-winning movie *Driving Miss Daisy.* Now, half a century after the bombing, that very sanctuary was the place where Jewish gospel prayer would come to life.

From the moment he takes the stage, you are forced to notice. For one thing, Joshua Nelson is a black Jew—he calls himself the KKK's worst nightmare. Following him on stage is a small gospel choir. You don't need me to tell you that this is not what the dais of a synagogue sanctuary normally looks like.

He starts to sing Adon Olam, a Jewish prayer that concludes the Sabbath service each week. The gospel choir answers "ah-ah-ah" to his "hey-ey-ey." After a few minutes of singing, Nelson swipes his arm and stops the music. "Wait a minute! Wait a cotton-picking minute," he yells, looking over to his band and backup singers. "In my synagogue, we do it just a little bit differently. Let's do it the way we do it up in Harlem." It's then that the real Joshua Nelson is unleashed and those of us lucky to be gathered here are introduced to an entirely new genre of Jewish prayer.

They start up Adon Olam again. This time Nelson pushes the piano man aside and starts banging on the ivories himself, screaming the soulful words into the nearby microphone and wiping sweat from his brow. I imagine Johnny Coltrane juiced up on steroids and Red Bull. And singing in Hebrew. "We just had to make sure you guys wake up," Nelson tells those in the audience, who are now rising to their feet.

His spindly fingers tickle the keys with such ease and enthusiasm. He's swaying. He's bouncing. He can barely contain himself. His entire body becomes one with the song. He's belting out Adon Olam like nobody's business.

He jumps off the stage, arms raised high and waving, and makes his way through the throng. The choir grows louder. Tambourines start shaking. The crowd is in a frenzy. If it wasn't clear before, it certainly is now—Joshua Nelson owns this room. This synagogue. This sanctuary.

I have sung Adon Olam my entire life, but never quite like this. No cantor I know belts out the prayer with such verve, such enthusiasm, such sheer joy. This was not the Jewish prayer I had grown up with. This was a whole new prayer. And it felt invigorating, as if someone had hooked me up to a spiritual IV and fresh Jewish blood was coursing through my veins. It was as if I was experiencing my religion in a truly new and unique way. I was singing Adon Olam for the first time. And it felt great. Good God Almighty, I had just witnessed one of the most spiritually uplifting renditions of Hebrew liturgy in my entire life.

The song comes to a rousing close and, flush from the experience, we all plop back down into the pews. It seems one of the central things I had been searching for this year, a meaningful Jewish prayer service, was embodied in this one performance.

Nelson's style mirrors that of his hero, the late Mahalia Jackson, widely regarded as America's most celebrated gospel singer. Ever since he was a little kid listening to her music on his grandmother's record player, Nelson has been following in her footsteps. He's collaborated with Aretha Franklin, Cab Calloway, and Dizzy Gillespie. He's performed for President Clinton and Oprah. He travels extensively around the world—to Poland, Italy, Sweden, Germany, Israel, England, Ukraine—carrying the novel concept of kosher gospel with him.

When he's not performing kosher gospel, he's the minister of music at a Baptist church in Hoboken, New Jersey. When he's not doing that, he's a Hebrew school teacher. I finally catch up with the overscheduled Nelson after the concert and ask him his thoughts on the current state of Jewish prayers, known as *davening* in Yiddish, and why it's normally not the electrifying experience we saw earlier tonight.

"It's sad how dry *davening* is these days," he tells me backstage as he sips some hot Tazo chai tea. "If you have a dry minister, you have a dry church.

If you have a preacher on fire, you'll have congregation on fire. The same thing is true for a synagogue."

Nelson believes the key to making prayer more meaningful is through song. "Music is a powerful phenomenon that God has given to people to help alleviate anxieties and to help comfort one another with," he says. "People are hurting today. They want to feel something. Gospel music can relieve some of that anxiety. When they leave synagogue, they want to feel closer to God."

As if to prove his point, he starts pounding the piano again, transforming popular tunes into spiritual ones. He plays Louis Armstrong's "When the Saints Go Marching In" and switches the lyrics to some Hebrew liturgy. He sings me a Jewish prayer to the tune of Harry Belafonte's "Day-O." He's practically giving me my own private concert.

The more Nelson performs, the more the Jewish community will be exposed to this style of Jewish prayer. "I'm surprised at my success, because I thought I'd have a lot of opposition to what I'm doing," Nelson tells me. "People are basically tired of sitting in synagogue and having no connection to God when everyone else is. People are waking up."

NELSON'S SINGING HAD certainly given me a wake-up call. But I wasn't the only one who wanted to see gospel dreams come true at Jewish prayers. A national nonprofit organization called Synagogue 3000 has a singular mission: to revitalize synagogue life in America. Its efforts cross over into many categories, everything from more inspiring prayer services to ways to attract new congregants. What's more, one of the ways it seeks to learn how to better a synagogue is by looking to churches to see what techniques can be brought back to the Jewish world. For example, a couple of years ago it invited megapastor Rick Warren to give a workshop to a group of rabbis on how they can do better outreach at their synagogues. Apparently, I wasn't the only Jew who had this idea.

And as it turns out, the organization had serendipitously picked Atlanta as the one city where it will focus its efforts this year, holding monthly seminars and workshops with the city's more than forty synagogues. "Jews need to be more quote-unquote evangelical," says Ron Wolfson, the co-founder of the Synagogue 3000 initiative and a professor at the American Jewish University in Los Angeles. "We need to do a better job of presenting

Judaism to our own people. The story doesn't get across that Judaism is a way to find meaning and purpose in your life. And that's another lesson I've learned from the evangelical model."

I met up with Wolfson for coffee to talk shop about my church visits, and he later invited me to the workshops as an honorary member. One event featured Bernie Marcus, the cofounder of the Home Depot, as the guest speaker. He was the last person I expected to be teaching me about the beauty of synagogue attendance. But there I was. And there he was. Teaching me about the beauty of synagogue attendance.

Marcus was telling a group of about forty rabbis that attracting members to a synagogue was no different than attracting customers to a Home Depot. "You're not giving people the product they want. It's no different than retail; it's the same thing," he said. "You're in the marketing business; you're selling a product. You're selling religion. It happens to be something that's good for people. But you can't get to them to sell them the religion because you're in the marketing business and you don't realize you're in the marketing business. You have to stop thinking in many respects like a scholar and start thinking like a retailer."

Wolfson knows it's going to take more than a few workshops to get the ball rolling. It's going to take some experiential teaching techniques as well. Which is why he plans on bringing Joshua Nelson back for a concert. To show my local Jewish community how powerful the synthesis of prayer and music can really be.

FIFTEEN

My First and Last Easter

The Bible addresses itself to four sons—one is wise, one is wicked, one is naïve, and one is unable to ask.
—*The Passover Haggadah*

WHEN I STARTED this journey more than eight months ago, I never thought I'd hear a pastor invoke the name of former *Playboy* playmate–turned–tabloid sensation Anna Nicole Smith to prove a point. But that all changed today on Palm Sunday. And this from the same church that gave birth to one of America's greatest orators, Martin Luther King, Jr.

Well, not exactly. The church where King (and his dad) used to preach is now part of the museum tour at the MLK history center in downtown Atlanta. It's rarely used for actual services because it's too small. Instead, a much bigger church was built across the street to accommodate the large weekly crowds that pack the building to partake in a bit of religious Americana. Both are called Ebenezer Baptist Church.

The new edifice is magnificent. Tall vaulted ceilings give the expansive sanctuary an even greater aura. African American women wearing matching black dresses, white gloves, and oversized bright purple bouquets on their lapels usher people to their seats.

The primarily black members of the congregation are grooving with the choir—standing, singing, clapping. The white members of the crowd, mostly made up of curious first-timers and parents looking for a quick history lesson for their kids, are wide-eyed and smiling. Some even awkwardly try to join in this cross-cultural experience. But as they are casually dressed in T-shirts and shorts, you can tell this is just another tourist stop for them.

As the choir settles down, Pastor Raphael Warnock takes to the pulpit. He starts to quote from the book of Matthew, but quickly digresses from his prepared text. "We have become comfortable bosom buddies with the worst things in the world," he proclaims. "All of us have our crosses to bear. For some of us, church is just another thing on our to-do list." *Amen, brother,* I think to myself after having gone to a different church every Sunday for nearly a year.

"The most important thing unfolding on the world stage is not Iraq, not genocide, not the firings of different federal attorneys. It's Anna Nicole Smith and who is her baby daddy," shouts Pastor Warnock to the crowd of three thousand in a rat-a-tat, Jesse Jackson–style verbal assault. "How much ink has been spilled? All of the television news time that has been spent on this! I'm sick of it!"

The pastor mops the beads of sweat from his shiny bald head with a cloth.

"I'm not worried about her babies," he continues in a booming voice, raising his arm. "I'm worried about the babies right here on Auburn Avenue."

The young woman next to me, dressed in a white peasant dress and lime-green straw hat, offers to share her Bible with me and places it on the bench between us. This can't be good. Jewish law dictates that I'm not supposed to sit on the same seat as a Bible, because it minimizes the book's holiness. Maybe, I justify to myself, this doesn't count because it's the New Testament. Or maybe because I'm in church and Jewish laws don't apply here. But then again, what would a church experience be without a little Jewish guilt?

"The cross is a complex symbol," Warnock says, pointing to the large wooden cross dangling from the ceiling by what appears to be nothing more than dental floss. "It's a paradox. It represents both evil and redemption."

I think about the timeliness of his words. In less than a day I'll be celebrating Passover, which commemorates the Jewish people's redemption from slavery at the hands of Pharaoh in Egypt thousands of years ago. Which is poignant considering that, in the wake of Rosa Parks and the ensuing Montgomery bus boycott, Martin Luther King's leadership role garnered him the nickname of the "new Moses." Our exodus narratives may differ in detail, but African Americans and Jews share a common theme—outsiders refused full citizenship.

Moreover, here I am in the heart of Martin Luther King's spiritual legacy. As a civil rights leader and humanitarian par excellence, King gave his life to ensure basic freedoms for his people. In an odd way, sitting here this morning before Passover, I begin to feel a connection to King I've never felt before.

Reverend Warnock's redemption sermon hits home. It's a common theme, I'm sure, in many religions. In Judaism, we're taught to see *beyond* the redemption. The important thing is not that we are free, but what we do with that freedom. Moses asked Pharaoh to "let my people go," but we often forget the next phrase in the verse—"so that they may serve God." Moses wasn't asking for freedom from slavery so the Jewish people could chill out at a Middle Eastern Club Med. Moses wanted the Jews to swap masters, to go from an earthly one to one of divine origin.

Being free, ironically, takes a lot of work. Freedom not bound to a moral code is a freedom divorced from what God really wants. My rabbinic brother Elie elucidated the concept further. Freedom, he told me, is not just about breaking loose. Our sages teach us to see purpose in not only the redemption, but also the slavery. Many of our commandments stem from that very concept. The Bible, for example, tells us to treat the stranger with respect because we were once strangers ourselves. Our experience as slaves should make us better equipped to empathize with the plight of others who are suffering. The Bible encourages us to find meaning in our suffering. Being a spiritual being takes effort, no matter the religion.

Martin Luther King, Jr., shared this collective vision. He wanted equal rights and freedom for African Americans, and he wanted them so that they would become full-fledged members of society, free to take on all the challenges that America had to offer. Freedom, King knew, is not to be squandered but to be relished.

I'm not the only one comparing black and Jewish history this Sunday. "Evil is determined," Pastor Warnock exclaims to the crowd. "Hitler and his attacks against the Jews, that's evil at its worst. Slavery in America, that's evil at its worst. The evil adversary is out to get you. That's why I'm so mad!" He pauses, and then growls, "And when evil is at its worst, God is at His best." He uses this as a launching pad to go through about two dozen incidents in biblical history when, as he puts it, "God moves, and Satan countermoves." It's like a sacred chess match.

From the stories of Joseph and Moses to the kings and prophets and all the way into the stories of the New Testament, *God moves, and Satan countermoves*. The farther Pastor Warnock goes down the line of biblical narratives, the more people in the audience get out of their seats to applaud. *God moves, and Satan countermoves*. With each passing example, more people stand up until finally he gets to the story of Jesus' resurrection and growls at the top his lungs, "But God had one more move!" At this point, the entire audience is up, going wild. Warnock plays off their emotion. "Stay tuned for next week," he says, laughing. "Same Holy Ghost time, same Holy Ghost place."

For the first time in a while, I am moved. Warnock has channeled the great oratorical style of his predecessor, Dr. King. His speech—its propitious timing, its content, its delivery—is inspiring. I've got goose bumps. I look at my watch and realize two hours have passed and I didn't even notice it. The choir starts up, and I find myself tapping my feet. I know it's heretical for me to say, but we could use a little of this Holy Ghost time in synagogue.

In accepting a humanitarian award from the American Jewish Committee in 1965, Martin Luther King, Jr., stated, "Freedom is one thing. You have it all or you are not free." I realize coming to King's church was the perfect way for me to start Passover. In the past, preparing for this holiday was something I tried to avoid. Today, it is something I am eager to embrace. *God, it's your move.*

CLEANING FOR PASSOVER is the annual rite for any obsessive-compulsive Jew. Non-Jews have spring cleaning. We have quarantine and hazmat suits.

Allow me to explain. On Passover, to recall the unleavened *matzah* cracker the Jewish nation ate during its exodus from Egypt, Jews are forbidden to own any leavened food products, collectively known in Hebrew as *chametz*. Sounds easy except when you consider that just about everything in the kitchen presents a problem—cookies, cereal, bread, Fruity Pebbles. But the fun doesn't end there. Check the bathroom too. Shampoos, toothpastes, and all sorts of other assorted household items contain minuscule traces of *chametz*. We even have to change our dog food for the entire week of Passover.

And it doesn't just mean locking those foods in a cabinet until after the holiday. We have to ritually sell them to a non-Jew, since we literally can't own them during this time. Last year, I saw a Jew selling his leavened foods on eBay—all for the cheap "buy it now" price of only one dollar. The Talmud spends an inordinate amount of space (an entire tractate to be exact) on all the nitpicky laws related to what foods we can and cannot have on our property during Passover.

Needless to say, many Jews (my family included) go a bit overboard with this food injunction. Not only do we clean our kitchen, but we go through all of our clothes looking for crumbs in the pockets, attack our cars with a fierce vacuuming, and—this I'm really not proud of—flip through all the books in our house to make sure no lone leavened crumb may have found its way in between any of the pages.

Okay, yes, I agree this is one of those laws (unfortunately of which there are many) that make observant Jews look about as sane as Jack Nicholson in *One Flew Over the Cuckoo's Nest* or Jack Nicholson as the obsessive-compulsive in *As Good as It Gets* (or, come to think of it, Jack Nicholson in any role). So unless we have a superbionic house mouse who grabbed a Cheerio, scurried to the top of the bookcase in the living room, and randomly cracked open that old John Grisham novel resting up there to page 234, I would venture to guess that we're pretty safe from stray leaven, but who am I to judge? There's actually a section in the Talmud that discusses this exact case (without the John Grisham reference, of course). The Talmud, not surprisingly, asks a myriad of follow-up questions. If you see a mouse run in your house with a piece of bread and run out a few minutes later with a piece of bread, can you assume it's the same piece of bread? What if it was a different mouse? The Talmud actually dives into a discussion of the different colors of mice at this point. I wish I was making this up.

But wait, there's more. The night before Passover there's an odd custom of checking your home for leavened products using nothing but a wooden spoon, a feather, and the burning light of a nearby candle. All we need is Ebenezer Scrooge, and we'd be characters in a Dickens novel. The whole concept is odd because most people have already spent the past month scrubbing their homes and ridding them of leavened food in preparation for Passover. This last-minute search is more of a token gesture than anything else, as the sages suggest purposely taking ten pieces of bread and hiding them throughout the house for other members of the family to find.

This poses one very basic problem. After spending the past month performing backbreaking labor (reminiscent of slavery in ancient Egypt probably) cleaning your house's every nook and cranny, the last thing you'd want to do is throw crumbs all over the place. You'd be insane—or an observant Jew (often the two are confused). So, with the 1968 invention of the Ziploc® bag came a long-in-the-making modern Jewish custom: putting the ten pieces of bread in hermetically sealed plastic bags before throwing them around the house.

Since it's just Elizabeth and myself, this rabbinically mandated search takes on an added awkwardness, because I'm basically hiding crumbs from my wife. (It was even sillier when I was single and tried hiding them from myself.) At least if we had kids it would be a fun educational activity. I can only imagine how bizarre this must seem to a convert like Elizabeth.

Quite to my surprise, though, she tells me it's actually not so different from the Easter egg hunts of her youth, in which the adults would hide colored eggs for the children to find. When she was growing up, her family held these holy versions of hide-and-seek at nearby posh Lake Lanier, where her step-grandfather was the commodore of the yacht club—which, to my knowledge, is just about the WASPiest thing I've ever heard in my entire life.

It's shortly after 4:15 a.m. and I'm driving in the pitch dark past a rather large antebellum plantation. It's not usually the type of activity I'd like to be doing this early in the morning, but today is no normal day. It's Easter, and if my year of living among my Christian neighbors has taught me anything, it's that this day is more than just a combination of brightly painted eggs and little girls in frilly dresses.

And although images of Civil War–era slave owners don't usually evoke anything remotely related to Jesus' resurrection, there's a reason I woke up way before dawn to be here. I don't even get up this early on Jewish holidays. Thanks to one of those calendrical coincidences that only God could come up with, Easter fell smack in the middle of the eight-day festival of Passover this year. On the sixth day to be exact. Yesterday, I got up around 7 a.m. to attend synagogue, and here I am up hours earlier for Easter. God would be proud. I'm just not sure whose God.

This plantation, I should explain, is in the middle of a theme park devoted to memorializing the Confederacy. And my car is just one among hundreds making their way through Stone Mountain Park.

Stone Mountain is the largest exposed mass of granite on the planet and the world's third-largest monolith, behind only Mt. Augustus in Australia and Peña de Bernal in Mexico. The bottom of the mountain extends for ten miles beneath the surface of the ground. At its peak it is 1,683 feet above sea level. And if you wanted to walk around the entire base of the mountain, get ready for a five-mile hike. Basically, this is one big rock.

It's also one giant Confederate memorial. On the mountain's northern face is the largest bas-relief sculpture in the world. C. Helen Plane, a charter member of the United Daughters of the Confederacy, had the brilliant idea to carve a monument with Stonewall Jackson, Jefferson Davis, and Robert E. Lee all on horseback on the side of the mountain. Think of it as Mt. Rushmore for Southerners.

The carving, larger than the length of an entire football field, is three acres wide and took nearly sixty years to sculpt. When we took class field trips here when I was younger, the sheer size of the carving was taught in terms we could understand: Robert E. Lee's shoulder was so big a school bus could park on top of it. This gem of Confederate propaganda was somehow supposed to make us nerdy Jewish kids feel proud of our Southern heritage. Keep in mind, I kid you not, we never studied anything called the Civil War growing up. We were taught about the War of Northern Aggression and, to be perfectly honest, we were never told that we lost, a sore point that got me picked on as a child at a Jewish summer camp in New York's Catskill Mountains.

For six months out of the year, when the weather is warm, the park puts on a nightly laser show on the face of the mountain. Our family used to go often, and it wasn't until I was older that I realized the cheeky music videos (e.g., *The Devil Came Down to Georgia, Georgia on My Mind*) displayed with lasers on the rock were a neon version of MTV for hicks. While my family was enjoying the show, Elizabeth, who grew up not too far from the mountain and whose great-grandfather actually fought for the Confederacy, worked at the laser show during summers in high school, selling neon glow sticks to the thousands of patrons who flow into the park each night at sunset.

The other odd piece of trivia that would make any little Jewish boy cringe is that Stone Mountain is famous for something else as well. For a long time it served as the base of operations for the Ku Klux Klan. After the lynching of Jewish businessman Leo Frank in an Atlanta suburb in

1915, the KKK reestablished itself by holding a ceremony atop the rock. The Klan continued to hold annual Labor Day meetings on the mountain's summit, where sixty-foot cross burnings were de rigueur, until just a few years ago. The strong anti-black sentiment associated with the place is why, many historians note, Martin Luther King, Jr., made the reference "Let freedom ring from Stone Mountain in Georgia," in his famous "I Have a Dream" speech.

Even nowadays, a faith-based presence pervades the park. A friend of mine who's doing his doctoral dissertation on religious groups at Stone Mountain recently tagged along on a field trip here with a group of home-schooled evangelical creation scientists who believe the mountain is not millions of years old, but a natural result of Noah's flood.

Native Americans, Wiccans, and dowsers working with earth energies have all tried to stake spiritual claim to this piece of nature for years. Not the least of which is the Herschend Family Entertainment Corporation, a Christian company to which the state of Georgia granted a long-term lease of the facility.

Before acquiring Stone Mountain, Herschend was most famous for owning Silver Dollar City, in the holy city of Branson, Missouri. Holy because Branson, it should be noted, is the promised land of Christian entertainment complexes, including the Studio City Café, where disgraced televangelist Jim Bakker now broadcasts a daily television show. And for some reason the small Midwestern town is also where Russian Jewish comedian Yakov Smirnoff, who gained notoriety during the Reagan era for his catchphrase "America, what a country!" has resurrected himself with a new stage show at the eponymous Yakov Smirnoff Theater. So come to Branson, where 1980s icons go to reinvent themselves.

Elizabeth worked for the Herschend Family at Stone Mountain throughout high school and college and invited me to the company's annual meeting one year while we were dating. It was the first time I had been exposed to a company that touts itself as one that is "consistent with Christian values and ethics" and the group prayer at the meeting's onset took me by surprise. But these are the people behind Dollywood, so nothing should've surprised me.

Today, I park my car and make my way to the skylift. I join about a thousand other people who are here to celebrate Jesus' resurrection on the top of a Confederate memorial as the sun rises behind us. Stone Mountain's sunrise Easter service dates back to 1944, when Lucile A. Lanford, a minister at Stone Mountain First United Methodist Church, decided to drag her congregation up there. It's been a tradition ever since.

A news camera chronicling the morning's event tapes me entering the skylift. Oy vey. I'm eating Passover dinner tonight at the home of the rabbi of my synagogue. I could only hope he wouldn't be watching the six o'clock news.

As I ride up the skylift, I recall the climactic chase scene in the little known and critically panned 1996 film *Fled,* starring Laurence Fishburne and Stephen Baldwin, the youngest of the acting Baldwin brothers. The action adventure flick, which took place in Atlanta, was an ill-fated marketing attempt to make our city look hip and cool in time for the Olympics, which were arriving that same summer.

Needless to say, when Fishburne and Baldwin, interracial prisoners who had been bound together for most of the film à la Tony Curtis and Sidney Poitier in the 1958 classic *The Defiant Ones,* enter Stone Mountain park chasing after the truly bad guys, you begin to get the feeling that this isn't going to be nominated for any awards. And it is from this very skylift that the villain falls and meets his untimely death. (I apologize to those readers who feel that I just spoiled the movie's ending. Believe me, you'll thank me later.)

I'm most likely the only Jew in the park this morning. Considering everyone is here to celebrate Jesus' rebirth three days after my ancestors allegedly murdered him, I hold on to the skylift railing a little tighter. As the skylift arrives at the top of the mountain, the first thing I notice is how cold it is. It may officially be spring, but it's only twenty-four degrees, one of the coldest April days in Georgia history, and at this elevation with the wind blowing it feels closer to fifteen. People are bundled up, thermos of coffee in one hand and Bible in the other.

The service finally gets under way around 6:30. A thousand people have gathered here to listen to Reverend Bob Bailey, Stone Mountain's chaplain (yes, this mountain has its own chaplaincy), welcome us. It's actually a picture-perfect sight. On a clear day you can see cities and vistas for hundreds of miles from the top of Stone Mountain. A large white cross has been erected for the occasion, and the good reverend speaks from a lectern in front of it. It's pitch-black outside, but soon the rays of the sun will begin to shine beautifully on this mountaintop.

"Welcome to Easter 2007!" yells Pastor Bob (that's what he tells us to call him). The crowd starts to shout and holler as if they're at the Stanley Cup. "Jesus likes the truth," he continues, "and the truth is it's cold out here. It's about eighteen degrees with a wind-chill factor that only God knows." He goes on to say that, owing to the freezing temperatures, he's going to make this service as short as possible. I wonder what Jesus would think of that. *Sorry, Christ. Congrats on the whole coming-back-from-the-dead thing. That's really great and all, but it's freezing up here, so God bless and we'll catch you back at the gift shop.*

Teeth chattering, Pastor Bob leads us all in a rendition of "Christ the Lord Has Risen Today." The song takes on new meaning, as we have all risen today earlier than we usually do to partake of this ceremony.

I miss part of the sermon because I'm distracted by a local television news reporter interviewing a bundled up family nestled together by a lamppost. She asks the mother why they came up here this morning. "I guess just to see it." And then the mother, perhaps realizing the reporter is looking for a good sound bite, quickly adds, "Because we're crazy."

It is clear, however, that many people have done this before, as evidenced by the fact they brought blankets and even lawn chairs up here. One family has even pitched a tent.

After the sermon, a woman sings "'Twas a Morning Like This," and I hear a backup choir, but upon closer inspection I realize she's just singing karaoke-style and the choir's voices are emanating from a nearby boom box.

As the sun begins to rise behind her, people whip out their cell phones to take pictures. Standing wrapped in blankets, the audience looks a little like biblical figures in robes atop an ancient mountain. Except with camera phones in their hands. I also notice three guys in kilts holding bagpipes. Next to them is a group of tattooed eastern European expats smoking. In one sense it's an oddly comforting scene. Jesus is not a one-dimensional character that only Southern Baptists can relate to. He's a global figure who's reached out to the masses, touching people of all shapes and sizes.

The service ends with a quick prayer. "This is going to be the fastest benediction in history," Pastor Bob says with a laugh and succinctly delivers on that promise.

We all shuffle back to the skylift. Pastor Bob is in my lift with about twenty other folks. He chats about the recent NCAA basketball tournament. As we start our descent, I see dozens of people still on the mountain-top having their pictures taken next to the cross as if it's some kind of Eiffel Tower, a tourist-trap monument to God.

Leaving the skylift, Pastor Bob catches my eye and says to me, "Thanks for getting up so early. God bless you." I don't quite know how or why he singled me out (did I look *that* out of place?), but it left a positive impression. My presence was noted—and it felt good.

Back at the foot of the mountain, at the skylift parking lot, the TV reporter is interviewing another woman who sums up the day as follows: "I think it gives you a better perspective to be out in the open to see God's creation and to see the sun rise and to know that the Son did rise and that He is alive."

Hokey? Perhaps, but I couldn't have said it better myself.

MY NEXT STOP on the Easter express is the Georgia Dome. The seventy thousand–seat arena is home to what is billed as America's largest Easter service. New Birth Missionary Baptist Church has been holding an Easter service at the Dome every year since 1993.

And people come from all over just to experience it. As I wait in a blocks-long line to park my car, I see license plates from North Carolina, Florida, Virginia, and as far away as Ohio and Michigan. I end up parking nearly a mile away from the entrance.

Entering the stadium a few minutes after the service begins, I quickly feel at ease. I've been going to church for almost a year now, and all the usual elements are present—a group of worshipers, a choir and a band, and large video monitors showing the goings-on. Except this church service is on steroids.

More than forty thousand people are here and, as far as I can see, I'm the only white guy. There is a concert stage with a two hundred–person choir standing in front of a large stone set reminiscent of the *Flintstones* (another great Stephen Baldwin film), which, I would later learn, is part of the Passion play. The screens lining the walls, which normally display the score of the NFL football games held here, simply have the words "Resurrection 2007!" flashing on them. Apparently, God's keeping score, and He's winning.

As I get my bearings in the hallway, I notice about a dozen burly men in black suits, white shirts, and black ties. They're all wearing sunglasses, and

their arms are crossed in unison. They seem like secret service men guard-
ing someone. And that's when I see him—Black Jesus.

He's tall and thin, with a closely cropped beard and long flowing hair.
A pair of dark shades just adds to his rock-star persona. If this had been
another time, another place, I would've thought it was Snoop Dogg. But,
no, it was Black Jesus. He's wearing a long black trench coat over his suit.
Think Morpheus from *The Matrix*. (Yes, I know, that's my second—and
hopefully last—reference to Laurence Fishburne in this chapter.) No frilly
ancient robes here. This is Modern-Day Black Jesus.

Just then "Jesus Walks," rapper Kanye West's popular hip-hop dirge to
the Lord Savior, blasts over the Dome's sound system. The secret service
men march into the arena from the top row of the main section single file
with Black Jesus. And the crowd goes wild. Teenage boys in baggy T-shirts
and one-size-too-big jeans pump their fists. Grandmotherly women wearing fur coats and wide-brim hats stand to their frail feet and wave their
canes with gloved-covered hands. Atlanta Mayor Shirley Franklin, who is
seated on the dais next to other local dignitaries, rises to her feet in defer-
ence to the one person in this room who's got more political power than she
does.

It's an odd bit of biblical boosterism that is completely foreign to me. As
Jews, we don't have biblical figures whose incarnations played by modern-
day actors would get us to turn into spiritual cheerleaders. I imagine if Val
Kilmer, who portrayed Moses in *The Ten Commandments: The Musical*,
walked into my synagogue, there'd be some head turning, but that's just
because most people in my synagogue don't know who Val Kilmer is. Perhaps it's to our detriment that our Jewish youth don't have a sense of hero
worship when it comes to biblical characters.

Black Jesus and his entourage (a.k.a. his twelve apostles) bounce as they
swagger to the beat of the music. It is surreal. Anywhere else this would've
been seen as a *Saturday Night Live* skit, but here this is a worship service
and the Lord is in the house. They make their way down the aisle and onto
the floor of the Georgia Dome.

A crowd of actors playing reporters (a.k.a. the Pharisees, a.k.a. the
rabbis, a.k.a. my people) clamor around Black Jesus, shoving cameras and
microphones in his face. Jesus stands on the steps to the stage and turns
around as if he's holding a press conference. The reporters, on cue, break
into a Broadway-style production number asking Jesus questions. A re-

porter from the fictitious *Entertainment Hourly* grills Black Jesus about his love for the poor and downtrodden.

"You have to learn to love the unlovable," Black Jesus responds in perfect made-for-television sound bite form.

Just then Black Mary Magdalene, dressed in peasant clothes, approaches Jesus as a slow song plays over the loudspeakers. She ascends the stage and dances an African-style ballet that would make Alvin Alley proud.

On the other side of the stage is an area cordoned off with yellow crime-scene tape. Apparently a little girl is dying and the father asks Black Jesus for help. "Your daughter will rise again," he says. "She's just asleep. She's not dead." He leans over her, and moments later the girl gets up, and the crowd erupts in applause. Some are even in tears. For the people gathered here, Jesus represents nothing less than humanity's hope.

Historically, Passion plays have been vehemently anti-Semitic and often whipped the masses into a frenzy that resulted in pogroms and other attacks on Jews. For a brief moment, I consider leaving, but decide to stay instead. The Passion performance continues as Black Judas bad-mouths Black Jesus. Roman soldiers lash Jesus and then carry the Son of God away on the cross amid rising plumes of special-effect smoke billowing from the stage.

One of the preachers grabs the microphone and starts shouting, "You're here because of the blood. You're at the Georgia Dome because of the blood. You're forgiven because of the blood. You're Christian because of the blood."

He means this as an inspiring message, but all I can wonder is why religion always has to be so violent. Many of the messages I have heard at church this year are based on one tenet: Jesus died for our sins. It's this one steadfast principle that guides all others. It's why Mel Gibson made a fortune not by telling the story of Jesus' life, but that of his torturous death.

In Judaism, we usually study the lives of the great sages as opposed to the details of their deaths. Although, one does come to mind. The famous first-century Torah scholar Rabbi Akiva was flayed to death by the Romans. (What is it with those Romans and their violent methods of torture and death for religious figures?)

But by no means does Christianity hold a monopoly on religious violence. One could argue that murder in the name of religion dates back to the dawn of time, when Cain killed Abel, in part to gain favor from God.

And for centuries we've seen countless examples of how religion begot the most bloody of body counts. Think about the Crusades. The sailing of the Spanish Armada. The missionaries sent to the New World to convert its inhabitants (or else). The Mormon massacre of Arkansas settlers in Utah on September 11, 1857, which (like all massacres) was eventually turned into a movie (this one featuring the all-star duo of Jon Voight and Dean Cain, in case you are interested).

These are but a few examples. Entire books and college courses are devoted to the subject. Heck, it's Passover. The plagues visited on the Egyptians, with their mass murder and man-eating frogs, could very well fit into this category. It seems that, for better or for worse, religious zealotry and violence share similar roots. Passion cuts both ways.

One of the Romans yells something about children at hell's gate and just then fifty kids come bounding onto the stage performing a big musical number, dancing and bopping up and down on the stage. The crowd is dancing now. About a hundred feet above the stage is a Cirque du Soleil–style performer in aerial silks twirling on purple drapes and flying around on high wires. If this is supposed to be reminiscent of something from the crucifixion story, I wasn't aware of it. Was there a trapeze Judas?

Just one week earlier this arena played host to another uplifting experience, March Madness, the NCAA college basketball tournament. The Final Four were held right here at the Georgia Dome. That bit of schizophrenic scheduling was not lost on the church. Bernice King, a church elder and the youngest daughter of Martin Luther King, Jr., pumps up the crowd before the offering by mentioning that the tickets to the Final Four event were costly, but this service at the Georgia Dome had no charge. "Salvation is free," she tells the throng, "but ministry is expensive."

"Our first family, as you know, is not on salary," she says, referring to the Bishop Eddie Long and his wife. As I'm jotting down this nugget of information, the guy next to me asks to borrow my pen and fills out his offering envelope, which includes spaces for tithes and offerings and allows people to use their credit cards. On the bottom of the envelope was this warning: "Please be mindful to charge/debit only amounts you have available."

Bishop Long (dressed in what I can only describe as a Michael Jackson–style dark military outfit with a gold New Birth logo over his heart) introduces the guest of honor—Jennifer Hudson, the *American Idol* alumna who went on to win an Academy Award for her starring turn in 2006's *Dreamgirls*. Even Black Jesus gets up to applaud her.

Hudson, dressed in a conservative dark dress with white pumps, sings three spirituals and, in between the melodies, speaks about her rags-to-riches tale. "I know the battle is the Lord's," she admits. "He took care of me. And here I am now." Her uplifting career arc—from virtual nobody to an Oscar winner in a year's time—is a resurrection tale in and of itself.

Here I am celebrating my very first (and most likely last) Easter, and it turns out to have nothing to do with a frivolous chase for chocolate eggs, but a chase for something much more meaningful.

The Haggadah, the sacred text we read on Passover, discusses four different types of children: the wise son, the wicked one, the naïve one, and the one who doesn't even know what to ask. For too long I had written myself off as the rebellious wicked son, gnashing my teeth at the myriad injunctions thrown at me by my religion. But all this time I was really someone else altogether. I was the son who had never figured out what to ask.

The seemingly pedantic search for leavened crumbs and Easter eggs has led to a greater search for my own spirituality. Jews are not merely looking for cookies and Christians for candy eggs, but we are looking inside ourselves. We are examining the unproductive directions our lives have gone in, in the hopes of finding a path to more meaningful faith. This is more than a mere physical spring cleaning, but a cleansing of our souls as well. This is a spring awakening.

Celebrating the great liberation story of Christians has helped me better understand the great liberation story of the Jews, not to mention my own personal liberation. During this process I've come to better grasp the notion of freedom. In a sense, I'm getting a fresh start and being reborn. At the Georgia Dome, among forty thousand Christians, on Easter, the day of resurrection.

Let freedom ring, indeed.

SIXTEEN

Latter-day Saints and Latter-day Ain'ts

And now, Joseph, my last-born, whom I have brought out of the wilderness of mine afflictions, may the Lord bless thee forever, for thy seed shall not utterly be destroyed.

—*2 Nephi 3:3,*
The Book of Mormon

I BOUGHT *A Mormon's Guide to Judaism* on Amazon.com. I bought it by mistake. It's a book by a Jewish convert to the Mormon Church who wrote a guide explaining Judaism to her new Mormon coreligionists. I meant to order the opposite book—a book by a Jew about Mormons. All this book has is stuff I already know. Kosher. Passover. Moses. It even has a dictionary of Jewish terms for the Mormon seeking to befriend the Jew. *Tateh* means "father." *Mameh* means "mother." A *bagel* is a hard, round roll. That last one, I kid you not, is actually in there. I wonder if Amazon has a return policy.

I admit that before hooking up with the local Mormon community, my knowledge of this religion could be boiled down to a few facts (and some myths). They are, in no particular order:

Mormons don't drink coffee.

Mormons don't have fun.

Mormons wear magic underwear.

HBO has a show about polygamous Mormons.

Gladys Knight is a Mormon.

Napoleon Dynamite is a Mormon. (Okay, *he's* not a Mormon, but the actor who plays him is.)

Orrin Hatch, for some unknown reason, is a Mormon. So are Donny and Marie.

And then there's this other piece of Mormon trivia I uncovered. In 1977 *Newsweek* ran a story about a Mormon missionary by the name of Joyce McKinney. She was beautiful, a former Miss Wyoming, and had an unrequited crush on Wayne Osmond (the older brother of Donny and Marie, for those keeping score at home). When Wayne didn't return her advances, she shifted her infatuation to fellow Mormon missionary Kirk Anderson. Anderson also rebuffed her advances and asked to be transferred to England.

It's there that McKinney tracked down Anderson, kidnapped him and took him to an isolated cabin, bound him to a bed with leather straps, and proceeded to rape him. For three days. Not surprisingly, the salacious episode made tabloid headlines around the world. Beauty queen! Religious cult! Forced sex! Leather straps! You get the idea. Solidifying her place in obscure Mormon history, McKinney reportedly said the following gem during her bail hearing: "I loved Kirk so much, I would have skied down Mt. Everest in the nude with a carnation up my nose." If only she had stuck around for the actual trial (she skipped town and fled back to America), the world would've been exposed to more of her unique aphorisms.

And yet, despite the sensational story, McKinney has long since been forgotten—save for a hard-core punk band whose members named themselves The Joyce McKinney Experience. They put out a CD called *Love Songs for Kirk*. Needless to say, that was their only release.

I'M NOT SURE what to expect as I pull up to a small ranch-style home in the town of Lilburn to meet up with a couple of female missionaries. I had met one of them while visiting a Mormon church recently and asked if I could tag along on one of her daily missionizing field trips. I had chosen her for two reasons: (1) The male missionaries ride bicycles door to door.

The female ones drive cars. I'm lazy. (2) She's a female missionary. See Joyce McKinney story above.

The first thing I notice about Sister Holloway and Sister Murphy is that they look strikingly like Jewish girls I would've dated ten years ago. They are short, have dark hair, and dress modestly in long sleeves and skirts. They could easily blend in at my synagogue, and nobody would be the wiser. Well, except for the fact that they're wearing "Church of Jesus Christ of Latter-day Saints" name tags.

Like me, Sister Holloway grew up in a religious family. Mormonism was all she ever knew, and she's just happy to be spreading the good word. She has a wide-eyed optimism about religion. I start to think she's one of those constant do-gooders, someone who doesn't have an evil bone in her body, someone who the rest of us can never dream of living up to.

But spend some time with her and you can tell she is a more complex young soul. As she got older and moved out of the house, she knew she had to define Mormonism for herself and not just live in the religious shadow of her family. "You can only survive on the borrowed life of your parents for so long," she tells me quite poignantly. She says she was invited to parties and offered alcohol, but turned it all down. She tells me how she used to be jealous of converts, with their rosy view of religion. Like me, she wished she could have chosen her religion instead of being born into it.

But our similarities end there. Sister Holloway's faith was strong enough to withstand those temptations, and now she's chosen her true path in life. She seems quite content, a feeling I've been angling for this entire year.

Sister Murphy, on the other hand, had a completely different upbringing. She was born a Catholic, rebelled in high school by joining a Wiccan group, and finally ended up a member of the Church of Latter-day Saints three years ago. "It's the best decision I ever made in my life." She tells me she has calluses on her knees from praying so much. The old Benyamin would've laughed this comment off. *She's just a newbie,* he would've said. *Give her some time. She'll soon become a cynic like me.* But I can no longer muster up that cynicism. If spending nearly a year immersing myself in other people's pathways to worship has taught me anything, it's that I'm no one to judge. Individuals relate to their religion on their own level. And just because I'm having problems connecting with God, it doesn't mean they are too.

Holloway and Murphy are two of more than fifty thousand missionaries worldwide who go out each year running errands for the Lord. These young Mormon missionaries are often referred to as God's army—which I find ironic, since it's the same name of a Jewish youth group I attended each Sunday as a kid. I guess none of us have a monopoly on pseudo-clever religious monikers.

Before they are released into the world to spread the gospel of Mormonism, the missionaries spend time at a training center, a spiritual boot camp of sorts, where they are immersed in Mormon theology classes and taught dozens of foreign languages. This reminds me a bit of the yeshiva environment, where Jewish young adults (albeit mostly males) dedicate some of their formative years to doing nothing but studying Judaism from morning to night. They immerse themselves completely—reading the Torah, deciphering the Talmud, memorizing the laws—often spending a year or two in Israel at an institution of higher learning, far away from the temptations of their life back in America.

Although these years for Mormon and Jewish young adults share some similarities, it's interesting to note their obvious theological differences. Besides the month or two spent at the training center, Mormons spend the majority of their missionary years proselytizing to those of other faiths. Yeshiva students, on the other hand, spend the entire time hunched over a Talmud in a study hall, often never even leaving the campus. Each group has its own way of seeking religious fulfillment, one not necessarily better than the other.

Like the yeshiva students, Mormon missionaries have stricter rules than "regular" Mormons. They have set wake-up and bed times, they must work within the confines of a buddy system, and they are allowed to call home only twice a year—on Christmas and on Mother's Day.

The home Sister Holloway, Sister Murphy, and I are missionizing at today belongs to a woman named Glenda. She was raised in Oklahoma and had a rough childhood. She was beaten up and abused. "I thought I wasn't good enough," she tells the three of us, just moments after we enter. "I had a hole and I wanted to fill it." This is their fourth visit to Glenda's house.

She's forty-nine, but her bleach-blond hair gives her the appearance of a much younger woman. She's been married for twenty-six years and has teenage children. The Mormon sisters and I comment on how good she looks for her age. She's led a rough life. She deserves the compliment.

Glenda says she's been having visions since she was eighteen and quickly runs to get the notebook she scribbles them in after waking up in the middle of the night. Visions of Jesus, of ladders, of black holes. She says she predicted the tsunami of 2004. Glenda is a little kooky.

A few years ago, while in Panama City, a drunk driver broadsided Glenda. She finally recovered after months of physical therapy. Then she found a tumor on her neck. I'm beginning to think Glenda has bad luck. When she seats me and the sisters at her small kitchen table, I make sure to sit as far away as possible from Glenda.

From my vantage point, I can see her teenage son washing clothes by hand in the next room. Glenda sees me looking and tells me her washing machine is broken. Apparently, so is her air-conditioning. It feels like the depths of hell in here. Windows are open and fans have been brought in, but they're not making much of a difference. I'm sweating profusely. Glenda hands the three of us bottles of cold water. Despite my best efforts, my slippery, sweaty hands can't open the bottle. I feel like a complete idiot. I keep trying, under the table so I don't draw attention to my utter incompetence, but to no avail.

They each have a *Book of Mormon* in front of them. The words "Church of Jesus Christ of Latter-day Saints" is stamped on the cover. I saw a documentary about Mormons explaining that in recent years the Mormon Church has changed the font it uses for the logo, putting the words "Church of Jesus Christ" in all caps with "Latter-day Saints" much smaller, to convey to mainstream America that Mormons also worship Jesus Christ just like other Christians.

The girls are lucky. Glenda is an easy person to missionize to. For starters, *she* approached them. Glenda's friend Fabiola had taken Glenda to a Mormon church and gotten her interested. All the sisters had to do was follow up.

We hold hands around the small table as Sister Holloway recites a prayer thanking God for bringing us all together today. She mentions me by name, and I twitch. I feel a little unnerved being blessed by a Mormon. For decades, Mormons have been posthumously baptizing tens of thousands of Jews, including many Holocaust victims. (For the record, the church claims to have stopped using rolls of Holocaust victims' names in the mid-1990s.) What was I doing here? She wasn't baptizing me, but somehow I felt as if I was doing something wrong. As if I was somehow playing for the other team. Me and the sisters trying to convert Glenda to Mormonism.

I feel a kinship with the sisters. Most of America thinks of Mormonism as a truly fanatical religion and, as an Orthodox Jew, I can *so* relate. We're

both perceived as nuts. They used to have polygamy. We used to have polygamy. They don't drink caffeine. We don't drink tea on the Sabbath. Six
of one, half a dozen the other.

We both seem crazy to the rest of the world. For example, they apparently wear special Mormon underwear to prevent them from sinning.
I once heard a devout Mormon woman refer to it as "wearing a hug,"
which is, all at once, an accurate and disturbing metaphor. But who am
I to judge? As an observant Jew, I'm required to wear a special under-
garment called *tzitzit* to constantly remind me of the Almighty and,
like the Mormon underwear, prevent me from sinning. The point is any
non-Mormon or non-Jew reading this paragraph will think we should be
placed in a straitjacket. We've both got horrible PR problems, and we're
both constantly debunking myths and odd traditions to a mouth-a-gaped
public.

But the similarities don't end there. Like the Jews wandering the desert
in search of their homeland, the Mormons made a similar spiritual trek in
the 1800s. Between 1846 and 1866 an estimated fifty thousand Mormons
traveled from Illinois (from which they had just been expelled) to the foot-
hills of Utah (Mormonism's American Jerusalem).

Sister Holloway begins by reading a verse from Ephesians and com-
ments on it. Something about finding a home in the gospel of Christ.
"That's what we want to talk to you about today," she says to Glenda.
Which seems odd. Glenda is already a Christian. She's just not a Mormon.
This theological difference never would've made any sense to me growing
up. We were taught that we were Jews and everyone else was not. They
were Christians. Catholics, Protestants, Pentecostals, Baptists, Methodists,
and even Mormons were all one in the same, all simply Christians in the
mind of a naïve Jewish kid.

Jewish schools teach children about Christians as *goyim,* a Hebrew word
that literally means "the other nations." It's kind of like when Mormons
refer to all non-Mormons as "Gentiles." Even Jews are included in that
term. Simon Bamberger, a Jewish former governor of Utah, once pointed
out that his state is the one place on the planet where Jews are called Gentiles. So, for once, I was among girls who thought I was a Gentile. Problem
was, they didn't think that was so cool.

Sister Holloway bounces around in her Bible. One verse here. Another
there. "I was reading this really cool verse today," she says in a Valley Girl

cadence, referring to a story about Elijah. After each verse, she attempts to draw out a meaningful lesson for Glenda. "Elijah went up and did the job he was told to do," she explains. "He didn't say, 'I'm too tired.'" Of course the same could be said about Abraham, Moses, Joshua, and any number of other Old Testament examples. I find myself wanting to interject between Holloway's seemingly simple explanations of the verses the more in-depth biblical exegesis I had learned growing up. Not sure what that would prove and also remembering that I am here as a guest, I opt to keep my Torah tidbits to myself.

"This verse shows *amazing* obedience," Sister Holloway continues. She uses the word "amazing" a lot. She's doing a fine job for someone her age, but she's obviously no expert. At one point, she tells Glenda there are 708 commandments in the Old Testament. There are actually 613, but again I feel reluctant to chime in. It's not my place to correct or, for that matter, to induct myself as an honorary fellow Mormon missionary.

You've got to admire Mormon founder Joseph Smith (who, little known fact, was born on the eighth night of Chanukah, 1805). We should all wish we had his youthful vigor. Consider this: With barely any education or social status, he published the 584-page *Book of Mormon* at the ripe age of twenty-three. By twenty-four, he had already organized his church, founded cities, built temples, and attracted thousands of loyal followers. It was a good thing he did this while he was still young; he was murdered by an angry mob when he was only thirty-eight.

I am thirty-two years old as I type this. By my calculations, I haven't accomplished nearly as much as Smith in any area, let alone religion. I've still got a few years left to reach these goals, and Smith's untimely demise is making me rethink my priorities. (Should I really be wasting so much time watching *Deal or No Deal*?) Sure, many thought Smith was a lunatic. But didn't we say the same thing of other maverick revolutionaries? Who in Philadelphia thought a bifocal-wearing, kite-flying Ben Franklin had all his wits about him?

As fate would have it, I've got a family connection with Mormons. I actually married into Mormon royalty. My wife, on her father's side, is a direct descendant of Brigham Young, the man who led Mormonism into the modern era after Smith's murder. For weeks after Elizabeth told me about this odd familial connection, I wore this as a badge of honor—the rabbi's son marries the minister's daughter and their child will have the same DNA as a Mormon leader. It was only a matter of time before the inevitable call came from *The Jerry Springer Show*.

My own personal genetic link to Brigham Young, barely tenuous at best, was shattered, though, when I took the time to consider just how many wives the polygamous Brigham must've had (for those curious, it was in the neighborhood of fifty). I realize my marriage to one of his myriad descendants might not be such a statistical big deal after all. There are probably hundreds of Brigham's great-great-grandchildren marrying Jews named Benyamin Cohen.

Sister Holloway tells Glenda that those who leave the church are doomed. Like Holloway's heretical uncle who's been divorced three times and can't hold down a steady job. The example is meant to bring fear to Glenda's eyes. It does. But not too much. She smiles at us. Her battered soul is just happy people are here spending time with her. *You are important enough* is the message the women keep conveying to her. We could probably be selling her an Amway membership, and she'd likely be thrilled. And after the life she's led, who's to blame her?

The two missionaries explain what becoming a member of the LDS church entails. "God will never command us something unless He provides us a way to do it," Sister Murphy starts. "So it may be hard to give up your sweet tea habit, but God commanded it, so it must be possible."

Glenda doesn't want to kick her sweet tea habit. Glenda says she was a vegetarian back in the 1970s, so curbing her diet should be a plausible feat. But it was her wallet and not her ideology that kept her from eating bison burgers and Italian meatballs. She was on welfare and simply couldn't afford fresh meat.

"We can give back to God," Sister Murphy explains. "We tithe, giving 10 percent of our income. It goes to build up the kingdom."

"Do I have to?" asks Glenda.

Sister Holloway, the more trained of the two, pipes in. "Well, you don't have an income right now," she says very politely. "But when you do, it's a commandment."

This mandatory 10 percent tithing has made the Mormons, per capita, the wealthiest church in America. They are a veritable fount of charity. Mormons were one of the first relief groups on the scene after Hurricane Katrina. Mormons have a custom of fasting the first Sunday of each month—money saved by not purchasing food that day is donated to the poor (a concept, by the way, also conceived by Jewish philosopher Maimonides back in the twelfth century). Sister Holloway tells me that her missionary car is paid for in full. Missionaries are counseled to stay out of debt. All of the buildings belonging to the church are reportedly paid for in full. This is certainly something other religions, including my own, can learn from. Most synagogues are heavily in debt and often struggle to keep the lights on and make payroll.

I'd be remiss if I didn't note here that, technically, Jews are also required to give 10 percent of their earnings to charity. But, unfortunately, many Jews do not take this injunction as seriously as their Mormon counterparts. Moreover, Mormons are all giving their 10 percent tithes to one central pot, making it the sole beneficiary of their benevolence. Viewed strictly through a business lens, if the Mormon Church were a corporation, it would be one of the richest in the nation.

For better or for worse, American Jews give their charity to hundreds of organizations, both large and small. There's even a concept in Judaism called a *meshulach*, someone who is sent to cities all across the world to collect funds for whatever small nonprofit they may work for. When arriving in a town, they scour the membership directories of the local synagogues for Jewish names in the community and go knocking door-to-door asking for donations. In my neighborhood, it's not a strange sight to see a different *meshulach* each night of the week, each one representing a different orphanage or school. For all our rules, there's no rule in Judaism that requires us to give our tithes to a specific charity.

But this discussion brings up a larger point—the structural differences between a religion like Mormonism (or even Catholicism), which has a centralized church hierarchy, and the sometimes anything-goes, maverick ways of a religion like mine. Again, this is simply a comment on the organization of the religion and not its actual rules and regulations. Of course we have rules in Judaism (indeed, we have more than our fair share), but when it comes to, say, opening up a new house of worship, we don't have to go through the paperwork and yards of red tape that Mormons do.

Unlike most other Christian denominations, if some Mormons want to start a new church, they have to get it officially sanctioned by the church leadership in Utah. Of course, one obvious benefit to this is that if a new Mormon church opens up, it will start day one completely operational with a fully funded bank account courtesy of the mother church. In Judaism, however, any random guy and nine of his closest friends can open a synagogue in a basement if they want—or, as my father did, next to our dining room.

But, surprisingly, Mormonism and Judaism also share much in common. Most fundamentally, *The Book of Mormon* relates how families from the Jewish tribes of Menashe and Judah left Israel for the holy land of North America, wrote *The Book of Mormon,* buried it for Joseph Smith to eventually unearth, and thereby set the stage for the birth of the Church of the Latter-day Saints.

Mormons, like Jews, believe in a human prophet who spoke directly to God. Mormons, like Jews, pray in a house of worship solely based on what neighborhood they live in. Mormons, like Jews, have been persecuted since their religion's inception. The only extermination order in American history was given by Missouri governor Lilburn Williams Boggs to expel all the Mormons in that state.

And Mormons, like Jews, have persevered. With thirteen million members, they are the world's fastest-growing religion. Rodney Stark, a noted sociologist, believes nearly three hundred million Mormons will populate our fair planet by the end of this century. All those caffeine-free faithful don't bode well for Starbucks' bottom line. But those facts don't tell the whole story.

Although their ranks are growing worldwide, their number in America—only about six million—roughly equals the number of Jews in this country. Bundled together, our two faiths only make up about 5 percent of the entire U.S. population. In reality, Judaism and Mormonism are both looked upon as minorities, with one foot in the mainstream and one foot just outside it. Outside Utah (which has a population that is two-thirds Mormon), Jewish and Mormon communities face a lot of the same sociological issues with their mainstream Christian neighbors. Maybe visiting with members of my local Mormon community (of which there are only about twenty thousand) will prove that we have more similarities, at least communally, than we have differences.

THE HOUR PASSES quicker than I expect. "Learning is not a one-time thing," Sister Holloway says as she schedules their next visit with Glenda.

As we leave the house, I ask Glenda what she's gained from her Mormon guests. "I'm a lot happier," she says, eyes widening. "I was searching for something, and I don't feel that hole anymore."

I walk the sisters to their car. Holloway pops open the trunk of her paid-in-full Toyota Corolla and hands me leaflets and a *Book of Mormon.* She also hands me a card with a Web address (mormon.org) and says I can chat live online with a missionary anytime I want in case I have follow-up questions. We Jews have a similar site (askmoses.com) staffed by an army of rabbis and their wives twenty-four/six (they're not open on the Sabbath). We just don't have cards printed up that we keep in our trunk.

I ask for their advice on how someone like me, who grew up in the cradle of a religious lifestyle, can find God and spirituality anew as an adult. "The Lord speaks to us quietly," Sister Murphy tells me. "As it says in the book of Kings, it won't be through major miracles, but through a still, small voice. God plants seeds."

It's a nice conceit, but is it true? Was God still planting seeds with me— or had He long ago given up on me as a lost cause? I am a member of the chosen people who, at times, wished to be unchosen. Surely, God would not still be investing in me? Or would He? Was that the point of an all-loving God? That no matter what, God was always throwing seeds around hoping we would eventually grow?

"Nothing we say will convince anyone of anything," says Holloway modestly. "We're just vessels. The spirit needs to be with us. And the more obedient we are, the more the spirit will be with us." What she seems to be saying is something I've obviously heard throughout my life. But, for some reason, at this moment in time, told to me by a twenty-two-year-old Mormon missionary, it's like hearing it for the very first time. The more I obey and honor God, the closer He will be to me. By those standards, God wasn't even in the same time zone as me. No wonder I had felt so astray, so distant from a spiritual epicenter that I didn't see God's guiding hand in my everyday life.

Holloway was offering a possible solution for my spiritual malaise. Follow the commandments and, instead of feeling jilted (as I had felt growing up for being obligated by all the laws), you can actually feel the warmth of God's presence in your life. Go to synagogue. Even if you don't want to. Eventually you'll go because you do want to. It never made any sense previously. But here, in front of Glenda's house in Lilburn, a Mormon missionary had made it lucidly clear to me. *Obey God and His spirit will be with you.*

In her ten months of missionizing so far, Holloway has already helped six people convert to Mormonism. "Each has been a miracle in my life." I consider saying "seven" and thanking her for the insight that is reconnecting me with my Judaism, but I think better of it.

She sees me jotting this figure in my notebook and quickly adds: "Your mission year is not about the number of baptisms. It's about missionizing yourself, to make *yourself* a better person." She pauses, and then adds, "It's a year of growth."

It's as if she had just given me the subtitle to my journey. Yes, this was most certainly a year of growth. I'm not a Mormon. But I am also on a mission. A mission that started at about the same time Sister Holloway started her own mission. It had been a year of growth for her, one that certainly strengthened her for years to come. My year has seen its up and downs, but as it nears its completion, I'm beginning to see the light at the end of the proverbial tunnel. I guess sometimes we just need a little Mormon to show us the way.

SEVENTEEN

Monk'd

Throughout the period of his separation he is consecrated to the Lord.
—*Numbers 6:8*

RANDOM RELIGIOUS EPIPHANIES aside, this year of cross-cultural experiences has been draining. It's wearing on me emotionally in ways I hadn't even imagined. And it's just plain physically tiring. I go through the entire Jewish Sabbath on Saturday—prayer services, religious rituals, and time spent with the community—just to wake up and do it all over again on Sunday for the Christian day of rest. And rest it's not. It's work.

But more to the point, these denominational day trips are giving me a holy headache. Bouncing around from one church to the next, from one religious group to another, is making my mind spin. I need to get away. Away from the noise. Just for a day. To catch my breath. To rejuvenate myself.

I'm not the only spiritual seeker looking for silence. About an hour south of Atlanta in the rural town of Conyers, Georgia, are forty-eight monks who live on two thousand acres of land in complete peace and solitude. It may not be the Club Med–style of rest and relaxation that most people would opt for, but for me this sounds like the vacation I need.

I wholly admit I know very little, if anything, about monks. My prior knowledge of the monastic community is limited to two disparate pop-culture references. The first is from the world of cinema. That infamous scene from Mel Brooks's *The Frisco Kid* in which Gene Wilder, portraying a rabbi, wakes up in a monastery and wonders if he's in the right place. My second and only other reference comes from the world of music. Who could forget the spring of 1994, when monk fever swept across the nation?

Cobain had committed suicide. O.J. was on the run. And the World Series was canceled. During this season of national turmoil, the Spanish Benedictine Monks of Santo Domingo de Silos rescued our souls with their hit album elegantly titled *Chant*. It was wildly popular, bestowing upon the unassuming monks a certain ascetic chic.

The album went triple platinum and peaked at number three on the Billboard 200 music chart. But believe me when I say it could've been number one, had it not been for dance pop group Ace of Base, whose "I Saw the Sign" (which, come to think of it, also evokes religious imagery) merely rode the mid-1990s wave of 1970s nostalgia by bringing back memories of that other Swedish family band, ABBA. The other album that topped *Chant* that year was the soundtrack to *The Lion King,* and all I have to say about that is two words: Hakuna Matata. Case closed. So, in my humble opinion, the Benedictine monks were robbed of their top slot. (Their inevitable sequel, *Chant II,* released in 2004, didn't fare as well. I'm pretty sure they deserved that. Maybe it was divine retribution for the rockstar monks who favored fame over humility. The only thing they're missing now is the requisite VH1 special "Where Are They Now?")

Gregorian chants notwithstanding, I had no clue what to expect as I embarked on a visit to the monks of middle Georgia. My home state, at first blush a bastion of Southern Baptists and Confederates, didn't seem quite the right location for monks pursuing a classic route to spiritual depths and communion with God. But if this year of seeing how people connect with God has taught me anything, it's to each his own. And expect anything.

THE FIRST THING you should know about the Monastery of the Holy Spirit is that it's located on a former cotton plantation. I guess, when you think about it, most things in Georgia are built atop the tarnished remnants of a bygone slave era. But as we are so comfortable in doing in modern society, we merely sweep away the dusty memories of an undignified past to make way for a more suitable present. Like a Pottery Barn. Or, in this instance, a monastery.

There's a concept in Judaism known as *Malin bekedusha vlo moridim bekedusha,* which is translated "Go up in holiness, but don't go down in holiness." The modern-day application of this Hebrew dictum usually refers exclusively to houses of worship. For example, a synagogue sanctuary should never be turned into something less holy. So when a synagogue closes down or "goes out of business," the custom is to sell the building to another synagogue, so it doesn't get razed to make room for, say, a night-club. Or a Gap. By the same token, it's considered honorable to take a place used for unholy endeavors and to elevate it into a sanctuary of God.

This is exactly what the monks of Conyers have done. They've taken a parcel of land where slavery was once king, where people suffered greatly, and transformed it into a resting place for God on earth. In fact, they have come full circle and are now giving back to the impoverished by turning part of their property into a food bank. Which is why I notice a wide range of non-monks lining up in the parking lot as I pull up next to battered pickups and the like.

Before driving down here I e-mailed one of the monks to get some advance information. (Yes, monks use e-mail. Some of them, anyway.) Brother Callistus was more than helpful and offered to give me a personal tour of the grounds. He meets me at the front gate wearing a long black and white robe, his denim jeans peeking out from the bottom. Callistus stands out among the monks here. For one, he's only fifty-eight years old, a veritable whippersnapper by monastery standards. Second, he's black, a native of Trinidad, where he grew up the eldest of ten children.

He moved to the United States at age nineteen and eventually ended up working on Wall Street. "I led a hedonistic life of worldly pleasures," he admits to me as we start the tour. Most of the monks here, of course, have led previous lives, including a former Brooks Brothers salesman, a Philadel-phia politician, and a New York City cop. Eventually they, like Callistus, felt what they refer to as a calling or a nudge. "I was dealing with the vicis-situdes in my life, whether it was a broken heart or a death in the family," he says. "It was that level of dealing with life that led to a search for truth."

This search would've led people like you and me to synagogue or to church and perhaps, if we were nudged just enough, a more observant life. At least until the next time we stumbled. But for Callistus, that call-ing led him to a Trappist monastery; he first tried out ones in Massachu-setts and Kentucky before ending up here in Georgia. He says that out of every hundred people who enter a monastery seeking to become a monk, "you'll be lucky if you get five." The reason? Many look to the monastic lifestyle as a way to escape their everyday problems, a way to outrun debt or avoid relationships in upheaval, kind of like a witness-protection program. "This is one lifestyle you can't fake. We're married to this," Callistus proclaims, noting that it's the only thing he and his fellow brothers are allowed to wed.

The long six-year process of becoming a full-fledged monk (as well as a battery of psychological examinations performed on inductees) weeds out the insincere. "If you don't have things to distract you, you'll be stuck looking at yourself. That's tough stuff," he explains in a particularly Nietzschean moment. "But those who embrace it encounter God here. But you first have to go through all that stuff, all those little peccadilloes. We come face-to-face with our real human nakedness. That can be scary. It's frail. It's weak. In a sense, it's powerless."

Early monks lived their solitude in the wilderness of a physical desert, a sacred place that was quite familiar to my own ancestors, who spent forty years wandering that same sandy terrain. As Brother Callistus is giving me a tour of the monastery grounds, I picture us as the ultimate odd couple. I'm a white, short Jewish kid with a BlackBerry attached to my hip. He's a black, tall monk in a flowing robe ripped right from the Middle Ages.

I've only been here for an hour and already Callistus has dashed my grandiose dreams of relaxing at a monastery. This is a hard life, all that looking at yourself and self-examination. I'm not sure my American comfort-at-all-costs ethos would last even a full day here. What's even more strange, Callistus refers to his life as hectic and says he's been "working his butt off" as of late. So he took a break from the monastery last week and spent some time living alone in a cabin deep in the forest. Which seems strange. Wasn't this serene two thousand acres of solitude enough?

"The ultimate is to be alone with God," he explains of his Walden Pond escape from the apparent hustle and bustle of monastic life. "There ain't nothing else there but you and your Maker," he says in his Caribbean accent with a Southern twang.

As you can tell, Trappist monks are serious folk. They're the ones who, in 1664, broke away from mainstream Cistercian monasteries because they felt those joints were too lax. I once heard Trappists referred to as "the Marine Corps of monasticism." That would probably explain why there are only forty-eight monks here at the Monastery of the Holy Spirit. Their number has clearly seen better days. Close to a hundred called this place home when they opened their doors more than sixty years ago. In a sense, monks are a dying breed, an endangered species. They're getting older, and the next generation isn't clamoring to get into this fraternity of the highest order. Think about it—you don't see too many Trappists with Facebook pages. I guess the whole social networking trend is kind of antithetical to the life of solitude.

In the past two years alone, seven elders have passed on. The infirmary, located above the scriptorium, is always staffed with nurses to care for the aging monks. There is a growing cemetery on the grounds, which marks the final resting place of Holy Spirit's brotherhood. At least forty of the original monks are buried on the property.

But Callistus takes a glass-half-full outlook. While places like Canada and France (countries he believes are becoming less religious) are seeing a drop at monasteries, other areas are seeing growth. In South America, Africa, and Asia—all in Third World areas—the Trappists are rebounding. "Our house in Nigeria has so many monks," he beams with pride, "they're literally turning people away."

Perhaps it's due in part to the relaxed reformations of Vatican Council II in the 1960s. In the early days of Holy Spirit, all monks took a vow of silence and had to learn sign language just to communicate with one another. (One monk tells me this made little sense, since you always knew what people were talking about, even in private conversations.) Now, there are designated times and places for silence, but it is not all-encompassing.

Besides relaxing the laws surrounding silence, the monks have cut out another of their particularly harsh regimens. In the past, every monk at Holy Spirit took "the disciple" on Friday mornings, flogging himself on his bare shoulders with knotted cords. Considering the octogenarian ages of many of the monks here, nixing the self-torture was probably, as Martha Stewart likes to say, a good thing.

The monastery is still no Pleasure Island, but it has been upgraded to include some modern amenities. Once a week, for example, the monks gather in the library to watch an hour of television—usually a nature documentary pretaped by a monk with the commercials edited out. While *Nova* may be on the now-playing list, past selections have included the George Burns religious comedy *Oh God* and even the Super Bowl. Somehow, I just can't picture these monks in La-Z-Boys downing nachos while watching the big game.

We stop by a trailer. It's the temporary digs of Father Methodius, the monastery's famed stained-glass maker, whose regular workshop was recently the victim of a fire. Methodius (who dyslexics may confuse with jazz great Thelonious Monk) is a genial old man, bald with a bushy white mustache, his glasses dangling from a chain necklace. He's been here for more than fifty years.

I tell him about my quest to spend the year learning from my Bible Belt brethren and start peppering him with queries. But as I've found out many times in this travelogue, the Christians I speak with are often more interested in my religion. "I really enjoyed *Yentl*," he tells me for no apparent reason.

He asks me a battery of questions about Judaism. Do I know how to read Hebrew? What's the deal with all the black clothes worn by the Chassidim? What about those long, curly sidelocks?

I tell him that the Jewish custom of growing our sideburns (some Jews grow them longer than others) is based on Leviticus 19:27, which forbids us from cutting them above the jawbone. More recently in history, many rabbis suggest the sideburn-shaving prohibition stems from some Jews' desire to be different from their Christian counterparts in medieval times—specifically the monks of yore who rounded off their hair and had no sideburns at all. I feel utterly stupid giving a spiritual sartorial lesson to more religious men twice my age. They smile graciously and don't seem to mind.

Methodius takes great pride in his work, showing me photos of windows he's made and sketches of ones to come. One drawing was originally for a white church but is now going to be used for an African American one, so Methodius had to make Jesus and the other biblical figures black.

We bid farewell to Methodius, and Brother Callistus takes me to the cloister, an area demarcated for no talking. "We're the Zen of Catholicism," he informs me. Though the official vow of silence has been lifted, a peacefulness still pervades the premises.

The next stop on our tour is the sanctuary. Its nave, outlined by cavernous archways, is a Gothic vision. The sanctuary walls feature stained-glass windows by Methodius that transform the light from the blazing Georgia sun into ethereal rays from heaven. Even in their solitude, the monks represent all sinners. Within these sanctuary walls, the Trappist monks pray for those who don't have time to pray. And they do that a lot. Starting when they wake up at 3:30 A.M., the monks pray seven times each day. Viewed through that prism, who am I to complain about the Jewish tradition to pray a measly thrice daily? "It's like a prayer factory here," Callistus laughs.

I pop into the Abbey Store, the monastery's gift shop. Walking through the aisles is a shock to the senses. The food section alone would put any synagogue gift shop to shame. There's Monastery of the Holy Spirit gourmet fruitcake (now back in stock!). There's Hawaiian Hazelnut and Georgia Southern Pecan gourmet coffee. There's a *Cooking with the Saints* recipe book. There are even Noah's Nugget Bars, something I have never seen, and they even bear a kosher seal of approval on the packaging.

There are sculptures, lamp oil, picture frames, and trinkets. There's a *Catholicism for Dummies* book. Holy water bottles. Religious robes. There are even some Judaic items. Maybe there's a Monastery of the Holy Spirit home board game I can buy. A Hallmark section boasts cards for religious occasions like a nephew's First Communion. I pick up one card under the category of "Quit Smoking," which has a funny drawing of a nun with an ugly head covering. The tag line on the front is "About that bad habit of yours . . . ."

Trappist monasteries are required to be self-sufficient, as mandated in the forty-eighth chapter of the sixth-century Rule of St. Benedict, which states, "You are only really a monk when you live from the work of your hands." To this end, each Trappist monastery (of which there are around 170 worldwide) produces some retail item to help financially sustain it. In European ones, Trappist beers are quite popular. In the United States, it's mostly food items. Which explains the Abbot's Table Jamaican Marmalade I spot on the top shelf.

As for the monks in this particular monastery, their expertise is fudge. Yes, fudge. All kinds of fudge. Monk's Fudge comes in a variety of flavors and is made in the on-site "fudgery." It is sold here at the gift shop and through the online store at www.abbeystore.com.

But putting their future in the fudge sector is proving troublesome. Sales have slipped in recent years and now only spike around the holidays. "They're seasonal items," Brother Callistus grumbles. The bonsai trees, which the monks intricately tend to, are also no longer a huge moneymaker.

The Monastery of the Holy Spirit had some luck thrown its way during the 1990s when Nancy Fowler, a former nurse, bought a farm nearby and told people that the Virgin Mary came to speak to her on the thirteenth of each month. (Her monthly messages are now conveniently archived at www.ourlovingmother.org.) Close to a hundred thousand pilgrims made the trek to Conyers each month, often dropping busloads off at the monastery to purchase various Catholic knick-knacks from the Abbey Store. But, sadly, Fowler's visions ended in October 1998 and with them, a reliable source of income for Holy Spirit.

Now they find themselves in desperate need of finding a new industry to sustain them. A while back they survived on cattle ranching like the typical Southern farm. But their agrarian culture hasn't stood the test of time.

They've tried launching several new products over the years, with varying degrees of success. In the early 1980s they had a large bakery business selling more than six thousand loaves of bread weekly. More recently, their attempts to corner the market on stained-glass windows have also proved unsuccessful. (Sorry, Methodius.) And their crackpot idea of selling ostrich eggs didn't really pan out either. But to the monks' credit, that last one wasn't their fault. An entrepreneurial visitor to the monastery had promised them ostrich eggs would be the next big thing. They were not.

One area where the monks are starting to see a profit is at their retreat house, which can hold dozens of guests at any given time. During my visit, I see a group of Presbyterian ministers who make an annual pilgrimage to the monastery. They pay for the privilege of staying on the premises and bask in the innate holiness of this place. They also contribute by working the fields and planting in the garden.

The monastery's latest big idea is hopping on the bandwagon of a new eco-friendly trend called "green burials." These simple burials, which resemble what's already being done throughout Israel, include no embalming. Families are given a choice of no casket or a biodegradable wooden one. This ensures the least amount of impact on the environment. "Most coffins are not biodegradable," explains Callistus. "And neither is formaldehyde." The monastery takes great pride in this newest initiative, feeling it's important for their holy fraternity to be good stewards of God's green earth.

And they have plenty of green earth, thousands of acres they've promised to never develop. So it's here in their forest that people can purchase plots in which to bury loved ones. A small marker will designate each grave site. The monks are already accepting presales of plots and, with any luck, this will prove more profitable than ostrich eggs.

And if people are not in a frenzy to have funerals here, Callistus has one more idea up his flowing sleeve. The Rockdale County Chamber of Commerce has told the monks that their ninety thousand annual visitors to the monastery make them the number-one tourist attraction in the county. Number two? A nearby horse park.

Consultants have told them the obvious. You have all these people coming here. You might as well offer them some things to do where they can spend some cash. Callistus points to some architectural renderings laid out across a folding table in the monastery library. The new plans call for a nature center, a butterfly reserve, a restaurant, and a museum, among other things. Silent zones are marked on the drawings as well. In 2006, Congress signed into law the Arabia Mountain National Heritage Area, which ties together seven thousand acres of green space from the monastery all the way into neighboring Alabama, with hiking paths and camping grounds. The monks are launching a capital campaign to raise the several million dollars needed for the major renovations.

If Trappist monks had a Bono it would be a guy by the name of Thomas Merton. He was the most respected Trappist monk of the twentieth century. What's most intriguing about Merton is that, saintly as he was, he wasn't perfect. And this made him all the more accessible to the masses.

Rumors of his excessive drinking and womanizing before finding faith abound. And he was interested in all sorts of things—at one point he even joined the Young Communist League. He was searching for himself. And he eventually found faith at a Trappist monastery. At twenty-six, he entered the Abbey of Gethsemani in Kentucky. That's where he really hit his stride.

He wrote fifty books within the secluded confines of that monastery's walls including his autobiography, which attracted national attention. Fan mail flooded the monk's mailbox, and royalty checks for all his writings filled the monastery's coffers. His increasing mainstream popularity led to a mad rush of wannabe monks who wished to join the monastery. At one point, Merton's Kentucky monastery housed a whopping 148 monks, some forced to live in tents on the property. This spike in enrollment led to the birth of three daughter houses—Mepkin Abbey in Berkeley County, South Carolina, the Abbey of New Clairvaux in Vina, California, and the Monastery of the Holy Spirit, in Conyers, Georgia, where I am today.

I'm certainly no saint, but I see a lot of myself in Merton. We both lost our moms when we were kids. We both were editor of our high-school newspaper. Like me, he didn't like the sanctuaries of his youth and tried out other churches—like an Episcopal one and even a Quaker meeting-house. While in college he was so turned off by organized religion that he stopped going to church altogether. It's his spirit that permeates these hallowed grounds, and it is poignant that I've come here as part of my spiritual journey.

Unfortunately, Merton's life was cut short in the winter of 1968 when the fifty-three-year-old was electrocuted while stepping out of a bath in Bangkok.

Brother Callistus hands me a booklet, *Cistercian Life* by Merton, a meditation on monasticism. Unlike the other branches of Christianity, which seek out as many converts as possible, the monastic life is one that seeks to rejuvenate from within, to work on the man himself. "What counts is not to count," Merton writes. "And not to be counted."

Merton further explains that not everyone is cut out for a monastic vocation. (That's an understatement.) Indeed, he admits, it's not the exclusive way for attaining closeness to God. There are many pathways that lead to the Almighty. This has been a theme underlying my yearlong spiritual quest. No one group holds the copyright on a connection with God. Not the Catholics. Not the Episcopalians. Not the Baptists. And not the Jews.

Monks and Jews go together about as well as oil and water. But Judaism actually has the ancient tradition of the *nazir,* one who "separated" themselves from the community not physically, but ritually, by taking additional obligations upon themselves to become more "holy" to God (Numbers 6:1–21).

The urge to find God outside the confines of community is as old as humankind itself. By stripping themselves of all secular and familial influences, the monks of Holy Spirit attempt to experience their faith as a solitary journey. Monks are the Michael Jordans of solitude. As I contemplate this, I realize I will never experience that level of aloneness. Any solitude I experience comes from my own doing, my own desire to escape the sometimes strangling clutches of my religion.

The Jewish community in which I was raised remains—whether I want it to or not—ever present in my life. As much as I may try, I cannot escape its grasp. In Judaism, solitude is not an option. A Jewish man is not an island. Even the *nazir,* probably the closest concept we've got to a monastic life, was not a bachelor living far away in a cave. On the contrary, *nazirs* were married, participating members of the larger society. Indeed, the magnetic pull of a Jewish community is an integral part of the fabric of our religion. Many Jewish laws cannot even be performed unless they're done in the presence of a community. We can't even hold a prayer service unless we've gathered at least ten people.

Perhaps nowhere is this notion more evident than in the aftermath of losing a loved one. When a close relative dies, Jews must sit in a house of mourning for an entire week. But they are not allowed to go through this alone. During this time of searing personal pain, when all they want to do is shut the door and be left alone to cry in unbearable pain, the Jewish custom is for the community to come on over.

I experienced this when my mom passed away. During a time of personal tragedy like this, we are taught to express, not repress, our raw grief. For seven days, friends and strangers streamed in and out of my house. Likewise, when Job experienced a succession of disasters, the Bible says his friends came to comfort him. Some scholars say this custom mimics God's behavior, as the Almighty Himself came to visit Isaac to console him after the death of his father, Abraham (Genesis 25:11). As Rabbi Maurice Lamm eloquently writes in *The Jewish Way in Death and Mourning,* "The purpose of the condolence call . . . is to relieve the mourner of the intolerable burden of intense loneliness."

The *nazir* only existed in biblical times. There hasn't been a *nazir* sighting for at least a thousand years. He's like Bigfoot.

The nazir chooses to take his own road to holiness, but it is not the only way to become closer to God. As Brother Callistus tells me, "This is not the *only* vocation, it's *our* vocation. We're not more elite than anyone else. God can use any walk in life for His glory." This interfaith message hit home. I'm not a *nazir* or a monk. I'm not a Baptist or an evangelical. I am a simple Jew seeking to find God. And that's a perfectly fine path for me to take.

In the vast sea of solitude, each monk here at the monastery is confronting his own naked humanity. They separate from society in search of a closer connection to God. In a way, this is what the journey has been about for me as well. Except, in my case, I'm doing the opposite of the Trappist monks. Instead of going into seclusion, I have gone out into the world. I've left the confines of a cloistered environment, jumped the denominational fence, and sought solace from the society around me. I've left the stability of my own religion in search of other ways to find intimacy with the Almighty.

• • •

BY ALL ACCOUNTS, the monks at Holy Spirit lead an uncomfortable life. No, they don't have many of modern society's technological advances and, yes, they spend hours each day working the land. But that's not the kind of unease I'm talking about. They may look serene to outsiders, but they are in constant internal turmoil, madly pursuing an intimate relationship with God. This ceaseless struggle for faith is what keeps them awake at night.

In a way, this is what Judaism has become for me. Uncomfortable. Uncomfortable not only in so many physical ways—from dietary restrictions to sexual restrictions, from monotonous prayers to monotonous holidays—but uncomfortable in an existential way as well. And what I've learned from the monks is that this feeling of unease is not a bad thing. When God makes us uncomfortable, He's doing us a favor. He's allowing us the opportunity to wrestle with our faith. To conquer our inner demons and emerge victorious on the other side. There's a Hebrew phrase, *Liphum tzara agrah,* which means "According to the investment is the return." The greater the struggle, the greater the reward.

As I head into the homestretch of my yearlong journey, I'm beginning to gain new appreciation for my own personal religious battles. Growing up a rabbi's son whose siblings all went into the family business, I could have easily slipped into that predetermined role as well. But I tussled with the Torah, thrashing about like a rebellious child. Now I'm starting to see that this struggle is itself a blessing. Without it, I would continue to walk through life a religious zombie. Like the monks, I needed to separate myself and go through this process of self-examination to emerge a better, stronger Jew on the other side.

Jesus' Medicine Cabinet

*The Lord said, "Throw it on the ground." Moses threw it on the ground
and it became a snake, and he ran from it.*
                                                    —*Exodus 4:3*

THE GUY IN the wheelchair is walking. Yes, it's true. I can't believe it
either. The guy in the wheelchair is actually walking. It's either a miracle
from on high or the most clichéd act you can witness while attending a
Holy Ghost–infused Pentecostal revival. Which, by the way, is where this
miracle of miracles is taking place. I'm here with Elizabeth's grandmother.
At the moment, she has her eyes closed, arms raised high, as she prays for
the guy in the wheelchair to start walking. Which he's now doing. The guy
in the wheelchair—I'm seeing it with my own eyes—is walking.

I'll admit, the whole "guy in the wheelchair magically getting healed"
routine was something that didn't actually shock me tonight. If I was going
to attend a "signs, wonders, and miracles" service (which is what Grandma
Martin called this event), you bet I'd expect to see a guy jump out of his
wheelchair and start walking. I'd feel cheated if I saw anything less. I half
expected him to take off into a sprint or at least dance a little jig. After all,
this was a Pentecostal revival. Guys getting up out of wheelchairs are, I
suspect, the lifeblood of these Pentecostal parties. It probably happens here
every week.

I should point out that this is not technically a church service; it's a
workshop. Like the self-help seminars that word evokes, the term should
have been my first clue I'd be exposed to an odd hybrid of Christ and
Carnegie (that would be Jesus and Dale, respectively). But this isn't just

any workshop; this is a place where people are promised the elusive nectar of restorative power. In plain English, that means they are told that if they come here tonight there's a good chance they can finally get rid of that pestering tumor. And, by all accounts, that's exactly what's going on in here. Sick people are wandering the halls feeling they've been cured, and the guy in the wheelchair, well, you know what's happening to him. He's walking. Praise the Lord.

The evening actually starts rather uneventfully. We're in a nondescript office park where close to a hundred people have gathered in a dimly lit room. Stackable black chairs serve as makeshift pews. On one chair, I spot a book called *Fighting Cancer with Christ*.

The ratio of women to men is inordinate. I'm one of only a handful of guys. I feel as though I'm at Loehmann's. The all-female band is playing "Draw Me Close" by Kelly Carpenter, a tug-at-the-heartstrings Christian pop song that sounds like a Fiona Apple number gone Jesus acoustic. Grandma Martin, dressed in sensible white pants and a white sweater, has her palms facing heavenward. She has a beatific look on her face. Many people are twirling in place. A few are making a halfhearted attempt at starting a dance circle in the corner of the room. A woman next to us is shaking her head as if she either is enraptured by the Holy Spirit or has a really, really bad case of the chills.

The woman leading the service is giving spiritual rejuvenation tips. "The best beauty plan is to put on Jesus," she says, as the mostly female crowd blushes. This seems like an oddly erotic and disrespectful way to refer to the Son of God. As if the rugged carpenter Jesus was just nominated to be in *People* magazine's fifty-sexiest-men issue.

Things gets stranger when a small boy ascends the dais and blows a shofar, a ram's horn and—I might add—a traditional symbol used by Jews to remind us to repent for our sins (like, say, attending a Pentecostal workshop). After the trumpetlike blasts of the shofar, someone mysteriously embodying Mel Gibson's *Braveheart* character yells "Freedom!" at the top of his lungs. I later find out the shofar-blowing boy's name is Israel Klein, which, according to the latest census figures, is the most Jewish name you can come up with. Unless, of course, you're name happens to be Benyamin Cohen.

Continuing to resemble an overzealous Oprah, the woman in charge asks, "We've got to kick the devil's booty! Amen?"

"Amen," we shout back with an underlying "You go, girl!" sentiment. Any moment now she'll be giving us all a free car or a home makeover.

Tonight's service—sorry, *workshop*—is a special one. They've brought in a preacher who, apparently, is known worldwide for his uncanny ability to heal the sick. He's an itinerant minister who's been to India, Africa, Israel, Ecuador, and South America. And tonight, he's here in Atlanta, in a non-descript office park north of the city convincing a claque of mostly older women that he can make all their physical ailments magically disappear. All for a small donation to his nonprofit organization.

I checked out his Web site before coming tonight. It features a couple of videos. One is of a blind woman claiming the minister restored her sight, and the other shows the minister's minions magically finding gold fillings in their mouths. The video explains that the Angels of Dentistry were resurrecting people's teeth. My research (a.k.a. five minutes on Wikipedia) shows no evidence of the existence of any Angels of Dentistry, but maybe this guy can call up the Angels of Bowel Dysfunction for my Crohn's.

"Atlanta is where we eradicate disease," the woman in charge says as she introduces the Minister of Medicine. "After all, the Centers for Disease Control is based here."

The pastor runs to the front and grabs the microphone. He's a dapper man in his fifties, with wavy blond locks, wearing a black faux turtleneck and dark slacks. He reminds me a little of Patrick Swayze if Patrick Swayze was a slick self-help guru (which he actually was in 2001's *Donnie Darko*). "I was planning on teaching something first," he tells the crowd, "but I feel His glory is already here, so I'm just going to move right into miracles." Then he says something that completely befuddles me. "I'm starting to feel a little juice. I've already got oil dripping from my hands."

My first thought is that this guy is being a little too transparent. He looks slick, even a little greasy, but now he's literally got oil dripping from his hands? If he was trying to shed any likeness to a used-car salesman, he wasn't doing himself any favors. But, as I later found out, he was actually invoking the spiritual healing powers of Jesus that are prominent through-out Christianity. In Catholicism, for example, the bishop anoints people during the sacrament of Confirmation with oil that's been blessed. As a matter of fact, in the lobby here tonight they're selling bottles of healing oil. Elizabeth once told me her minister dad used to carry a spare bottle of holy oil in his glove compartment. For emergencies, I guess.

Faith healers are nothing new. Jesus, Our Lady of Lourdes, and St. Jude are all well-documented classic Christian examples. But their modern incarnations have sometimes been shady characters. LeRoy Jenkins, whose faith-healing practices brought him fame and fortune in the 1970s, was eventually sent to a South Carolina prison for a whole host of crimes—including, but not limited to, conspiracy to burn down the home of one of his creditors.

Back at the Pentecostal revival, America's health-care problem is finding a new solution: the restorative touch of Jesus Christ. "Some of you are already getting healed right now," the preacher says. This all seems to be happening rather rapidly. Just five minutes ago we were listening to a little boy blow a shofar; now we're already getting medical attention. "Someone who has a bad gland, check it. It's healed. Someone here is having lower back pain. It's being healed right now." As if on cue, someone who says she had lower back pain now bends down and touches her toes. And, as if on cue, we all clap.

Someone in the crowd says she wants a tumor fixed; she says it as if she just drove up to a mechanic and asked for some new brakes. "Tumor, shrink in the name of Jesus," the preacher yells into the microphone. He pauses for effect. "Run to the bathroom," he tells her, "and see if it disappeared." The woman waddles off, her now benign tumor most likely as befuddled as I am.

Another woman tells the medicine man she also has a tumor. Without hesitating, he waves his hand and says it's been healed. She looks down her shirt at the tumor and shakes her head. "It's still there," she says with a worried look on her face.

His response? "Miracles happen now. Healings happen in a few days." Man, this guy is good.

"We're going to release another wave of glory," he tells us. "Begin to watch your hands to see if you have any oil. Look inside your mouth. Anyone see any gold dust?" Some women take their compacts out and use the mirrors to check for traces of precious metal.

His campaign against the demons of dental work now turns toward the curses of cataracts. "Eyesight, come back in the name of Jesus! Twenty-twenty vision, in the name of Jesus!" I wonder what Jesus would think of his name being used for this myriad of medical miracles. It's like the scene in Woody Allen's *Hannah and Her Sisters* when someone says, "If

Jesus came back and saw what's going on in his name, He'd never stop throwing up."

"Some of you will be able to read without glasses tonight," the preacher proclaims. A few in the audience, including Grandma Martin, pull out random receipts and slips of paper from their purses. Lifting their glasses off their faces to the top of their well-coiffed dos, they attempt to read the tiny print. Most struggle.

His response? "If you can't read now, then check it again in a few days." Perhaps, and I'm just guessing here, that's how long it takes for the placebo to take effect.

This feels like an emergency room. Disease is rampant. Everyone here seems to have some sort of medical dilemma—tumors, cancer, arthritis. People are checking their pulses. A kid with an earache says, thank the good Lord, he's now feeling better. All the while Pentecostal whoops and hollers spout forth. "Go Jesus! Go Jesus! Go Jesus!" This is part Holy Roller tent revival, part *Marcus Welby, M.D.*

An Asian student wearing a university sweatshirt runs to the front of the room carrying his cell phone. "My girlfriend has a nasty cold," he tells Swayze. The minister grabs the cell phone and screams into the mouthpiece. "In the name of Jesus, heal your cold." Then he adds, ever so eloquently, "Call us back when you're healed."

Now I know what it must've been like to live in River City, circa 1912, watching the Music Man come to town.

People in the front of the room are twisting and convulsing. The band continues to play haunting, mood-appropriate music. The preacher is crying. The audience is crying. I'm still wondering what the hell happened to that tumor. I look like a deer in headlights.

This is about the time that everyone starts gathering around the guy in the wheelchair. Everyone else has been healed—or is going home with promises of future recovery—and he's the only one left. I guess it's no surprise he's the grand finale. I saw this final act of faith coming a mile away. It seems everyone wants to heal this guy. Everyone, including Grandma Martin, is touching him. I can't help but think how far Elizabeth's grandmother has come from her Quaker ancestors who arrived on the shores of Pennsylvania with William Penn in 1677. What would they think of tonight's festivities?

And this is when the preacher says something I've never heard before. "Shababoomba!" This is a word, it should be noted, that is not found in any reliable dictionary of the English language. He shouts it again. "Shababoomba!"

I pull at Grandma Martin's sweater. "What was that?" I ask her.

"He's speaking in tongues," she responds. "He's slain in the spirit." She says it as if this kind of thing is normal.

It turns out it actually is quite normal. According to a recent study published by Baylor University, 37 percent of Americans say their house of worship would allow or encourage speaking in tongues. Another study found that nearly 20 percent of Christians in America speak in tongues several times a year. There's tradition to this seemingly loony lingo. Apparently, they're hearkening back to the babbling Christians in the book of Acts. They believe their bodies are taken over by the Holy Spirit, which forces them to speak an unintelligible word salad.

"Shababoomba!" the minister repeats.

"Shababoomba! Shababoomba!" the women respond, almost trancelike.

"Shaba-laba-laba-boomba," the minister says, expanding his tongue-tangled repertoire.

To me, this sounds like Flintstones-speak. Dr. Seuss talk. Any moment now I half expect to hear cries of "Yabba-dabba-doo" or "Horton hears a who."

A FEW DAYS after the healings and miracles workshop, Elizabeth and I found ourselves at the hospital. Simon, a close friend of the family, had suffered a cardiac arrest. The paramedics said he had actually stopped breathing for a full four minutes. The survival rate for something like this is less than 5 percent. And those that do survive usually end up with severe brain damage. For all intents and purposes he was already brain-dead when they picked him up and rushed him to the hospital.

Simon's not that old a guy. He's only sixty, but he should've died years ago. I mean that with no disrespect. It's just that he's already the recipient of a double transplant—both a liver and a kidney—and has a long laundry list of health problems. And now he can add a cardiac arrest to that list.

At the hospital, Simon's organs began shutting down one by one. The doctors said there was no hope. For the time being, he was only being kept alive with the help of a breathing machine. Simon's wife and children began making funeral arrangements and consulted clergy. He remained in a comatose state for a week and, as the sun set on Friday evening, we left the hospital to go home for the Sabbath. Since Jews don't use the telephone on the Sabbath, we had to wait until Saturday night to find out the latest—what time he passed away, when the funeral would take place, if there was anything we could do to help the family in their time of need.

But when we called the hospital upon the Sabbath's conclusion, we got a startlingly different message. Simon had woken up during the past twenty-four hours. His heart, which once emitted only a faint murmur, was now beating on its own. The doctors were dumbfounded, family members were pleasantly puzzled. Simon didn't remember much from the morning of the attack. Indeed, he didn't even believe he had suffered a cardiac arrest. When asked why he was in the hospital, he thought he had eaten some bad popcorn at a movie theater and was rushed to the emergency room. He may not have had all his wits about him, but he was alive and his vitals were showing that he was doing remarkably well. Especially for a guy who was practically pronounced dead a day earlier. It was a cardiac miracle.

Or was it? Unlike the Pentecostal revival service, Jewish theology goes out of its way to dissuade its adherents from believing in grand miracles. At the hospital, a rabbi is visiting Simon, and I ask his take on this apparent medical marvel.

"We all sometimes see the hand of God in statistics," he explains matter-of-factly as we settle down into two chairs in the waiting room. "We believe in the hand of God miraculously performing things within the confines of natural law. We want God to miraculously manipulate statistics. We pray to God that someone like Simon will be that 1 percent statistic that comes out of this situation alive. We simply pray to God to bias stats in his favor."

I tell the rabbi about the tongue-tied "healings and miracles" revival.

"There's nothing wrong with that," he says diplomatically, "but we have no tradition of the rabbi coming in and rubbing your pancreas and—poof—you're cured."

"But didn't God perform overt miracles in times of old?" I ask.

The rabbi's response is long and windy (aren't they always?), so I'll try my best rabbinic impersonation and attempt to paraphrase.

In Jewish tradition, the Almighty, the rabbi explains, only performs miracles within the confines of nature. Just look at the Bible and take the classic story of the ten plagues or the splitting of the Red Sea. On the surface, these seem like blatant miracles delivered from on high. But examine the verses. To initiate the eighth plague, for example, God "guided an east wind through the land all that day and all the night. It became morning and the east wind brought the locusts" (Exodus 10:13). Why does the Bible emphasize the east wind? Couldn't God have snapped His celestial fingers and just made the locusts appear out of nothing?

The same could be said a few chapters later when God similarly employs a "strong east wind all night" to part the Red Sea to enable the Israelites to escape from the pursuing Egyptians (Exodus 14:21). If Cecil B. DeMille could get the sea to part without an all-night east wind, couldn't God? If you look at the text, it seems all of the plagues were brought about through somewhat natural phenomena. What is the reason for this?

The Bible, it appears, is reiterating the rabbi's point—miracles occur within nature. In Judaism, we believe that God uses nature as a tool to implement His will. Rather than bringing locusts to Egypt out of thin air, God causes the wind to guide them. In modern times, this kind of divine fancy footwork may manifest itself in a variety of ways. Take the corporate world, for example. Instead of dropping a bag of money out of the sky onto a deserving person's lap, God causes the man's business to skyrocket.

Another Old Testament example can be seen in the story of Noah. When he was commanded to build an ark, Noah was given specific details for its construction. The verses describe its dimensions in painstaking detail. It had to be made of gopher wood—three hundred cubits long, fifty cubits wide, and thirty cubits high. It was to include three floors, a window, a door, and it was to slant upward to a pointed roof (Genesis 6:14–16). This reads like something out of *Architectural Digest*.

As we know, the main purpose of the ark was to hold at least two of every animal species on earth and enough food to last all of them for a full year. If you think about it, it is physically impossible for everything to have fit into such small dimensions (approximately the size of two football fields). Even fifty such arks would have been too small for such a load. Only through an overt miracle could everything squeeze into the relatively small vessel.

Rabbeinu Bachya, a fourteenth-century Jewish biblical scholar, asks the obvious question. If the animals were being saved through a miracle anyway, why did Noah have to build such a specifically designed ark? God could have suspended the animals in the air high above the floodwaters or performed some other miracle instead. Why make Noah go through all the trouble and effort? Rabbeinu Bachya answers his own question with the same fundamental principle as the rabbi at the hospital. God designed the world to run within a natural law. When miracles must be done, He hides them to whatever degree is possible within that natural law. Thus, when people are involved, God commands them to do whatever is in their power to accomplish the desired task, and whatever is left God fills in with miracles.

The prime example in the Jewish canon for this is the book of Esther. This is the one book in the Hebrew Bible that doesn't mention God's name. For the uninitiated, here's the Cliff Notes version of the story. A king gets drunk at a party and consequently orders his wife's execution. His new queen (Esther) happens to be a Jew and has an uncle (Mordechai) in the nobility who foiled a plot to assassinate the king. An anti-Semitic viceroy (Haman) lobbies to have all the Jews executed. The king, ignorant of the ethnicity of his wife and of the person who saved his life, allows his viceroy to make plans to execute the Jews. The queen reveals her roots and turns the king against his wicked viceroy. The Jewish nation is saved. A big party ensues. We celebrate the festival of Purim each spring to commemorate the episode.

All these events seem to occur naturally without any grandiose divine intervention. There's no mention of God anywhere. The miracle that occurred in the book of Esther seemed to occur as a result of a bunch of political machinations merely happening in favor of the Jewish people.

The rabbi at the hospital was explaining that, yes, certainly it was a miracle that the Jews were saved from Haman's wicked plot against them. And yes, certainly God had a hand in that. But the story is constructed in such a way that, if you want, you can explain away everything as having occurred just through human and political causes.

Interestingly, the cloaking of God's guiding hand during this episode may have all been predetermined serendipity. The name Esther derives from the Hebrew word *hastir,* which means "hidden." Divine intervention was like the Wizard of Oz, working behind the scenes to manipulate public perception.

The rabbi takes the discussion one step further. Miracles happen every day, and we just don't realize it, he tells me. Three times each day Jews around the world recite the Modeem prayer. In it, we thank God "for Your miracles that are with us every day." Last I checked, plagues of locusts aren't arriving on any semiregular basis. For which miracles, then, are we thanking God? The fact that we wake up, that the sun rises, that nature works the way it does.

An apple growing on a tree is no less miraculous than a plague of locusts; a baby being born is no less awesome than the splitting of the sea. A person can grow to love and believe in God just by observing nature at work, and that is why the Jewish mystics gathered by the rivers and in forests to find inspiration for their prayers.

The rabbi gets up from his chair and walks toward the waiting-room exit. He pauses for a moment and then turns around to tell me one more thing. "You don't need the sun to stand still in order to know God; God is in every sunrise, in each waterfall, in the wind and the rain. You just have to care enough to see Him there."

THE PENTECOSTAL REVIVAL had left a bitter taste in my mouth. And it wasn't gold pixie dust in my tooth fillings. All the cancer curings and the guy in the wheelchair walking seemed to me like a carnival sideshow, not an authentic view of a growing denomination. I know the show put on by this charismatic one-man miracle machine shouldn't prejudice me against all of Pentecostalism. In my opinion, what I had seen was not religion, but merely a human footprint on it. Like the sex scandals of the Catholic Church or the financial escapades of many televangelists, the purported healings do not necessarily embody God. They are merely earthly manifestations of people hijacking religion for their own purposes.

It's like the Pardoner episode in Chaucer's *Canterbury Tales*. (For the record, I am not a Ye Olde English snob. I recall this only because my dad who, in addition to being a rabbi, has a Ph.D. in British literature.) The Pardoner's Tale is about a guy who's selling fake religious trinkets to unsuspecting commoners. The items are supposed to be indulgences (pardons for sins, hence his name) sanctioned by the Roman Catholic Church. Instead, they are meaningless charms. Adding to his holy charade, the Pardoner wears a cross that appears to be studded with precious stones but is merely a piece of scrap metal.

This was most likely Chaucer's social commentary on the ills of religious profit. But even though the Pardoner was a thief, that still couldn't taint what he was selling. He may have been selling false hope, but it was hope nonetheless. The unsuspecting customers didn't know that they were receiving pig bones instead of the relics of revered saints. Despite his insincere efforts, the Pardoner was indeed offering religion to the kind villagers. Like the minister of miracles healing tumors right before my very eyes, you can't keep the faithful down. Those gathered there that night honestly believed they were having a religiously invigorating experience. Despite the apparent hucksterism that I witnessed, the preacher was doing God's will in spite of himself.

Watching the Minister of Medicine perform "miracles" on senior citizens, I couldn't help but think that this is one of the most hypocritical manifestations of religion. A seemingly pious man using God for the ungodliest of things—not only stealing money from innocent people but, worse, giving them a false sense of hope. Granted, Grandma Martin was having a good time. She didn't feel as though she was being cheated. Indeed, for her, this was a night of enjoyment. So what if it cost her a hundred bucks? What's the difference between that and someone spending the same amount of money on a ticket to a Broadway show? In both instances, people feel they've gotten their money's worth.

I don't know. Maybe there were real miracles happening right before my eyes that night, and I was just too cynical to see them. The people gathered there sincerely thought they were witnessing miracles and the true hand of God. They weren't going to allow someone I thought was a huckster to taint that. These people were revival junkies.

And, truth be told, it's not the house of worship, but the worship itself that brings people closer to God. No matter how mesmerizing a minister, his minions move toward a more religious life because of their own faith, their own inner dialogue with the Man Upstairs, whatever shape that may take.

Look at 1980s televangelist Jimmy Swaggart. Even with his odd penchant for prostitutes and plagiarism, he still managed to inspire millions through his ministry. And now, Jay Bakker, the offspring of Jim and Tammy Faye (those other famous televangelists from the bygone 1980s), is leading the charge among alternative religious practices. Call it savage grace. His Christian ministry, aptly titled Revolution, is described by the *New York Times* as "one of several thousand alternative ministries that have emerged in the last decade, meeting in warehouses, bars, skate parks, punk clubs, private homes or other spaces, in a generational rumble to rebrand the faith outside of what we think of as church."

In one sense, I embrace Judaism's "no miracle" policy, as it washes away any potential for false hope. False hope would be my downfall. I know that, for me, it would stunt my maturity. I would be, forever, the kid standing at his mother's hospital bed waiting for her to wake up.

And yet Simon's children did see that miracle. And Grandma Martin and her fellow Pentecostal cohorts see miracles in their lives all the time. But somehow I can't seem to bring myself to such a raw and vulnerable state. I'd be too afraid of getting hurt. Instead, I'm unable to let even the slightest miracle in. Unfortunately, I find myself living in a cocoon of my own making, safely tucked away from the whims and fancies of a benevolent and involved deity.

My rational mind tells me that God is not going to suddenly strike me with lightning and—poof—I'll magically be religious. Like Noah, I need to go through the motions. Build my ark. Have faith that God will provide the rest and intervene on my behalf. Whether it's an outright miracle or the faint murmur of a beating heart, God is trying to speak to me. I just need to listen. That's what Grandma Martin has taught me—to open myself up to possibilities, to embrace the potential miracles in life.

When God turned Moses's staff into a snake at the beginning of Exodus, what did Moses do? He ran. That sounds a lot like me, running from God's signs when He tries to make Himself known.

In the end, I guess, it all boils down to taking a leap of faith. When my ancestors arrived at the shores of the Red Sea, God did not part it immediately. The Jewish nation stood motionless, the raging waters on one side and Pharaoh's army barreling down toward them on the other. The Talmud explains that it wasn't until Nachshon, a prince of the tribe of Judah, bravely jumped into the crashing waves and the water reached his neck that the sea actually split. The Israelites, like me, were unsure if God would intervene. But Nachshon was prepared to welcome God's helping hand. As a result of Nachshon's literal leap faith, Jewish sages teach that he was rewarded by having the noble King David descend from his bloodline.

I may not be surrounded by outright miracles, and I may not enjoy a preacher whose only training seems to have come from Harry Potter's Hogwarts School of Magic Spells. But I'm beginning to understand the need to *choose* to believe in God. To choose to see His hand in my everyday life. To choose to take a leap of faith.

Confessions of a Catholic Pretender

When anyone is guilty in any of these ways, he must confess in what way he has sinned.

—*Leviticus 5:5*

VINCE IS MY only real Catholic friend. I say *real* because I know plenty of fictional Catholics. The Sopranos, the Corleones, and a whole host of other Italian mobsters. And I know plenty of actual Catholics as well. Like Regis Philbin. And Mel Gibson. And the pope. They're just not in my Rolodex.

Catholicism has always intrigued me. Even though I didn't know an evangelical from an Episcopalian growing up, I was aware (somehow something must've seeped in) that Catholics were different. In my sheltered Jewish brain, I stereotypically imagined Catholics as upper-crust white-bread WASPs—which, I now realize, makes about as much sense as Mel Gibson's Mayan epic *Apocalypto*. By definition, Catholics can't be White Anglo-Saxon Protestants. I now know that. I see the error of my ways. But, for some reason, Catholics stood out for me from other Christians. They almost seemed liked royalty. Maybe it's all their robes and crowns. They represented Camelot; they were (literally) the Kennedys of Christianity.

Spending some time at Catholic churches this year, I now understand what the big deal was when JFK became the first Catholic president. Catholicism is remarkably different from other brands of Christianity. I see how non-Catholics could look at it as a completely separate religion, what with the whole Vatican thing and all.

Vince and I used to work together at, of all places, a Jewish newspaper. He was the editor at the time. Which may sound odd at first, but when you think about it, it kind of makes sense. Catholicism and Judaism have much in common. In the history of the United States, Jews and Catholics were both immigrant groups who made their way en masse to American shores roughly between 1830 and 1930. We were both huddled masses, impoverished and fleeing persecution. Once here, one type of persecution was replaced with another, as we were both discriminated against by main-stream Protestants.

Catholicism and Judaism share theological threads as well, of course, putting aside Jesus Christ. Both are riddled with ancient rituals and ob-scure prayers. As Vince puts it, both religions are full of demands, threats, fears, and obligation. "Catholics, like Jews, are hard-core."

But Jews and Catholics haven't always been bosom buddies. Our inter-faith history is littered with bloody massacres. And in 1492, the Catholic monarchs Ferdinand and Isabella were so fed up with my ancestors they expelled all the Jews from Spain. Which may possibly explain my distaste for gazpacho.

But Vince and I are attempting to single-handedly rectify centuries of ill will between our two faiths. Besides the fact that he grew up in Brooklyn not far from the Chassidic hood of Williamsburg and attended what was then an overwhelmingly Jewish Brooklyn College, Vince's affinity for Jews could stem from the fact that his ex-wife is Jewish. As is his absolutely non-Jewish named daughter, Gabrielle Pia Coppola.

I told Vince I wanted to go to confession. I figure after a year of going to church and abandoning my own religion for other faiths, it's the least I could do.

Sacred Heart Catholic Church is located in bustling downtown Atlanta, so finding a parking space is a bit tough, but I eventually do and make my way inside the building. It's Friday around noon, and according to the church's Web site this is one of the three times during the week when priests listen to parishioners confess their sins.

Including me and Vince, whom I meet up with inside, there are about ten of us lining up just outside the confessional booths in the back of the sanctuary. I had come to this church a few times this year, and each time the pews were packed. Once, actually, it was so crowded I had to squeeze into one of the confessional booths in the back because it was the only available seat. But today the sanctuary is mostly empty save for the small group of us who have gathered to reveal our deepest and darkest secrets to a man of the cloth.

Most everyone in line is quiet, just standing here, perhaps a little embarrassed. After all, we're here to confess our sins, not to proudly boast of our latest successes. Standing in this line, I feel as though we've all been collectively sent to the principal's office.

Hey, what did you do?

Threw a paper airplane at the teacher. What about you?

Adultery.

To be honest, I expected there to be more people here. Maybe there's only a small crowd because of the difficult downtown location or because it's the middle of the workday. Or maybe it's because people are confessing their sins elsewhere. Like on the Internet. While researching confession, I found a number of Web sites that offer the ability for online confessionals. The Florida-based and cleverly named ivescrewedup.com gets about a thousand hits a day, where confessions range from the somber—"I had an abortion and I am sorry, God, for not keeping that baby"—to the silly—"I have done enough drugs to make Keith Richards envious!!!!!" (sinner's exclamation points, not mine). This site, which accepts anonymous confessions, is actually sponsored by a real church (although not a Catholic one). Mysecret.tv, another church-run site, boasts thousands of confessions and millions more who have logged on to read them. Another site, Dailyconfession.com, was launched by a former Disney executive.

These guilt-bearing Web sites shouldn't surprise anyone. According to a recent Pew study, 82 million Americans use the Internet for faith-related reasons. That's more than the number of people who use the Net for online banking or even online dating. The popularity of GodTube.com, the evangelical equivalent of YouTube, is soaring. And it's not only Christians who are hanging out at the nexus of divinity and the digital world. Muslims have news and information pages, and even comedy sites (check out allahmademefunny.com). In Judaism, we have tens of thousands of Web sites traversing our religious spectrum from blogs and social networks to educational and news sites. A bunch of sites offer practical services such as having your e-mailed prayers tucked into the crevices of the Western Wall in Jerusalem.

But, to my knowledge, no Jewish Web site offers online confessions. And that could be for one very simple reason—Judaism doesn't have the same concept of confession as Christianity. At least not confessing to another human being. Sure, we confess to God. We do that a lot. In fact, three times a day Jews recite "Forgive us, our Father, for we have erred. . . . We have willfully sinned . . ." during our prayer services. And on the High Holidays, seeking forgiveness is practically the entire liturgy. The Yom Kippur prayers alone list dozens of potential sins. Eventually they all jumble together and start to sound the same. Forgive me for gossiping. Forgive me for slandering. Forgive me for leering. Forgive me for watching *Gossip Girl*.

But these forced confessions are so rote and scripted, there's no room for creativity or personalization. Where's the scripted confession for journalists who turn in articles past their deadline? Where's the one for watching too much reality TV? The one for actually enjoying the guilty pleasure that is MTV's *My Super Sweet 16*?

At Sacred Heart, we may not be discussing with each other the many sins we committed, but the mere fact that we're here speaks volumes. It says not only did we do something wrong, but we feel bad enough to take some time off from work, trek downtown, and tell some guy on the other side of a partition our most embarrassing sinful moments. We've got a conscience. Or at least the others do. I'm just here for anthropological reasons, studying Catholics in their natural habitat.

Vince keeps telling me I should actually use this opportunity to confess something. I ask him if I can preemptively confess for conning a priest into believing he's pardoning a fellow Catholic when, in fact, he's absolving the son of a rabbi. I'm going to go out on a limb here and say that's probably not something the Son of God would approve of. Thinking about it, I actually begin to feel bad about my con job. That's another thing Catholics and Jews have in common: guilt.

I should explain that I wanted to be honest with the priest, to tell him I'm a Jew who's lost his way. After all, that's what I had done at all the other churches I visited. The introductions were like those at Alcoholics Anonymous meetings. *Hi, my name is Benyamin Cohen, and I'm a Jew.* But Vince said I couldn't do that here. Only Catholics were allowed in these booths, so if I wanted an authentic confession experience, I'd have to do it undercover. Pretend to be someone I'm not. Adopt the guise of a guy who grew up somewhere in New England, graduated from Notre Dame, and made contributions to Ted Kennedy's many reelection campaigns.

I could do that.

The truth is the whole notion of being alone with the priest scared the hell out of me. In a large church setting or while at a Christian rock festival,

I could blend in with the crowd. Well, for the most part anyway. I admit, wearing a skullcap and looking, for lack of a better term, innately Jewy made me feel like the *Where's Waldo* character of church excursions. *Where's the rabbi's son? Oh, there he is.* But the confessional booth is different. Here, I not only had to perform an act, but I had an audience of one.

In a way this makes Catholic confession harder than the contrition I'm used to in my own Jewish prayers. I recite those before an invisible deity, silently so nobody can hear the remarkably stupid sins I so often continue to commit. But Catholics have to say them out loud to a fellow human being. Judaism allows me to admit my crimes to an ethereal being with no chance of being laughed at, which, you know, makes it easier. A year ago, I never would've thought Judaism was easier at anything.

Although one thing that makes the confession of Catholics more practical than that of my own religion is that they get instant pardons. Say a couple of Hail Marys and sins are magically absolved as you walk out of the booth. That's like a "get out of hell free" card with every visit. I kind of like this concept. I can do anything. I feel indestructible. I feel all-powerful.

Vince tells me that when he was a teen, he used to try to listen in on the girls when they went into the confessional, so he could find out which ones were sinners—and, presumably, help them sin a little more. He didn't take confession that seriously. Vince says that when he and his fellow Catholic high-schoolers didn't have any interesting sins to confess, they would embellish their minor infractions for dramatic effect. "We use to make up sins just to make it exciting since our lives were so boring. It was like we had to fill our quota."

The person at the front of the line walks in the booth and shuts the door behind him. Like in an airplane bathroom, an "Occupied" sign lights up. As we continue to wait, a handful of people stream into the church and pray silently in the pews.

An old woman comes into the church, falls to her knees, and proceeds to shuffle down the aisle on them. Vince says he's seen the peasants of Mexico City's Cathedral of Guadalupe do this for hundreds of meters. "That custom is from like three hundred years ago," he explains. She's barely moving. She's like a turtle. A Catholic turtle. She removes her coat and continues to scoot down the aisle on her knees. This is going to take awhile.

Meanwhile, our confession line is inching forward slightly faster than the old woman on her knees. A beautiful young blond woman who walked in the booth about fifteen minutes ago is taking an unusually long time in there. I wonder what she's confessing. "That woman must have a lot of sins," Vince says.

One by one the people in front of us take their turns in the confessional. Eventually it's Vince's turn. "I'm actually afraid of this," he confides to me before he enters. "Every time I do this, I start to cry. I'm reminded of my mother who was an observant Catholic, and also of the long-ago years of childhood." He goes into the booth and leaves me to my thoughts. I've got to say, I'm a little nervous too. What if they find me out? Jew in the house! Sound the bell tower!

A few minutes later, Vince exits the booth wiping his nose with a tissue. My turn to become a faux Catholic has finally arrived. As I walk to the booth, I eye the sanctuary exit and—for a brief moment—consider high-tailing it out of here. But I opt not to. Perhaps it's my newfound Catholic guilt. A feeling of trepidation rushes over me. I shouldn't be doing this. But I enter anyway.

The confession booth reminds me of a closet from the 1970s. Its soft lighting and wood paneling are something out of a different era. It's also colder in here than I had imagined. I guess I just assumed it would be cramped and stuffy. I can see the priest—a young man in his thirties with glasses and a goatee—through the screen. Vince had told me that at this church the booths have options—you can talk to the priest through a screen or you can actually speak to him face-to-face. I don't need to tell you that I went directly for the chair in front of the screen.

"Forgive me, father, for I have sinned." I had heard that phrase in dozens of TV shows and movies, yet I never imagined I would ever utter it myself. I had been rehearsing these words for the past hour, yet they still come out awkwardly. I don't own them. Would the priest see right through my thinly laced facade? Would the jig be up?

It isn't. The priest's piercing eyes meet mine through one of the holes in the meshed metal.

"How long has it been since your last confession?" the priest asks in the calmest voice I've ever heard that wasn't on an NPR broadcast.

I look down at my hands and stutter. "Um . . . it's been awhile." I figure that is, at the very least, a half-truth. It *had* been awhile. I didn't want my first (and most likely only) interaction with a priest to start with a blatant lie. Of course, that's not including this entire charade of pretending to be a Catholic going to confession. I'll have to worry about confessing for that particular sin a little later.

"What would you care to tell me?"

I don't care to tell him anything. I feel as Vince did when he was a kid making up sins. After all the research and preparation I had done, I had neglected to remember the most integral ingredient of any good confession: a sin. How could I have forgotten such a fundamental part of the process?

My mind is drawing a complete blank. I sin. I sin all the time. But for some reason, at this precise moment in the space-time continuum, I can't come up with any of them. *C'mon, Benyamin. Gossiping. Coveting. Lying. Cheating. Paper. Plastic. Pick any one. For God's sake, just say something.*

Anger. Anger is all I can think of. It's like the pink elephant in the room. Sorry, the *confessional booth*. Anger is all I can think about. And not anger at myself for being so stupid. I am consumed with anger at someone I had been doing business with recently.

Some brief background. I was recently taken advantage of during a rather expensive business transaction. The whole episode had left me reeling, full of anger at the shady businessman. I woke up angry. I went to bed angry. I harrumphed at breakfast. I harrumphed at dinner. Being the geek that I am, I actually created a "Don't do business with this man" Web site that explained, in excruciating detail, why nobody should ever use his services. (Elizabeth wisely convinced me to take down the site just an hour after I posted it.) But I couldn't stop seething with anger anytime I thought of this charlatan. I had been full of pent-up anger for days and, so, with my mind unable to string together any other cohesive thoughts, I was left with nothing else to mutter to the priest.

"I've been feeling overwhelming anger lately." It's really all I can come up with. For dramatic effect, I add, "I'm often filled with rage." Rage—that was good for confession, right? Makes me sound like a psychopath. A real bad seed. A rebel without a cause. That's got to be worth something in a confessional booth, right? Anyone? Hello? Is this mike on?

The priest looks at me funny. I knew it. I knew I should've practiced this more with Vince before I arrogantly attempted this sham before the Father of all Forgiveness. I am a fraud, and this man of the cloth is certainly going to bust me.

But he doesn't.

"Anger can become all-consuming and destroy people's lives," he explains, his soothing NPR voice calming me. "It will drive you insane. Whatever it is that's causing this emotion in you is simply not worth it. You don't want to carry the burden of anger around with you. Think about how much more meaningful your life would be if you weren't angry all the time."

He has a point. The duplicitous businessman isn't worth the trouble. I have other things to worry about. Like getting through the rest of this confession.

"Yes, yes, you're right. I should know better." Was that what I was supposed to say? Aren't you supposed to feel sorry at confession?

"Is there anything else you want to confess?" Through the grate, I can see one of his eyebrows arch up as he asks this glaringly obvious question. He and I both know I didn't shlep all the way to Sacred Heart's confessional booth just to talk about my anger-management issues. This isn't therapy. No, this is my one opportunity. I will never be in this booth again. I need to actually confess something meaningful or this whole exercise will be a waste. I need to embrace the situation and take advantage of it.

And so, after several minutes of procrastinating, I relax, take a deep breath, and tell the priest what is really bothering me.

"Father, I have sinned a great sin, a sin against myself. I have allowed myself to slip away from the religion that raised me, and this psychic distance is haunting me." Okay, I'm pretty sure those were not my exact words. In hindsight, as I type this I may be trying to make myself sound more articulate and emotionally honest than I actually was, sitting there, sweaty and nervous, in the back of the confessional booth. But I'm a writer, I have a license, and I'm going to employ it.

I roll on.

"Father, recently I've been feeling disconnected from my faith." Once again, this is a half-truth. I *had* been feeling disconnected from my faith. It's just that the faith I was feeling disconnected from was Judaism, not Catholicism.

As if to further make my case that this is indeed a sin worth confessing, I add, "I haven't been going to services much lately." Okay, I admit this was not even a half-truth. It was an outright and utter lie. I had been going to services. Catholic ones. Baptist ones. Jewish ones. I'd been going to all kinds of services. I'd been hanging out with gospel singers and Christian wrestlers, with Mormons and with monks. I was more connected to religion this year than I have ever been in my entire life. If anything, I was overstimulated, overconnected to the religious world. Sparks were shooting out of my spiritual synapses. So not only was I now blatantly lying to a priest, but I had done so in a confessional booth of all places. I wonder what kind of penance I will need to do for this transgression.

I allay my worries with the thought that there is actually some truth to my confession. I *had* been feeling disconnected from my faith and, although I attend synagogue services regularly, I had not really taken advantage of them. I had been praying in a synagogue since I was a little boy, but for too long I had been absent—if not in body, than certainly in spirit. Jewish services had become rote rituals that weren't doing anything for my soul. I was in synagogue, but at the same time I wasn't. I was in another world wishing for more religious rejuvenation. In that sense, my confession rang true. I hadn't been *attending* services lately.

The priest, thank God, sensed my sincerity.

"I encourage you to go to services more frequently. They're only once a week. It's really not that hard. Pray for God to make you feel more connected."

I want to tell the priest that Jewish prayers happen three times a day, not once a week, but I think better of it. That would most certainly blow my cover. Opening up some more, I tell him it's all the rituals that are driving me batty. Once again, I should point out, I was referring to the ancient Jewish rituals and not the Catholic ones. Regardless, his advice is prescient.

"These rituals are powerful stuff, man." Yes, he actually referred to me with the surfer-dude colloquialism "man." "And even if you don't understand it now, just come to services anyway, because it eventually will have meaning for you."

At first, his pat response seems like a brush-off. *Just come, and we'll figure out the rest later.* But I allow the message to seep in for a moment, and it finally hits me. I stop hunching over, perk up, and look at him. My eyes open wide, and a smile breaks across my face. This priest had just given me some much needed advice. He was actually echoing a Jewish concept known as *Shelo lishmah bah lishmah*—even if you do something desirable for the wrong reason, you'll eventually end up doing it with the right intentions. Go to services (at a synagogue, in my case) even if you don't get much out of them. Just know that the more you go, the more you will get out of them.

Which is what's been happening. I've been going to services my entire life, and nothing has been making them more meaningful. Until this year. This year, I've opened myself up to change. As a rabbi once told me, *Motion creates emotion*. Or, as Nike likes to say, *Just do it*. Don't stand still; stagnation is the enemy of spiritual growth. And so this past year, I started attending a different Sabbath service, one that better suits my personal style. And, as the priest predicted, it's been working. Attending the early morning *hashkama* service has been helping. I've become actively involved in those services, and I've felt closer to God in that more intimate environment.

But when the priest said those words, it got me thinking about another aspect of my church field trips. It's something that truly needed confessing. Starting something for the wrong reason was, in some way, the initial underlying theme of my entire journey. Despite my sincere desire to grow this year, I think there was always a part of me that wanted to experience a year of living among the Christians as a way to merely access the many things that I never had as a child. I got a rabbi's permission slip to go to church to see what I could learn, but deep down there were other, less noble, reasons for my trip as well. I was envious of the Christian community. I was envious of them for their Christmas presents. I was envious of them for their Easter baskets and parades down Fifth Avenue. I was envious of them for how easy their lives looked compared to my law-obsessed religion. In essence, I must confess, I had started this mission partly for the wrong reason.

But as the Jewish dictum and the priest were telling me, even if you start something for the wrong reason, you'll eventually end up doing it for the right one. Which, I'm finding out, is actually true. Despite my initial greedy intentions, this year was about so much more than living out a childhood fantasy. This was more than a tour of the Wonka factory of faith. What I had gone through were life-altering experiences. I had truly come closer to God. I had found a renewed connection to my Judaism. And I had Jesus to thank for it.

AFTER MY CONFESSION, the priest helps me recite the official "Act of Contrition" formula. Vince had gone over it with me before, but of course by now I had forgotten all the words. I repeat each phrase after the priest, at which point he responds with his own formula, and, before I know it, my first and only confession is over. The priest absolves me from all my sins. It feels good, as if a big weight has been lifted off my shoulders. I walk out of the booth a new man, a man with a clean slate.

And then I remembered I wasn't Catholic. As a Jew, I must confess in the way dictated by my own religion. But this confession here at Sacred Heart, admittedly done under false pretenses, was still worth the visit. Confession of any kind contains within it a cleansing power. I had emerged from this confessional booth a better person than when I first walked in.

Depending on the severity of your sin, the priest will give you instructions on what you need to do. This is known as penance. I ask the priest what my sentence is, and he simply says I need to come back to services more often. I guess my confession wasn't as bad as I thought it was. Vince, on the other hand, must've committed some pretty horrible sins, ones that were a little more noteworthy. His penance is that he has to stick around for the Mass about to be conducted. I notice the beautiful blond woman who had spent so long in the confessional booth before us sticking around as well. Now I'm even more curious what her sins were.

I decide to voluntarily stick around for Mass. Maybe my presence will impress the priest. After all, he did tell me to go to more services. During the Mass, the priest quotes from Genesis about the Garden of Eden and the fall of humankind. Original sin seems very apropos for this penitent crowd. Although not everyone is taking the subject so seriously. One guy a few pews in front of me isn't paying too much attention. He's doing a crossword puzzle. Another guy is reading *Spires,* the church bulletin. I wonder if this irreverence negates their penance.

The service comes to a close with the taking of Communion and the elegant sounds of bells ringing. This is all happening in a building in the middle of downtown in the middle of a workday. It's cool to see how faith can transcend time and place. The service ends exactly thirty minutes after it started. The Sunday Catholic services I attended this year were themselves only an hour, by far the shortest of those of any of the churches I had visited. Catholicism, I'm finding out, is for people on tight schedules.

Vince and I shuffle out of the sanctuary with the other sinners. For now at least, we are better people than when we first entered. As I exit the church, I notice that everyone parked for free in a nearby church-owned lot. "Jesus Christ," I say to myself. "I didn't have to pay for parking."

Taking the Lord's name in vain. Oh, well, another sin to confess.

TWENTY

A Man for All Seasons

When the whole community learned that Aaron had died, the entire house of Israel mourned for him thirty days.
—Numbers 20:29

I DON'T REMEMBER much from my circumcision. I highly doubt most people do. Jewish law dictates that it be done eight days after birth and, I've got to tell you, I don't really have many memories from that far back. All I know about that fateful spring Tuesday morning is from what friends and family have told me. Like how good the catering was. Or like the fact that I was tiny, so tiny they had to take me to a butcher's scale to weigh me to ensure I would be able to handle the minor medical procedure that would forever tie me to Abraham, Isaac, Jacob, my dad, my brothers, and Joe Lieberman.

I have only one photo from my circumcision ceremony. (Look, I was my parents' fifth child. I guess by that point, they stopped taking so many pictures.) The photo shows a rather large crowd in attendance. It wasn't because I was some golden child or the next Dalai Lama. If only my birth was such a momentous occasion. No, it was because my dad was the community rabbi, and so hundreds of people gathered for the event. The photo shows my grandfather, my mother's father, in the center of the synagogue sanctuary amid the throng of people, clutching me in his arms as the rabbi snips away. My circumcision was the act that first connected me, whether I wanted it or not, to my ancestors' ancient religion. It's what first defined me as a Jew and would bind me as a part of this religion for all eternity.

But I'm also sure that being in the safety of my grandfather's embrace was a comforting feeling. The noise, the light, the snipping, it all was surely frightening. But there's my grandfather, holding me tight, placing a pacifier between my pursed lips.

And, of course, he continued to be there for me as I went through the highlight reel that was my life so far—my bar mitzvah, my mom's passing, my wedding. I think about my grandfather and how he has always been there along the way. No matter what I was going through, he remained a constant source of comfort in my life. I often think about that photo, how I came from that point in time to where I am today.

Today I am looking at that photo and it has, unfortunately, new meaning. The photo, its sepia tone reminiscent of far simpler times, is laced with sadness. My grandfather, at the ripe old age of ninety-two, has just passed away.

IT IS TWO days later and, at the moment, I am standing next to my grandfather's grave shoveling dirt onto his casket. There is a torrential downpour, the mother of all downpours, and only a few people had the foresight to bring an umbrella to the cemetery in upstate New York. Even those few umbrellas proved worthless as the rough winds mangled them beyond use. (In our defense, it was perfectly sunny just an hour ago.) Water is seeping through our finest clothing, rain drips from our hair, and our shoes are covered with mud. I can't help but think of the irony. My grandfather, a dapper man whose shirts were always pressed and Italian loafers always shined, is probably looking down at us shaking his head.

Shoveling the dirt onto a loved one's casket is the duty of survivors. It's a traditional Jewish custom whose basis is actually quite poignant. This is, as Jewish scholars describe, the ultimate act of kindness one can do. But the shoveling is not only for the deceased. Psychologically, the thud of the earth hitting the casket marks the finality of death, a last farewell to our loved ones. After all, if heaven is all it's cracked up to be, then the dead do not need our shoveling; it is for us, the living, as a source of closure.

I've always shied away from shoveling dirt onto a casket whenever I could. Even though the custom has good intentions, I just always felt it was a bad thing, as if I was somehow helping put a dead person six feet under. But here, standing next to my grandfather's grave as his casket is being lowered into its earthly retainer, something inside me pushes my hand toward the shovel. I pick it up and, along with my grandfather's other eleven grandchildren and nineteen great-grandchildren, start scooping.

I wipe away the rain from my face with each heartrending thud of dirt on his casket. This will be the last thing I can do for my grandfather. From the moment of my circumcision he protected and comforted me. Now it was my turn to do the same for him.

As we stand in the pouring rain, I look over at my grandmother, huddled with my dad under one of the only working umbrellas. Her frail body is shivering. She was married to my grandfather for sixty-nine years and, by all accounts, their love was one for the ages. A telling detail: My grandfather would shave twice a day—once in the morning for the public and once when he got home after work just for my grandmother.

In synagogue, the Five Books of Moses are divided into fifty-two parts, and a section is read each Saturday morning. Around the world, every synagogue reads the same section each week. This past Saturday, just two days before my grandfather left this earth, we read from the book of Numbers in the exact section that discusses the death of Aaron, Moses's brother. This is, for lack of a better word, poignant. My grandfather's name was Aaron.

The Torah states that Aaron was a man who brought harmony between husbands and wives. My grandmother once told me that grandpa was no fun to fight with because he was a man of peace, dignified and even-tempered.

My grandfather was a man for all seasons—kind, noble, soft-spoken. He was a gentleman in the truest sense of the word, a personification of the Yiddish term *mensch,* a stand-up guy, a man of integrity. In a word, my hero.

At the burial, my grandmother is wearing the same black dress she wore to my mother's funeral more than eighteen years earlier. In Jewish tradition, it is a custom for mourners to rip a part of their clothing as a way to express their utter anguish at this time of unbearable loss. Like the biblical Jacob, who tore his garments when he thought his son Joseph had died. Or David, who rent his clothes when he heard of Saul's passing. This is a tradition that has been passed down for generations.

I've asked rabbis why we do this. On the surface, it seems like a perfectly bad idea to ruin a good piece of clothing. In his fascinating book on the laws of Jewish mourning, Rabbi Maurice Lamm writes that the rending of the garment is an "opportunity for psychological relief. It allows the mourner to give vent to his pent-up anguish by means of a controlled, religiously sanctioned act of destruction."

I recall doing this. I wore my bar mitzvah suit to my mother's funeral and tore a gash right through its collar. This suit, which was purchased for such a happy occasion, would forever be marked with death. In many ways, my grandparents have been surrogate parents to me and have been a constant connection to my mother. I have now lost part of that too. Today, my grandmother's black dress is already torn in one area from when she performed this ritual at my mother's funeral. Today, her glass cane in one hand, she rips it again for her dearly departed husband of nearly seventy years. "I'm throwing this dress away after today," she whispers to me. "I won't be needing it again."

As we continue to shovel dirt onto my grandfather's simple pine casket, we read Psalm 23 aloud. "The Lord is my shepherd, I shall not lack. God restores my soul, and guides me to righteous paths. Though I walk through the valley overshadowed by death, I will fear no evil, for You are with me."

My grandmother and uncles recite the Kaddish, the prayer recited by Jewish mourners for centuries. And, at this precise moment, the rain suddenly stops. The clouds part, giving way to ethereal rays of warm sunshine. My grandfather, the man who spent his life comforting others, is now himself at peace.

THE FUNERAL ACTUALLY took place a few minutes away from my dad's childhood home, so afterward we drove through the town and my dad showed us the sights—the pharmacy he worked in as a teenager, the movie theater where he saw Burt Lancaster portray a con man turned man of God in *Elmer Gantry* a half-dozen times. As we're driving down the main thoroughfare, my dad points to an intersection. "I was in the car with my mom right here when we found out JFK was shot."

We drive past his childhood home, a three-story brick walkup not far from the center of town. He shows me where he played basketball, his walk to school, and the synagogue that turned him on the path to an observant Jewish lifestyle as a teenager. Seeing all this gives me new insight into my father's personality. He is more than the dictator who chastised me for rebelling as a kid. He had once been a kid himself, surely going through a lot of the same experiences and challenges I had gone through. Seeing all this history humanizes my dad in a way I've never seen before.

The synagogue that made my dad a more religious Jew is no more. Mt. Vernon's Jewish population has, for the most part, fled to more suburban utopias. My dad's childhood synagogue is now the White Plains Deliverance Evangelistic Center. The synagogue's stained-glass windows depicting various Jewish symbols still remain. As do a couple of Hebrew verses etched in stone on the front of the building. Passersby probably wonder what architect with a multiple-personality disorder constructed this interfaith edifice.

I've spent the past year leaving my comfort zone of the synagogue and going to a different church each week. And here, my dad's childhood synagogue was following a similar path, taking the same trek from Moses to Jesus.

As we drive by my dad's childhood synagogue, the house of worship that defined the rest of his life (as well as mine), I can tell it pains him that it is no more. As if its transformation from Jewish icon to Christian one somehow marks the retelling of a greater American tragedy.

But as I tell my dad how going to church has made me appreciate my own Judaism more, I see my story gives him a sense of comfort. The building that had once made him religious is now, in its new incarnation, working its same magic on his son.

My dad knew about my crazy plan to spend the year gallivanting through Bible Belt churches. Believe it or not, he was actually cool with the idea, after he learned I had gotten permission from a fellow rabbi he respected. I begin to tell him the various stories from my journey. About the Braves' Faith Day. Pastor T. D. Jakes at Megafest. Spending the day with the polygamist prince. Going to Ultimate Christian Wrestling and a Christian rock festival. About Christmas and confession. About Easter. About Grandma Martin. About the monks, the Mormons, and the miracles. It is as if a weight is being lifted off my shoulders. I tell him about my face appearing on the jumbo screen at a megachurch and how my first and only thought was what he would think. His response surprises me.

"This would make a great movie," he says, laughing. "You know who would be good to star in this? Ben Stiller." He pauses. "Although, come to think of it, he may be too old to play you." Sorry, Ben, your agent is not on speed dial.

Movie deals aside, I tell my dad how meaningful this year living among the Christians has been, how it has put my Judaism into clearer focus, and I can tell that makes him happy, filling him with a long-lost sense of pride.

I recently discovered a copy of the sermon my dad delivered at my bar mitzvah. In it, he talks about the meaning of my name. My middle name is Akiva, in honor of the great first-century rabbi whom the Talmud refers to as the "Head of all Sages." You'd think with that kind of name, my parents were practically begging for me to become a world-renowned Torah scholar. But perhaps they had something else in mind. Rabbi Akiva is also known for starting his religious journey late in life. It wasn't until he was forty years old that he began studying the Torah. "He saw water dripping on a rock," my dad said in his sermon, "and it inspired him to persevere, for just as slowly dripping water eventually makes an impression on granite, so too does consistent effort over a long period of time bring results." Rabbi Akiva, like me, was a spiritual late bloomer. It was as if my dad somehow knew that of all his children I would be the one that would take the longest to see the light. But that eventually I would.

I THINK BACK to Psalm 23, which we read together at the funeral. "The Lord is my shepherd, I shall not lack." We echo this sentiment in the liturgy of the Yom Kippur service when we recite, "We are your sheep and You are our shepherd." This notion has special resonance for me today. I feel as though I've gone astray, off the path of my flock of fellow Jews. The divine shepherd is probably wondering where I've been heading.

And yet.

The Psalm continues: "God restores my soul, and guides me to righteous paths." Eventually the sheep returns to the flock, and the shepherd guides him to where he needs to go. Almost a year after I started this journey, I am now grasping the true meaning of this verse. My faith was lacking, but now it's restored. God, like a shepherd, is leading me down a righteous path. After a brief layover in Jesus town, I'm finally coming to terms with who I am, with my connection to my ancestors, and where I need to go.

I return from my grandfather's funeral a different man. I once heard death referred to as the night that lies between two days. This is where I feel I've been, stuck in a dark fog for far too long. But, finally, I am seeing the light of the new day ahead.

TWENTY-ONE

Paradise Lost, and Found

In the middle of the garden were the tree of life and the tree of knowledge of good and evil.
                                                    —*Genesis 2:9*

IT'S THE FINAL Sunday of my churchgoing extravaganza, and I've woken up early in a sweat and a state of spiritual confusion. Is today the Sabbath? And whose Sabbath would that be? I guess suddenly breaking my church habit, going cold turkey on Christ, isn't going to be as easy as I thought. They should really make some sort of patch for this.

With nothing on my schedule for a few hours and Elizabeth still blissfully asleep, I decide there's time to make one last stop. I'm still jonesing for Jesus, and need one more fix of faith to make this spiritual odyssey come full circle.

The church across the street from my childhood home looms over me like an evil spirit from my past. Although I've been at times both tempted and repelled by it, I've felt a strange connection to this edifice my entire life. It was my archnemesis, Alexander Hamilton to my Aaron Burr, the Road Runner to my Wile E. Coyote. I couldn't go blazing through local churches on an inspirational rampage without going back to where it all began. To the building that first coaxed me toward Christianity, whose insatiable lure thrilled me with youthful visions of sugar plums dancing in my head.

And there it stands. Cokesbury Methodist. My Everest, just the way I remembered it.

If you're reading this paragraph cinematically, as I assume you are, this is the point when the camera pans out and shows a tiny Benyamin standing at the looming steps of this monumental church, its steeples stretching far into the heavens. Think of me as Dorothy at the gates to the Emerald City. (Better yet, don't think of me as Dorothy.) The clouds break, allowing the bright sun to shine down on this holy piece of architecture, its heavenly rays blinding me. A loud dramatic overture, probably one with choral accompaniment, is playing ominously in the background as I reach up to open the oversized creaky door.

The day after Thanksgiving, when I was growing up, I would watch the janitor at Cokesbury Methodist climb a ladder and place beautiful wreaths in each window. In the church's front yard more than a hundred Christmas trees were erected and put up for sale. I saw happiness being bought in the form of a fir tree. I considered, on more than one occasion, sneaking out from under the watchful eyes of my rabbinic house to pretend to be a patron. For just one moment, I wanted to be part of what I thought was a wholesome holiday tradition.

Too scared or perhaps too guilt-ridden, I never ventured across that street—the small divide a vast abyss in my spiritual psyche. Instead, I stayed home and flicked on the TV, only to be bombarded by messages of yuletide cheer (*A Charlie Brown Christmas* comes immediately to mind) and commercials for Christmas CDs that featured happy families sitting by a piano or fireplace (or sometimes—heavens to Betsy—both) drinking eggnog while wearing tacky red-and-green "seasonal" sweaters.

I'm no longer a little Cohen kid looking to purchase a Christmas tree at this church. I'm here to do nothing less than slay my inner demons. To emerge victorious from the Battle of Cokesbury Methodist. Delusions of psychological grandeur aside, I need to enter and see if it actually lives up to all the hype in my head. If it indeed is the awe-inspiring Christian merry-go-round I had dreamed of for so many years, as I looked longingly at it from my bedroom window.

This time I don't need to justify my presence here by "accidentally" kicking a ball across the street merely to stand on these forbidden blades of grass. I am standing here as an adult, and this time nobody's stopping me. My father has long since moved away, and there's no chance of one of my siblings running after me, grabbing me at the last moment before I step over into Christendom, and drag me safely back to the *shtetl*. This time, despite still being scared of this church, I can actually go in.

And so I do.

I enter and almost instantaneously the orchestral choir in my head stops singing its song. Their hymn books drop to the floor in disbelief, and one of the sopranos shouts, "What the . . . ?" You'll have to excuse the orchestral choir in my mind; it has a flair for the dramatic.

I should've known that no church, no matter how magnificent, could live up to the wildly grand expectations I had set in my head. This was not the Vatican.

Only about thirty people have gathered here for the service, held in a nondescript sanctuary that looks like a dozen churches I've seen before. I had been worshiping (metaphorically, of course) at the edge of this church ever since I was a kid. All this time I had thought it was something completely different, a veritable fantasia of fun-filled faith. But this was not the imaginary wonderland of faith that I had built up in my mind for the past three decades. This was not the mighty adversary that should've stunted my spiritual growth for this long. I want a refund. I almost wonder if someone tipped them off to my impending visit and they decided, for some reason indiscernible to my Jewish brain, to play a prank on me. *Quick, the rabbi's son from across the street is coming. Hide all the shiny objects. Let's make this look as plain as possible.*

The church's less than remarkable impression on me today is not the fault of Cokesbury, but more likely the result of my having spent the past fifty-two weeks going to church. Like my synagogue attendance, churchgoing had become old hat. This house of worship, even though it is the Great and Mighty Cokesbury Methodist, wasn't ever going to live up to all the hype. This was, of course, not the first church where the parishioners seemed to be simply trudging through the motions of their own service. I had seen bored congregants at many of the churches I visited. In fact, it made me feel good, and not in some twisted *Schadenfreude* way. But it felt comforting to realize that frustration with faith is not religion-specific. At some point, I guess we all lapse to some degree. What I've found out this year, though, is it's how we rebound that will ultimately define us.

I had basically spent the last twelve months in a Disneyland of Christianity, a creation of my own making. I had cobbled a string of Christian fantasies together into a Jesus theme park whose sugary confections drew me in, but ultimately turned me into a person more serious about faith. I had ridden the roller coaster of resurrection and instead of its multiple loops leaving me nauseous, I hopped off invigorated. Like inhaling a deep breath of fresh air for the first time, it was truly exhilarating. I could've easily turned out like Lampwick, the naughty character in *Pinocchio* who overindulged at that haven for wayward boys known as Pleasure Island. He partook of all that the island had to offer—smoking cigars, gambling, vandalizing, all without fear of being punished. But none of that sat well with him and, well, he eventually grew a tail and turned into a donkey. I, for one, have returned home more human.

A HEAVYSET PASTOR hobbles up to the pulpit with the help of a cane. He makes some random announcements and what I could swear is some reference to celebrating deodorant month but (a) I shouldn't swear and (b) after a year of doing this, I still don't have a clue about some things. After a few prayers and a hymn, another church leader comes to the pulpit and delivers a lesson from the Old Testament about Laban, Jacob, and Rachel. Had this been several months ago, this Old Testament chatter would've irked me. You know, the whole "It's my Testament, not theirs" thing. But now, instead, I listen.

My religious rage, the one I felt back at the Milestone Church when they sermonized from the Old Testament, has since been tempered. If Cokesbury Methodist wants to use a Torah story to impart a lesson to its congregants, you won't see me stopping them. Preach, preacher, preach.

After the sermon, the service rounds third base and finishes surprisingly quickly. And that's it. Like the rapid ripping off of a Band-Aid, thirty years of inner demons are slayed in under an hour.

After the service, as we exit the church, Cokesbury Methodist has "Lemonade on the Lawn," a social gathering consisting of mingling and some random prayers. I introduce myself to a few young couples with babies and ask how long they've been coming here. I get the same response from most of them. They grew up at this church and they've decided to bring their children here now, despite the fact that the church membership is mostly old and dying. They're hoping, and praying, for a rebirth.

Their cause is a noble one. For decades, Cokesbury has inspired them, uplifted them, and brought them closer to their Creator. And now they want to pass that spiritual experience on to the next generation. What could be better than that? I've got to give them props.

I look past them, to the bottom of the lawn, and see the ghosts of Christmas trees past lined up neatly in rows by the curb. I was standing, finally, in my Garden of Eden. But no longer does its fruit tempt me.

I WATCH THE congregants get in their cars. I owe Christianity a huge debt of gratitude. After all, this year of cross-pollinating with Christianity has taught me to appreciate my Judaism more.

And so, as my newfound Christian friends have taught me, I will say grace. Thank you, Jesus, for making me less of a cynic. Thank you for teaching me that prayers can be recited in many ways and in many languages and that God listens anyway. Thank you for miracles, even those of the golden dental variety. Thank you for small synagogues. For big churches. For gospel choirs. For holidays. Thank you for gratitude. For sickness and health. For repentance. For the lessons gleaned from death and loss. And, most of all, thank you for rebirth.

When I set out on this journey, I had been comparing our boring Yom Kippur service to the high energy of a gospel choir, but you can't equate the two. What I should have been doing is looking beyond the synagogue's walls. There's more to being Jewish than what goes on in the confines of the sanctuary. And that's true for any religion, not just my own. Indeed, although prayers play an integral part, my Judaism is so much more than the sum of my synagogue attendance.

Judaism dictates my entire life. How I'm brought up, whom I marry, how I raise my children. I'm Jewish when I wake up and recite the morning prayers. I'm Jewish when I go to the grocery store and buy only hermetically sealed kosher sushi. I'm Jewish when I laugh at anything that Woody Allen writes just because we share the same DNA. Judaism, for me, is a life-cycle religion that encompasses more than I can ever fully fathom. More than just prayer. More than just a moral code. More than all the myriad commandments it requires of me. Judaism's black hole of laws is something I may not ever completely understand, but at the very least I can now appreciate their profound complexity. They are the ancient rhythms of my faith.

My Judaism, as religion is for most Americans, is multidimensional. Religion is about more than just where we pray or where we convene. In its purest incarnation, it is the belief in a Higher Power, the collective notion that we are all here on earth for the purposes of good, not evil. In our best moments, we are a society mimicking the divine—benevolent, patient, forgiving.

For all of my religious road-tripping, the answers I had been seeking were right in front of me the whole time. Apparently, I just needed Jesus to show me the way back to my Judaism.

CHRISTIANITY, AND I mean no disrespect, is like Starbucks coffee. It comes in many flavors and sizes: Baptist, Catholic, evangelical, grande, venti. Taking this metaphor to its logical conclusion, this past year I drank from the trial-size cups of Christianity. I am, by no stretch of the imagination, an expert in each denomination—but I can tell you what each tastes like. And this caffeine-induced rush of religion awakened me to the many paths we all follow toward faith.

I learned that God can be found in the unlikeliest of places. I learned not to judge others. I learned that people of faith have more similarities than differences. I learned that the first step is always the hardest. The many lessons I've learned over the past year have already started to help me become a more serious Jew, someone who looks to religion not as a burden, but as a source of hope. And when my faith occasionally wanes, as it does for all of us, I can draw on these experiences to bolster me.

I leave Cokesbury Methodist and head home. For now, I will be putting away my traveling shoes, hanging up my cross necklace, and redonning the prayer shawl of my Jewish faith. Driving home, I feel like the prodigal son returning after his long trip away. Like that biblical character, I went off to experience the world and did what I wanted to do. And now I'm coming back home a better man. Like the prodigal son, I feel both my heavenly father and earthly father are welcoming me back with open arms, loving and forgiving. As it so eloquently states in the book of Luke, "For this son of mine was dead and is alive again; he was lost and is now found." Or, as my own Testament in Jeremiah puts it, "Return, O wayward sons, and I will heal your waywardness."

The return of the wandering son is a biblical motif, one I have found myself identifying with this year. Tales of intergenerational turmoil are not unique, but for me, thank God, it's been a year of reconciliation with my father. He had also traveled a similar path of religious growth, and I can now see past the immaturity of my youth to a more enlightened view of his fatherhood. The tormentor of my past has become the mentor of my present.

The prodigal son has taught me to believe in the power of a second chance, the power of redemption. For more than three decades, I have lived a life mostly bereft of true spiritual joy. But now I've reached a point where my doubts and concerns have finally been allayed. In their place, the embers of true religious enthusiasm have been ignited, warming my soul with their glow. I went through an emotional catharsis and, like Catholics leaving confession, I now feel cleansed. I am returning to the fold a wiser man, a more settled man.

Pulling up our driveway, I see Elizabeth through the living-room window. She's in her robe, sipping coffee from a mug. She is waiting for me. She, along with my family and my faith, is waiting for my return.

At the end of the day, I just wanted to be the Jew I always knew I could be, one who's jazzed about his Judaism. But I had to choose it. I had to make it my own. I had to find my way back to the synagogue of my youth. I had to find my way back home.

Epilogue

COKESBURY METHODIST IS now closed. A month after I visited the church, it held services for the very last time. Then the doors were shut, never to be opened again. The anemic attendance on that Sunday I visited was apparently the final straw in the slow decline in membership. Old members had moved on, and very few new ones were moving in. It's the inevitable cycle of any church, the death knell for any business. Customers die, so make sure you keep their kids happy. Or something like that.

The large church sign that was staked in the ground for so long at the corner of my childhood street has now been torn down. It once stared at me, tempted me. It called out to me with its times of services, sermon topics, and pithy quotes. (In particular, I remember "Our church is like fudge—sweet with a few nuts" as well as "A lot of kneeling will keep you in good standing." But my personal favorite is still "Under the same management for over two thousand years.") Now the sign sits lifeless and lonely by a nearby dumpster. It's a sad ending to a once prosperous life. I thought about bringing home the sign as a memento, a keepsake from both my childhood and my year of going to churches. But I'm not sure where in my house filled with Judaica I would place a large piece of metal that proclaims "Cokesbury Methodist, Happy Hour Here Every Sunday at 11:00."

Although the sign, without its accompanying sanctuary, would be an appropriate metaphor for my trip. Looking back at this year, I realize that I have just been toiling in the margins of others' religions. My wanderlust had led me to merely be peripatetic, popping ever so briefly into various churches, just enough to learn a lesson and move on.

Spending a Sunday with evangelicals and another with Episcopalians doesn't make me an expert in either of those. It makes me, like many of you, a pilgrim of faith. They were just visits, stops, guideposts, signs along the path of my spiritual journey.

But what I did learn was that there are many paths people take to find faith in God. The gestalt of religious practice in America is simply this: Between the Buddhists and Baptists, the Muslims and Mormons, the pagans and Pentecostals, I found more similarities than differences. Despite the gospel choirs and Christian rockers, despite the baptismal baths and Christmas trees, despite the wine, wafers, and confessional booths, and even despite our theological and philosophical differences, there is a deeper thread running throughout. There are many roads leading to spiritual maturity and even to God Himself, and all of us have to find our own way.

Judaism, I guess I've always known, is the true path for me. Although I certainly learned a lot from my religious field trips, I've found the old adage to be true: The grass is not always greener at the house of worship across the street.

It took going out of my comfort zone, being a stranger in a strange land, to make me realize just how much I cherish my faith. I now have newfound appreciation for the prayers, the people, and the public rituals. It seems odd to say it, but I guess it's true. Hanging out with Jesus has made me a better Jew.

Hallelujah. Praise the Lord. And Amen to that.

Acknowledgments

IT'S NOT OFTEN I'm given the opportunity to quote a man in spandex so please allow me this rare chance to replay the words of one of the athletes I met at the Ultimate Christian Wrestling event—gratitude is an attitude. With that aphorism in mind, I'd like to publicly thank the following people:

To Rabbi Emanuel Feldman for being the original inspiration. To Rabbi Benjamin Blech for reigniting that inspiration. To Chaim Saiman for teaching me how to think critically (and humorously) about Judaism. And to Rabbi Michael J. Broyde for helping me beyond words.

To the entire Christian community who opened their arms and hearts, allowing me into their lives with nothing but curiosity and a reporter's notebook. In particular, Deeta West, Ron Peterson, Atlanta's Mormons, Brother Callistus, Rob Adonis, TD Jakes, and especially to the Martin and Palnau families who have warmly welcomed me into their family. You are all fine exemplars of Jesus' teachings.

I am forever indebted to my journalistic mentor Vincent Coppola for teaching me how to spot people's inner demons and, more important, how to write about them. To AJ Jacobs for being a Godsend in all that I do. And to Mark Pinsky who, as a fellow Jewish journalist in the trenches of Christianity, served as an invaluable sounding board during this process.

To Chana Shapiro for being my number-one cheerleader. To Jennifer Spring for introducing me to Benyamin 2.0. To the Rosenheck family for their kindness and hospitality while I was writing this book. To Joel Babbit, Mark Goldman, and Michael Jacobson who are not afraid to think outside the box and allowed me to do the same. To Yoel Spotts and Josh Feingold for always being there and not thinking I was insane. To the late

Jeff Hodes for inspiring me to look at life and laugh. And also thanks to Neshama Carlebach, Alyssa and Elly Berlin, Lisa and Lawrence Stroll, Brion Grossblatt, Jeff Jarvis, and the totally original Chuck Klosterman.

To my darling Wikipedia for being there 24/7.

To Ed Bean, Niles Goldstein, Jay Kaiman, Jonathan Kesselman, Bradley Lowenstein, Bradford R. Pilcher, Jimmy Baron, Joey Raab, Lauren Sandler, Joseph Skibell, Hella Winston, Ron Wolfson, and my sister Chanie for taking early looks at the manuscript as I wrote and offered terrific insight on ways to make it better. They get all the credit, not me.

There is no way to properly thank Farley Chase for going above and beyond the call of duty for an agent. He spent an inordinate amount of time helping craft the perfect proposal and held my hand through the entire process. Without his faith in me, you wouldn't be holding this book in your hand. His generosity knows no bounds.

To Eric Brandt at HarperOne for taking a chance on a first-time author and offering his kind and insightful wisdom throughout the writing of this book. You have him to thank for this book not being a hundred pages longer. And I mean that as a compliment. Thanks also go to the other fine folks at Harper, namely Mickey Maudlin, Alison Petersen, and the entire graphics and marketing teams who helped shepherd this project from start to finish. To Kelly Hughes, the world's best publicist. And to copyeditor Ann Moru for reading through the book with a fine-tooth comb, having sound judgment, and doing her best to make me not look stupid.

To all my siblings who, whether they knew it or not, have constantly been sources of encouragement to me—not to mention good fodder for stories included in this book. To my stepmother Meryl who bore the brunt of my teen angst (I'm sorry). To my father who deserves more than a mere sentence in the acknowledgments. And to my late mother who still inspires me to this day.

Last, but certainly not least, I express the deepest sense of gratitude to my wife, Elizabeth. Brought up in the Christian faith, she brings to our marriage a fresh perspective of Judaism that allows me to look at my religion through a new lens. She was the first person to read each chapter (including this thank-you to her) as I typed it, and her unique perspective helped give the manuscript both its depth and genuineness.

And to you, the reader, for buying this book. Thanks.